P9-EDQ-028

Honest Politics

Ian Greene and David P. Shugarman

James Lorimer & Company, Publishers
Toronto, 1997

© 1997 Ian Greene and David P. Shugarman

All rights reserved. No part of this book may be reproduced or transmitted in any form or by any means, electronic or mechanical, including photocopying, or by any information storage or retrieval system, without permission in writing from the publisher.

James Lorimer & Company Ltd. acknowledges with thanks the support of the Canada Council and the Ontario Arts Council in the development of writing and publishing in Canada.

Cover illustration: Dan Murphy

Canadian Cataloguing in Publication Data

Greene, Ian
    Honest politics: seeking integrity in Canadian public life

Includes index.
    ISBN 1-55028-535-1 (bound) ISBN 1-55028-534-3 (pbk.)

1. Political corruption - Canada. 2. Political ethics - Canada.
I. Shugarman, David P., 1943–   .
II. Title.

JL86.C67G74 1996   354.71009   C96-932172-4

James Lorimer & Company Ltd., Publishers
35 Britain Street
Toronto, Ontario
M5A 1R7

Printed and bound in Canada

Contents

AUGUSTANA UNIVERSITY COLLEGE
LIBRARY

To our children, Sarah, Julie, Christina, and Philip
with the hope that ethical politics will become a fact of their lives
and
To Linda and Eilonwy, who promote mutual respect by example

Preface

This book presents a framework for sorting out right from wrong in politics. We don't claim to have all the answers, and reasonable people will sometimes disagree about the right course of action in a particular situation. But sustained with good will and democratic sensibilities, Canadians can make progress. Canada has already contributed more to ethical democracy in terms of developing procedures that work, we believe, than most other countries. In typically Canadian fashion, however, we Canadians have done little to publicize these innovations.

This book is primarily about ethical expectations and standards concerning the conduct of elected officials. In this respect we concentrate on the ethics of political processes and the behaviour of politicians and not, except in passing, on ideological disputes over the content and direction of public policy. With regard to elected officials, we have focused on three key areas of misconduct that need to be checked and repaired: conflicts of interest, undue influence, and "dirty-handed" politics. Other facets of ethical politics, for example, gender and ethics, and the ethics of public policy generally, are so important they deserve separate books. We focus on conflicts of interest, undue influence, and dirty-handed politics because we are convinced that a clear understanding of these subjects is necessary to ensure a commitment to democratic procedures in serving the public.

Our views about ethical politics have been heavily influenced by our reflections on our own past experiences in active politics — which began when we were undergraduate students at the University of Alberta in the 1960s. Although we did not know each other at the time, we both became fascinated by the relation between ethics and politics as a result of taking political theory classes taught by Tom Pocklington, now president of the Canadian Political Science Association.

Shugarman was introduced to active politics by knocking on Alberta's doors for the NDP. In Edmonton West he campaigned on behalf of Pocklington, who was an NDP candidate for the provincial legislature. Shugarman and future Prime Minister Joe Clark became friends while classmates in Pocklington's advanced political theory class. However, Clark was unsuccessful in getting Shugarman involved in Davie Fulton's leadership bid for the Conservative party. As a lark Shugarman started a new party called the Constitutionalist Party for the U of A Model Parliament and campaigned against Preston Manning, then leader of the campus Social Credit party. Both Shugarman and Manning ended up sitting on the opposition side of the House, trying to bring down the "uppity" Liberals.

When Greene entered first year at the U of A, he got to know Clark through another Model Parliament. As a result of Clark's influence, Greene joined the campus conservatives and later served on the executive. He was an alternate delegate at the 1967 "dump Dief" Conservative leadership convention in Toronto, and a year later he became campaign manager for Robert Thompson in Red Deer after Thompson abandoned the leadership of the Social Credit party to join the Conservatives in time for the federal election. In the early 1970s, Greene worked as the executive assistant to a cabinet minister in Peter Lougheed's government for a year. But after finishing graduate school, he decided that for him, academic research did not mix well with active politics. Shugarman, however, has occasionally been involved in NDP campaigns in Toronto, though like Greene he is not a member of a political party. Lest Liberal supporters feel left out, we admit that we have both occasionally voted Liberal. And in graduate school at the University of Toronto one of us even had a room-mate who went on to become the leader of the Ontario Liberals and then Premier.

We mention these items not to indulge in name-dropping but to emphasize that both of us know and understand practical politics and politicians. The analysis and recommendations in the chapters that follow don't come out of an insulated ivory tower. Without our experiences in active politics — the hope of electoral victory, the remorse of defeat, the feelings of intense partisanship, the extreme pressure to make your candidate look good at all costs — it would have been difficult to analyse the relationship between ethics and politics from the perspective of participants in the political process. The academic world has given us the opportunity to reflect on these experiences and put them into a broader theoretical perspective.

Given this background, the present book opens in Chapter 1 with the argument that ethical politics is a requirement for democratic government. We then turn in Chapter 2 to the ethical duties that are the basis for the more specific codes of ethical conduct. Chapter 3 argues that conflicts of interest, patronage, and various lobbying practices are incompatible with the principles of democracy that flow from mutual respect. Chapter 4 presents case studies of conflicts of interest, including those of Michel Gravel, Sinclair Stevens, Bill Vander Zalm, Michel Côté, Ralph Klein, and Richard Le Hir. Chapter 5 considers undue influence and examines the cases of Patti Starr, the Pearson Airport controversy and the Airbus affair. Chapter 6 describes Canadian experiments in the enforcement of political ethics through ethics commissioners. In Chapter 7, we consider "dirty-handed" politics — unethical behaviour rationalized as serving the public good. Our recommendations for reform are included throughout the book alongside our discussion of particular kinds and instances of misconduct. In Chapter 8, we highlight some key proposals for new and/or stronger institutionalized supports for ethical conduct.

At several points we refer to a series of workshops on ethical politics held between 1992 and 1994 at York University in Toronto. Thanks to a grant from the Social Sciences and Humanities Research Council, we brought together leading politicians, public servants, academics, and journalists to discuss current ethical issues in Canadian politics. We have benefitted enormously from their insights. The contributors to these workshops are listed in Appendix I. Appendix II contains excerpts from some ethics laws and codes of conduct, while Appendix III provides examples of the opinions of Canadian ethics commissioners.

If there is a single factor most likely to sap the vitality of a nation, it is political corruption. It has eaten away at the people's trust in such provincial regimes as Bill Vander Zalm's in British Columbia and Grant Devine's in Saskatchewan to the point where their provincial parties have been devastated. And abuse of public trust is not unknown at the municipal level, as indicated by jail terms for corrupt municipal politicians in the Toronto area and the saga of Edmonton's former mayor, "Wild Bill" Hawrelak, twice thrown out of office for blatant corruption.

Many consider "ethical politics" to be an oxymoron. They want ethics in politics, but as case after case of wrongdoing is uncovered they consider it a lost cause. But however much the people may come to expect a certain number of instances of corruption, they don't find them acceptable. We have a long way to go before we can be assured that our children will inherit a country in which ethics in politics is as much a practised requirement of our democracy as are free elections, judicial independence, and human rights. Ethical politics will undoubtedly be a major preoccupation of democratic citizens over the next few decades.

Ethics tends to be a controversial subject among politicians, academics, and the public at large. The subject of ethics has profoundly personal overtones and is easily connected to feelings of guilt, self-righteousness, blame, and outrage. We certainly are not setting ourselves up as paragons of virtue. In fact, the more we have reasoned through ethical dilemmas, the more we have become aware of our own shortcomings — past and present. But it is better to treat these failings as opportunities for learning than as triggers for self-flagellation. As Rick Salutin has so aptly put it, ethics is "not about playing 'Gotcha'" — it's about respect for people. And unless we respect the right to be wrong while working for improvements in how politics is pursued, we are unlikely to make any progress toward a more honest political system.

We look forward to a time when Canadians are as adept in electing ethical politicians as they currently are in turfing out the corrupt ones they have unwittingly voted for. We also look forward to the time when universities and colleges will include the subject of ethical politics in their introductory political science courses, as well as offer more advanced courses in this area. We hope that this book will make a modest contribution in this regard.

Acknowledgements

We acknowledge full responsibility for any errors or omissions in the pages that follow. However, the manuscript has benefitted greatly from the help of dozens of friends or colleagues, a few of whom we mention here. We are indebted to all who participated in the ethical politics workshops at York University in the early 1990s. Those who took part are listed in Appendix I, but we would like to thank participants Hon. Gregory Evans, Donald MacNiven, Donald C. MacDonald, Charles Campbell, and Patrick Boyer for taking time to read our manuscript and to provide us with comments. Others who were kind enough to read the manuscript and advise us were David Baugh, Derril G. McLeod, Robert C. Clark, Mr. Justice W.L.M. Creaghan, and Andrew Heard. Howard Wilson, the federal ethics counsellor, his chief advisor Gordon Parks, and Cornelius von Baeyer, who was with the ethics counsellor's office prior to his retirement, all provided us with valuable insights. Peter McCormick has helped us to think more clearly about the recall and other aspects of democratic ethics. For help with a particular citation and discussions on the nature of fiduciary trusts we thank Mayo Moran and Douglas Cunningham. We are particularly indebted to Ken Kernaghan, who has done so much to promote ethics in the public sector, and who gave us a very detailed commentary. We have learned much from *The Responsible Public Servant,* Kernaghan and Langford's analysis of ethical standards for non-elected public officials.

More generally, we wish to record our appreciation and thanks to Tom Pocklington, who set us on our way, whose teaching and writing continue to inspire and who will no doubt find much to disagree with and criticize in what we have written. Others who have significantly influenced our thinking about ethical politics include the late Donald Smiley, who combined a deep sense of ethics and social justice with good humour, and Peter Russell, whose research, student support and public-service contributions have been driven by his commitment to mutual respect and democracy. We are also grateful for help received from Maureen Mancuso, Michael Atkinson, Neil Nevitte, and André Blais, whose work on the Canadian Political Ethics Project has informed and refined our thinking.

We are grateful to McLaughlin College's administrative assistant, Lilian Polsinelli, and secretarial staff Frances Tee, Vicki Carnavale, and Vicky Perot for helping us with the preparation of the manuscript and, in Shugarman's case, easing the burdens of a university administrator at crucial times.

For parts of the book, we relied heavily on Ian Greene's article, "Conflict of Interest and the Constitution," published in the *Canadian Journal of Political Science* in 1990; we thank the Journal for permission to use the article. The Social Sciences and Humanities Research Council not only provided the funding for the three workshops on ethical politics, but also support for related research that was invaluable in the preparation of this book.

At various stages in the organization of our workshops and the research for the book a number of graduate students in York's political science department were very helpful. In this respect, we thank Brenda Lyshaug, Graham Longford, Susan Ferguson, Tami Jacobi, and Pamela Leach.

No project like this can succeed without the support and patience of family members, and in this project those closest to us even provided editorial advice and research assistance: Eilonwy Morgan, Margaret Bertram, Doris and Monty Annear, and Linda Scott.

Most of all, we are grateful to Jim Lorimer for deciding to publish this book, to editor Diane Young for her tireless and thorough editorial assistance, to Laura Ellis, our copy editor, and to Paul Rynard, our Graduate Research Assistant. Rynard's assistance was invaluable: in many respects there are words, phrases, and sections of the book that are as much his as ours, and he also is responsible for assembling the notes and bibliography.

This book is very much a shared project. However, we did work out a rough division of labour. For those interested in such things, Chapters 3, 4, 5, and 6 are mostly by Greene, Chapter 7 is mostly Shugarman's, while Chapters 1, 2, and 8 are pretty much 50-50 efforts. That said, each chapter has been reviewed, revised, and edited by both of us. Where we had some differences, we resolved them through the kind of moral compromise referred to in Chapter 7. Co-authoring a book that places heavy stress on mutual respect was an instructive and gratifying lesson in the importance of practising what is being theoretically claimed.

Ethics and the Principles of Democracy

In September 1995 Lorne McLaren, Premier Grant Devine's labour minister, was sentenced to three and a half years in jail for his part in a scheme that defrauded the people of Saskatchewan of nearly $850,000. The strategy, which had been approved at the highest levels of the Saskatchewan Conservative caucus, diverted funds earmarked for constituency communications expenses to numbered companies, and from there into the pockets of Conservative MLAs and cabinet ministers as a form of personal reward.

Every one of the thirty-eight Conservative MLAs approved the diversion of 25 per cent of his or her communications allowance to the numbered companies, and at least eleven members received payments from the illegal fund before they were caught. McLaren admitted that he personally took $114,000. Four other MLAs have been convicted, three have been acquitted, and four others have been charged. One MLA committed suicide rather than face investigation. Former minister Joan Duncan said she participated in the fraud because she was angry about being dropped from the cabinet in 1989. She used the money for a trip to Hawaii.[1]

This expense-fund fraud is an example of what ethicists call an abuse of trust. When public officials abuse the trust that is placed in them in order to provide themselves or their friends with special benefits, or to achieve personal goals in violation of the principles of equality and respect, which are the cornerstones of democracy, we say they have acted unethically.

An abuse of trust is a fundamental characteristic of an unethical political act in a democracy. But some public officials justify unethical practices as the necessary means to achieve good results. For example, throughout the early 1970s Canada's security intelligence services were involved in a succession of shady, duplicitous practices which were known as the RCMP "dirty tricks" campaign. According to the McDonald Royal Commission on the RCMP, security officers of the national police force were involved in break-ins, wire-tapping, incidents of disinformation, illegal mail openings, and scare tactics; they also spied on political parties and members of Parliament. Members of the force who testified before the Royal Commission saw nothing wrong with these actions because from their perspective, they participated in these activities for the greater good of Canadians as a whole. Not a single member of the Liberal government then in power was willing to take responsibility for what happened, despite the admission of a former chief of security services in Quebec that certain illegalities, such as opening the mail and theft, "were so commonplace they were no longer thought of as illegal."[2]

We call this second type of ethical misconduct "dirty-handed" politics. It occurs when leaders feel embattled and regard politics as a form of warfare. Convinced that their cause is right and their opponents' wrong, they will do or authorize to be done anything that they believe is needed. They reason that it is often necessary for representatives to "get their hands dirty" by resorting to unscrupulous tactics to pursue their version of the public good. Compared to using public office for private purposes and siphoning off public monies into private hands, dirty-handed politics is clearly a different kind of political corruption. What these corrupt practices have in common is that they violate democratic procedures and undermine democratic values.

The Saskatchewan communications fraud and the RCMP dirty tricks scandal are only two blatant examples of political corruption. In fact, there have been many ethics scandals in Canada during the past two decades.

Ethics concerns the way people ought to act in their relations with one another. Throughout history, humanity has wrestled with tough ethical issues. The quantity of books related to the philosophy and practice of ethics is now so great that their study could occupy a lifetime. All of these writings have certain features in common. They discuss ways of acting and organizing social relations, and they argue that some forms of behaviour are more acceptable than others. Furthermore, they seek to state the principles that underlie ethical practices and that can be used to evaluate deviations from or improvements to them.

Because the opportunities for human action are enormous and change over time and in various circumstances, no set of ethical principles and applications can determine what ought to constitute appropriate behaviour in every situation. And reasonable people who accept the same principles can disagree about how those principles ought to apply. The value of an ethical approach is that it provides an opportunity to work out resolutions to difficult situations.

In addition, an important part of being content with ourselves is the extent to which we feel we have made our best efforts when faced with life's difficult choices. In this sense, our psychological well-being is connected to what ethical theorists call *moral autonomy*, a form of freedom whereby a person is essentially self-governing in regard to morally relevant choices without being selfish.

Mutual Respect

Democracy is founded on the principles of equality and respect for all individuals: what we refer to as mutual respect. Ronald Dworkin, a contemporary legal theorist, put it this way: " ... individuals have a right to equal concern and respect in the design and administration of the political institutions that govern them ... [T]hey possess [this right] not by virtue of birth or characteristic or merit or excellence but simply as human beings with the capacity to make plans and give justice."[3]

Mutual respect means that we owe the same consideration to others when making decisions that affect them as we feel we are owed when others make decisions that affect us.[4] Some would suggest that the fundamental principle of democracy is the concept of free elections for representative institutions, or the related principles of equality and freedom, or the postulate of individual autonomy.[5] Our thinking, however, is that mutual respect is a more basic democratic principle: it is the concept from which free elections, equality, and freedom are derived. David Held argues convincingly that the contemporary quest for democracy stresses individual autonomy, or the idea that the "individual ... is free and equal only to the extent that he or she can pursue and attempt to realize self-chosen ends and personal interests."[6] However, we think that Held's approach does not adequately convey the notion that others are as important as self, an ideal embedded in the concept of mutual respect.

There are several factors that have led to the ascendence of mutual respect in the world's democracies. First, the world's religions have undoubtedly played a major role. Not only do religions concern themselves with ethics, but the ethical principles held by most religions tend to have a lot in common. Among these principles is the belief that every human being has equal worth, and therefore is equally deserving of respect. There has obviously been a great gulf in many periods of history between religious belief and practice, but the tenet of the equal worth of all human beings is so pervasive that it has survived movements to quell it and has had a major impact not only on the institutional structures of religious organizations, but also on the thinking of their adherents about democratic government. Among the secular humanists who have rejected religion but still seek guiding principles around which to organize their lives and their society, there are few who would reject the "golden rule": do to others as you would have them do to you.

Second, the political philosophy of liberalism and the development of liberal societies have also contributed to the prominence given to the principle of mutual respect. Liberalism first developed during the turbulent seventeenth century in the United Kingdom, where civil wars were fought between those who believed that a peaceful and orderly society would result only through a monarch with absolute authority and those who held that government must exist by the consent of "the people." The liberals' victory in the Glorious Revolution of 1688 has had a profound impact on the history of the democratic world. The philosophy of liberalism is complex and has many variants, but the essentials are that mutual respect implies government by consent of the governed and as much individual freedom as is consistent with safeguarding the equal freedom and security of others. Liberalism broke the stranglehold that the upper, land-owning classes had previously held over the economy and established the sovereignty of the people in government. The ideals of liberalism powered the American revolution and enormously influenced Canada's evolution.

But with liberalism, as with any grand philosophy, there has always been a gap between ideals and reality. The liberal emphasis on equality of opportunity for material enrichment in a free-enterprise economy led to an increased inequality between rich and poor during the eighteenth and nineteenth centuries. Furthermore, early classical liberalism denied all women (except royalty) and men from the lower classes (who constituted a majority of the adult male population) any voice in government. The contradictions in the application of liberalism led to the rise of socialism in the late nineteenth and early twentieth centuries. Whereas liberalism had stressed equality of opportunity, socialism concentrated on equality of results. The appeal of socialism in the first half of the twentieth century led to reform liberalism, which encouraged expanding the franchise and supported the development of a democratic welfare state. Whereas socialists claimed that true equality could never be achieved in a capitalist society, reform liberals held that state intervention in the economy could neutralize the worst of the inequalities resulting from capitalism.

After the Second World War, state intervention designed to promote equality had mixed results: enormous advances were made in social security services through programs like unemployment insurance, minimum-wage laws, state pensions, public health care, and income support for those in dire need. The provision of such services, however, led to the development of large bureaucracies that were sometimes unwieldy and unresponsive to citizens' complaints and suggestions. While welfare-state programs helped alleviate the incidence and repercussions of the boom-and-bust aspects of the business cycle, they were relatively ineffectual in moderating the demands of capital for increased profits and growth. The rich got richer, the working classes and the poor got poorer, and the middle class struggled to maintain its position. Entrepreneurs and the corporate sector resented having to adopt regulations governing the workplace and product reliability, as well as practices providing equal access and equal benefits through universally applied programs like the Canada Health Act. And they were concerned that the increasing cost of such a system would ultimately force them to share a much greater tax burden than they had previously.

In the 1980s and 1990s, powerful business interests moved to support pressure groups and political parties that were committed to dismantling much of the welfare state. These forays into agenda-setting have been considerably successful. Consequently, both socialism and reform liberalism have recently been upstaged by neo-conservatism and neo-liberalism. Neo-liberals advocate smaller government and a return to many of the original principles of liberalism, as well as a reliance on market activity and corporate decision making. Neo-conservatives place a similar economic emphasis on marketizing and privatizing, but also promote what they feel is a need to recapture "traditional values," bringing religion back into public life and focusing on public order and discipline. In two studies of Canada's political economy published in the nineties, Linda McQuaig, an investigative reporter and political analyst, has argued, based on a great deal of supporting evidence, that these departures from reform liberalism represent a rejection of some elements of mutual respect and equality.[7]

The tension that neo-conservatives sometimes feel between a belief in mutual respect on the one hand and the perception that there is too much government intervention to promote it on the other erupted in a showdown in the Reform Party at the end of April 1996. Reform party MP Bob Ringma remarked that it is acceptable for a business person to move an employee whose colour or sexual orientation offends a customer to "the back of the shop." Another Reform MP, Dave Chatters, expressed similar views, and in the resulting furor Reform Party Leader Preston Manning suspended both MPs from his caucus. On May 6, Manning issued a statement defending equality and respect and inviting those who rejected these values to leave the party. He said that the Reform Party affirms "equality and tolerance, but we have done so too weakly ... It is because we have individual members who either do not agree with this principle or do not understand what it truly means when applied to real-life situations ... The party can no longer be placed in the position of defending ... situations that undermine the important principles of equality and respect for individuals. More importantly, if there are members who at the end of the day simply do not agree with these principles, they should leave the party, the sooner the better."[8] But it was MP Jan Brown, who had been suspended from the Reform caucus for her public criticism of Ringma and Chatters, who later quit the party. She apparently felt uncomfortable with the number of people in the party whom she perceived as having views similar to those of Ringma and Chatters who didn't quit. Ringma and Chatters have since been welcomed back into the caucus.

Many people tend to adapt various elements of ideologies to their own circumstances and hopes. We suspect that is the case with the Reform Party. The tension within and between political parties and among adherents of differing ideologies over the relative importance of mutual respect leads to various interpretations of that principle, and therefore, to different ethical judgements. But in our view, those for whom mutual respect is of little importance are unlikely to make consistent ethical judgements or conduct themselves in ways that are compatible with the needs of a democracy.

The practice of democracy is constantly changing. Representative democracy with a universal franchise is a relatively recent invention in human history. Its development coincided with the increasing importance of mutual respect in evolving liberal ideologies. But there is always a gap between ideals and practice, and this explains, in part, the fact that ethical practices do not always reflect the standard of mutual respect. As the protection of human rights and the maintenance of social obligations are taken more seriously, more attention ought to be devoted to ethics in government. It has only been since the enactment of the Charter of Rights and Freedoms that the creative energy of Canadian democracy has begun to focus on ethics issues, and so naturally there is still a lot of work to do. Democratic ethics concerns rights and responsibilities. A focus on the ethical misconduct of politicians examines the nature of abuses of the right to govern and derelictions of responsibilities to citizens.

Five Principles of Democracy

There are five principles of democracy that follow from mutual respect: social equality, deference to the majority, minority rights, freedom, and integrity. A familiarity with these principles provides a foundation for judging ethical behaviour in the public sphere and for resolving ethical dilemmas in a democratic context.

Social Equality

There is no doubt about the importance of social equality to Canada's political culture today. Although beliefs do not always translate into actions, and media stories about racism in police practices or sexism in the workplace are relatively frequent, the public's belief in social equality is probably at an all-time high.

The support for social equality can be traced in part to early liberalism, which advocated free and equal access to the marketplace by entrepreneurs, regardless of their social-class background. Although the early liberals felt that social class did not constitute a legitimate reason for limiting equality, they accepted the unequal position of women or men without property. But the rhetoric of equality that accompanied the campaign for commercial egalitarianism encouraged the lower classes to press for a broader application of equality. As Macpherson and others show, women and working-class men demanded equality in the right to vote and more equality in social and economic decision making than capitalism provided.[9] Ultimately, a more general application of the principle of equality transformed liberal societies into liberal democracies.

The equality principle in western political thought has been interpreted in a variety of different ways. The theories of equality can be divided roughly into two categories: formal equality and social equality. Formal equality, which has two aspects, is the narrowest approach. First, it suggests that those in similar situations should all be treated in the same way. For example, in 1973 the Supreme Court's decision in *Lavell* implied that as long as all Indian women in Canada are treated equally by the law, then the requirement of equality under the Canadian Bill of Rights is satisfied, even if Indian men receive more favourable treatment.[10] Second, formal equality emphasizes removing legal or institutional barriers to choice, but without providing the means to make choice a real possibility. Formal political equality grants everyone an equal right to vote and an equal right to stand for election. It does not guarantee everyone equal access to and influence on parliamentarians between elections. And unless one has the time, experience, and money, the chances of participating meaningfully as a candidate for election are slim. Formal legal equality and its limitations can be exemplified by a simple scenario: In a society that prohibits religious, racial, or sexual discrimination, everyone has the right to register at a first-class hotel. But of course the right does not mean much to those who cannot afford to stay at hotels. Much like the universal right to spend the night under a bridge, only some will avail themselves of the opportunity.

Theories of social equality begin with the assumptions that all human beings deserve to be treated respectfully as equals and that the real-life situations of disadvantaged groups need to be considered to ensure that equality is not just a hollow promise. There are many variations of this theory, ranging from those that propose only slight adjustments to the rules of formal equality to ensure equal opportunity to those that advocate affirmative action programs to encourage groups that have been the victims of unfair discrimination.[11]

The Supreme Court's decision in *Lavell* was vehemently attacked in the law journals for its narrow approach to equality, and after the Charter of Rights and Freedoms came into effect, the Court rejected formal equality and adopted social equality as a means of interpreting the Charter.[12] The Supreme Court's preference for social equality over formal equality appears to reflect the views of many Canadians today. A survey of the attitudes of Canadians toward civil liberties conducted by Peter Russell and others in the late 1980s found that 72 per cent of Canadians disagreed with the statement, "Some people are better than others," and 73 per cent disagreed with the proposition that "all races are certainly not equal."[13] There is undoubtedly much greater support for social equality in Canada today than there was several decades ago.

This concern with equality may be in part a response to the media coverage of the civil-rights movement in the United States and recent movements in Canada that have advocated equality of treatment for women, visible minorities, the disabled, and the elderly. It may also reflect the emphasis that liberal ideology has placed on a broader notion of equality since the late 1800s and which was furthered by the socialist movement in this century.[14]

Consistent with this trend, the wording of the equality clause in the 1982 Charter of Rights and Freedoms was an attempt to broaden the scope of legally enforceable equality provisions in Canada, expanding the more limited provisions in the 1960 Canadian Bill of Rights. In particular, section 15(1) of the Charter guarantees the "equal benefit of the law," which according to Bayefsky makes it one of the most far-reaching equality clauses of any modern bill of rights.[15]

Although there is an increased demand for and acceptance of practices that promote greater social equality, there is certainly no general consensus about how far social equality should go. The 1996 debate in the House of Commons over extending the protection of the Canadian Human Rights Act to homosexuals testifies to this lack of consensus. Such issues as pay equity, compulsory retirement, the segregation of juvenile sporting associations according to gender, and discriminatory auto-insurance rates have sparked controversy over how social equality should be implemented. The issue of government contracts and appointments could be added to this list. Should decisions be made impartially, that is, based on equal opportunity modified by merit, or should supporters of the party in power be given preference, and if so, in which situations? Although many of our governments in Canada are led by decision makers who believe that economic efficiencies should take priority over measures to lessen social inequalities and that moves toward greater equality are "too costly" at the present time, the overall trend in public expectations and attitudes seems to be an acceptance of higher levels of social equality.

With regard to gender equality, public officials have an ethical responsibility to treat women and men with equal concern and respect. There are a number of obstacles that stand in the way of this ideal. There remains a lingering legacy of earlier generations of men who considered themselves superior to women. This attitude has led not only to a tendency to pay men more for doing the same work as their female counterparts, but to various forms of unequal treatment in the political arena, from the near-absence of washrooms for women in many legislative buildings and court houses to a shortage of day-care facilities for parents who enter public life. The failure of too many men to accept an equitable share of the responsibility for child care has had a profound effect on the career opportunities for women in public life — both in elected and appointed positions. And masculine stereotypes of expected behaviour continue to dominate theories of political interaction, from international relations to domestic party politics. When "manly" virtues are emphasized in politics, as they are in competitive sports, the result is that women are discouraged from participating and encouraged to remain on the sidelines.[16]

Ethical politics clearly requires the full participation of women, as equals, in public life. However, this important and complex issue, like debates about ethical social or economic policy, cannot be adequately addressed within the framework of this book, which focuses on the conduct of politicians and the procedures that need to be followed to avoid abuses of power.

Sexual practices become relevant to the public sphere whenever public officials attempt to use their office to obtain sexual favours or as a safe haven for sexual harassment. The former Speaker of the Ontario Legislature, Al MacLean, resigned in October 1996 after allegations that he had misused his position for sexual considerations. Although the facts of this case were still in dispute at the time of writing, there is no dispute about whether sexual harassment is ever ethically acceptable.

The greater emphasis that the Canadian public has placed on social equality during the past few decades may explain why Canadians seem to be more concerned than ever before not only about gender-related breaches in political ethics, but about a whole spectrum of issues. In the past, if ministers exercised discretionary powers to reward their friends (personal and political), their relatives, or themselves, such practices were tolerated, if not applauded, as the inevitable consequences of the political process. Today, however, with less tolerance for the unequal distribution of benefits under the law, Canadians are less complaisant about such practices.

Deference to the Majority

The principle of mutual respect suggests that everyone in a particular community should have an equal opportunity to participate in community decision making. In small communities, decisions reached by consensus once everyone has had a chance to be heard make the most sense. The consensus approach has for centuries been an important part of the decision-making process in the democratic aboriginal communities of North America.[17] In most Canadian communities that are small enough to be governed by all their members, consensus decision making occurs naturally — for example, in families, parent associations in small schools, in academic departments, and in small churches, synagogues, or mosques. But when disagreements cannot be resolved through discussion and compromise, a majority vote is a fair, though not ideal, way of settling the issue. It is fair because everyone in the community has an equal right to vote. It is not ideal because the worth and dignity of the losers in a vote are sometimes treated as inferior to those of the winners.

Most communities are too large for consensus decision making about all issues, and the solution is to provide for intermittent elections to select community representatives for making decisions as trustees. From an ethical perspective, both the elections and the subsequent decision-making process must demonstrate mutual respect.

Deference to the majority is not as simple as "majority rule." Every effort must be made to find a broad consensus. When a consensus is not possible, then from a practical perspective the issue should be settled by a majority vote. But representatives must be selected fairly, and they need to be in a position to make fair decisions. Fairness means that speakers from all sides have a right to be heard, that the decision makers are not in a position to benefit personally (i.e., are not in a conflict-of-interest situation), that undue influence — pressure contrary to democratic principles — is not brought to bear on decision makers, and that no decision violates the basic principles of democracy. This latter point means that in order to treat minorities in representative systems with equal respect, their "rights," or their basic entitlements in a democracy, must be protected.

Minority Rights

Even when minorities are on the losing side of an issue, they still have the right to be treated with equal concern and respect. There is a tendency for majorities to forget about respect for minorities in their haste to achieve their goals, and so all democracies have developed mechanisms to remind us of our philosophic commitment to respect minorities. In Canada, these safeguards are to be found in the Canadian Charter of Rights and Freedoms, the Canadian Bill of Rights, the various provincial bills of rights, and the federal and provincial human rights acts. Minority rights are also reflected in parliamentary and legislative rules and conventions. The rules of debate and the practice of providing major opposition parties with official status and research resources are all intended to allow the opposition a full hearing.

Human rights legislation is an attempt to list the most important ways in which all members of society and in particular minorities and the less advantaged deserve to be treated with equal concern and respect. For example, the Charter of Rights highlights fundamental freedoms (freedom of religion, expression, and assembly), the democratic rights to vote and run for office, legal rights such as the right to counsel, to fundamental justice, and to an independent and impartial judge, and the right to equality without discrimination. The rights to use and to be educated in the English and French languages receive special treatment, and there are some safeguards for aboriginal rights and for the right to move within Canada for employment purposes.

The protection of minority rights is central to ethical politics, as the principle of mutual respect invests citizens in a democracy with a duty to ensure that minorities are treated with the same respect as majorities. The Charter of Rights confers a duty on all public officials — elected and appointed — to respect the rights listed in it. Failure to do so is a breach of the constitution as well as an ethical lapse.

One of the more interesting features of the Charter is section 1, which guarantees the rights set out in the Charter "subject only to such reasonable limits prescribed by law as can be demonstrably justified in a free and democratic society." The Supreme Court has decided that a law that violates a Charter right can survive only if the law has an important objective in a democratic context, if it sets out to achieve that objective rationally, if rights are limited as little as necessary to achieve that objective, and if the law overall does more good than harm.[18] Public officials have an ethical duty to undertake this kind of analysis whenever they are considering a policy that might interfere with a Charter right. Unfortunately, there is a temptation to avoid that ethical responsibility by trying to "Charter-proof" a law — that is, to devise a plan to prevent a Charter challenge rather than to take minority rights seriously.[19]

Freedom

Mutual respect accords individuals the right to make their own decisions about how to conduct their lives. Limits are placed on various freedoms only to help attain the higher goal of mutual respect.

Clearly, the plethora of federal, provincial, and municipal laws and regulations and the taxes we pay to support the programs authorized by these laws place important qualifications on our freedom. These qualifications fall into three general categories: negative restrictions designed to prevent harm to others (for example, the Canadian Criminal Code, the provincial Highway Traffic Act, and some municipal parking by-laws); positive measures designed to promote equality of opportunity (for example, medicare, social welfare entitlements, fair-trade laws, education systems, and libraries); and taxation requirements to pay for these programs.

Decisions about the extent to which it is necessary to limit freedom are difficult ones, but they always boil down to the question of how best to advance the ideal of mutual respect. Ronald Dworkin contends that in cases where claims to liberty and equality conflict, freedom must yield to equality.[20] A public official behaves ethically when considering limits to freedoms by seriously considering how mutual respect is best advanced. But if freedoms are limited for other reasons — for example, for administrative convenience or to provide special benefits to some at the expense of others — then freedom is limited in an unethical fashion.

Freedom of Expression

Although citizens in a democracy enjoy many freedoms, one that is central is freedom of expression. This freedom is a good in itself, but it also promotes mutual respect. In addition, full public discussion of issues is essential for the machinery of democracy to work. According to John Stuart Mill, Jean-Jacques Rousseau, and Carole Pateman, public debates about important issues help citizens to understand others' points of view and to enter into the kind of compromises necessary for democracy to function. Mill argues that an open dialogue about contentious subjects, in which no points of view are suppressed, is the most likely to lead to reasoned, enlightened policy choices.[21]

The right to freedom of expression is exercised only to the degree that Canadians permit and promote full and free public discussion of events and issues. Two recent major political cover-ups provide examples of the suppression of public discussion. The first is the Somalia affair. In 1993, members of the Canadian Airborne Regiment murdered a civilian whom they had captured while they were on a humanitarian mission in Somalia. Subsequently, according to testimony before a public inquiry into these events conducted by Mr.

Justice Gilles Letourneau, senior officials in the Canadian Armed Forces and the Defence Department ordered the destruction of official documents that would have shed light on the circumstances surrounding the killings.[22]

The second cover-up is the "bingogate" affair. From 1983 on, the Nanaimo Commonwealth Holding Society, a registered charity in British Columbia, raised money from bingos and other activities and then allegedly channelled as much as $200,000 into the local and provincial NDP organizations. Disturbing as the allegation itself was, of even greater concern to B.C. voters was what appeared to be an attempt in 1995 by NDP Premier Michael Harcourt and his cabinet to cover up the facts.[23] Even more troubling was the fact that the bingogate cover-up was not unique. In another instance the government tried to conceal the existence of its contract with a U.S. public-relations firm by routing payments through a B.C. firm.[24] These alleged cover-ups led to Harcourt's resignation as premier and his replacement by Glen Clark, who was able to distance himself from the incidents in time to narrowly win the 1996 B.C. election. Nevertheless, allegations of another cover-up continue to dog the Clark government. During Clark's election campaign, he maintained that the NDP government had managed to balance the budget in spite of protecting social spending. Shortly after the election, the finance minister admitted that in fact there was a deficit because the economy had not performed as anticipated, and so tax revenues were down. If this information was available during the election campaign, then Clark had an ethical responsibility to disclose it, but he claims that he was not aware of the deficit until after the election.

Those who have intentionally tried to prevent relevant information from entering the public realm have failed to live up to their ethical responsibilities as citizens of a democracy. Of course, it is human nature to try to cover up embarrassing incidents. These cover-ups often occur almost automatically, without any thought given to the ethics of the situation and with little concern about the consequences. This tendency can be combatted to the extent that public officials are able to reason through a personal ethical position. Because ethics has been neglected by most political scientists up to now, unfortunately, little effort has been made to think through these kinds of ethical dilemmas.

One of the safeguards of democratic government is the principle of openness or transparency. All information collected by governments should be open to the public — both because of the potential usefulness of much of this information, and to prevent corruption — except for information that for good reason should be kept private, such as individual health or financial records. During the 1980s and 1990s, the federal government and several provincial governments enacted freedom of information and privacy laws to further the complementary ethical principles of openness and privacy. In Alberta, the ethics commissioner is also the freedom of information and privacy commissioner.

But mutual respect as applied to freedom of expression implies more than simply getting all relevant facts about a public issue out into the open, and then carrying on a responsible public debate about those facts. The process of public debate itself needs to demonstrate a concern for mutual respect. The Supreme Court has found that Canadian anti-hate laws represent a reasonable limit to freedom of expression, in part because messages of hate violate the fundamental principle of equal concern and respect. The rules of debate in Parliament and Canadian legislatures are intended to promote an atmosphere of mutual respect. Unfortunately, this ideal has been buried in an avalanche of political self-interest. In his 1994–95 Annual Report, Ontario's integrity commissioner, Gregory Evans, wrote:

> My previous experience as a judge conducting judicial business in a courtroom where a certain decorum is demanded and a sense of dignity prevails, did not prepare me for the raucous behaviour in the Legislature which through the medium of television invades private living rooms ... [A former cabinet minister told me] it's just like a 'game.' I did not agree ... Most observers would welcome some flashes of wit and humour, some overheated rhetoric, and verbal jousting, if they were not carried to the extent that it interfered with the business of the Assembly ... Why provide a fertile field for the critics and the cynics?[25]

On November 1, 1995, Ian Greene testified before the Joint Committee of the Senate and House of Commons on a Code of Conduct, the committee charged with recommending an appropriate code of ethics for MPs and senators. Greene's main point was that ethical standards in politics are based on mutual respect. Having just witnessed a particularly stormy question period in the House of Commons prior to the committee meeting, he asked how the committee members could develop a meaningful code of conduct if they could not even treat each other with respect during a debate.[26] After the committee hearing, a committee member who had been a teacher said she was deeply embarrassed by the example — or lack of one — that members were setting for visiting school classes about the workings of democracy. And a Reform party MP was reminded of one of his original reasons for running for office: to bring some decorum to question period. The problem was, he said, that without participating in the vitriolic exchanges in the House, the Reform party did not get much television coverage. And without television coverage, their popularity ratings plummeted. This brings us to the question of the media and ethics.

In one of Canada's most famous judicial decisions, the media were described as "the breath of life for parliamentary institutions."[27] We rely on the media to provide us with the information we need for informed public debate about important public issues. We expect political news coverage to be comprehensive, balanced, accurate, and impartial.

Without media that are ethical and ethically attentive, it is difficult to have ethical politics. Most media outlets have codes of ethics for their journalists that stress impartiality in presenting news events and that prohibit conflicts of interest. Although many journalists take these codes seriously, they are often written in very general language and could be interpreted in widely different ways. As well, the media codes have yet to tackle some of the more difficult issues related to the impartial reporting of the news.

For example, impartiality is sometimes simplistically assumed to consist of presenting two different perspectives about the same issue. More moderate and balanced positions are often neglected. The emphasis on the entertainment value of a news story and the pressure to compete with other media outlets for readership or viewership can lead to subtle pressures to distort an issue. As well, some visible minorities claim that the news coverage of their community is biased either because there are not enough journalists from their community, or because a media outlet may be catering to the biases of the majority community. And other groups, such as gays, lesbians, and labour, sometimes claim that the media ignores events that are of concern to them.

Another problem is that the television news format, which most Canadians rely on for their understanding of public affairs, has severely limited the depth with which most issues can be treated. We were once contacted by a national television news program to provide background on one of the conflict-of-interest laws introduced into the House (but never passed) during the latter years of the Mulroney government. In the end, the correspondent handling the story concluded that the issues were too complex for the forty-five seconds he had been allotted, and so he decided to treat the event as a story about the "posturing" of the Mulroney government.

The media's tendency to comment incessantly on the "posturing" of politicians instead of analyzing the substance of public issues is targeted by James Fallows, the *Atlantic Monthly*'s Washington editor. He attributes the propensity of journalists to comment on political manoeuvres and avoid the analysis of issues to two factors: a lack of in-depth knowledge about public issues on the part of many reporters, and the widespread habit of imitating the most prominent journalists.[28] As a result, important public issues are not examined in depth, and therefore informed public debate is increasingly rare. And because of the importance of media coverage to political fortunes, politicians often feel forced to take a policy position that is likely to receive media attention rather than one that might be more thoughtful, nuanced, and fair.

Another potential threat to impartial news coverage is the concentration of media ownership. Even if the owners of newspaper chains such as Thomson and Southam exert no influence whatsoever over editorial policy or the impartiality of news coverage, the economies of scale that affect a chain's operation surely have an impact on the dissemination of a wide range of points of view. Rick Salutin, who held the Maclean Hunter chair in ethics in communications at Ryerson Polytechnic University for two years, claims that to most journalists, media ethics consists of "niggling personal dilemmas about whether to use sources or photos ... They eliminate the larger ethical context — the *social* ethics involved — that in their case includes questions about media ownership by a few individuals and corporations and the effect this has on the moral health of our polity ... [Media ethics ought to be] about respect for people, not about playing "Gotcha!" and it's inevitably tied to the state of justice in your whole society."[29]

Although this book focuses on ethical issues that impinge directly on politicians, it should not be forgotten that politicians and the media have a symbiotic relationship, and the ethical standards in one domain will always have a profound influence on the other. David Olive writes that in Washington, journalists "who condemn rampant influence-peddling ... accept undisclosed gifts and fat speaker's fees from groups seeking to influence pending legislation. Celebrity columnists and reporters hide behind anonymous sources of dubious credibility when imparting unverifiable 'truths' … Dialogue is fabricated when transcripts are not at hand, in order that high-ranking officials can be depicted as profane and ridiculous."[30] Any comprehensive attempt to raise ethical standards in politics is bound to fail unless there is a concurrent reform of ethical standards in the media.

Respect for freedom is clearly an essential ingredient of mutual respect, of which freedom of expression and freedom of the media are important elements. Nevertheless, in a democracy, freedom needs to be exercised with ethical responsibilities in mind.

Integrity

Integrity is honesty modified by concern and respect for our fellow human beings. As Stephen Carter puts it, "one cannot have integrity without being honest … but one can certainly be honest and yet have little integrity."[31] For example, a party could make a campaign promise that it would fight crime by doubling the sentences available under the Young Offenders Act and making them mandatory. If the party is elected and follows through with its promise, we would consider it honest. But many studies show that young offenders learn how to become better criminals in the places where they are incarcerated, and the longer they are jailed, the more effective they are as criminals when released. If party officials were aware of these studies and admitted their credibility but ignored them in order to gain easy votes, then these officials would lack integrity.

Telling a lie is dishonest. But telling the whole truth at every possible moment does not necessarily constitute acting with integrity. We all face situations where we must be the bearers of distressing news. But we can often choose the time and the circumstances for presenting the news to maximize the respect we can show for the recipient. Carter mentions the case of a husband, on his deathbed, admitting to his wife that he had extra-marital sex.[32] This admission might have made the husband feel the virtue of his honesty for a few minutes, but it would fill the rest of the wife's life with needless distress.

So integrity is actually a complex ideal, closely related to the political problem of "dirty hands." In a dirty-hands situation, a public official knowingly does something dishonest but justifies this action as being in the public good. Although it may sometimes be necessary during wars and other emergencies for public officials to act dishonestly in order to advance the public good, at no time can dirty-handed actions be justified as ethical in a peace-time democracy. Public officials may try to rationalize their dishonesty for several reasons. First, they may lack the creativity needed to resolve a difficult situation with integrity. Second, public officials may learn to act according to the norms of the political culture they find themselves in, and the Canadian political culture often justifies dirty-hands actions as necessary when, in fact, they are not. In other words, if everybody seems to do it, it's OK. Third, integrity demands courage: dirty-hands solutions are often easier, and sometimes less risky, than ethical solutions.

Integrity often arises as an issue in election campaigns. Not infrequently, a political party will make election promises, only to break them once elected. The flip-flop of the federal Liberal party on replacing the GST (Goods and Services Tax) after the 1993 election is only the most recent example of this tendency. In some cases, such scenarios represent dirty-hands problems: party loyalists feel so strongly that their party needs to be in power for the public good that they are willing to make irresponsible promises to win. In many cases, however, promises are made on the basis of an insufficient understanding of an issue, and it is not until after the election that party loyalists, provided with comprehensive information, realize that fulfilling a particular promise would be bad public policy. Certainly, political parties should be held accountable for breaking promises. But integrity is sometimes better served when a party admits it was wrong and breaks a promise, than when it proceeds to implement a promise that it has discovered would lead to harmful results.

Another complicating factor is that few people who vote for a particular party support every single plank on the party's campaign platform. Moreover, studies of voting behaviour show that most voters base their decisions on factors other than the party's policy, such as the personal attributes of the the leader and local candidates, and very few voters are aware of more than one or two of the issues forming a party's campaign.

In early 1996, Sheila Copps resigned as deputy prime minister and as the MP for Hamilton-Mountain because she had made a categorical promise during the 1993 federal election campaign to resign if the Liberal party did not abolish the GST. After 1993, the Liberal government had come to believe that in spite of problems with the GST, there was no better tax to produce the kinds of revenues the government needed to reduce the deficit. During the week before her resignation, Copps made light of her 1993 promise as simply being an example of her "big mouth." In the subsequent by-election, Copps was re-elected, but she talked very little about the GST, and she garnered a lower level of support than in 1993.

The Copps case illustrates the kinds of complex ethical issues often associated with an integrity question in politics. If Copps's 1993 promise was an example of dirty-handed politics, then we would have to assume that she made this promise to get votes, even though she knew that abolition of the tax was doubtful. On the other hand, as seems more likely, she may have believed sincerely that the Liberal party *would* abolish the GST once in office. From this perspective, Copps acted with integrity by resigning, although making light of this promise during the week prior to her resignation certainly did not show integrity.

What are we to make of Copps's original promise to resign if the GST was not abolished? We could argue that politicians who promise to resign if their election promises are not kept act with integrity; after all a promise is a promise. But it may be that Copps and the Liberal party made their promise to replace the GST on the basis of insufficient information, which was irresponsible and therefore not ethically sound: taxation policy is certainly one of the most complex of public-policy fields, and Copps and her party erred in treating it so simplistically. In interviews after her by-election win in June 1996, Copps said as much. But the replacement of the GST was so central to the Liberal platform that from an ethical perspective, the Liberal government ought to have obtained the electorate's permission to be released from the promise. This could occur through a referendum, or through a debate about the GST in a subsequent general election. From our perspective, Copps should have requested her constituents' permission during the by-election to be released from her promise. By ducking the GST issue during the by-election, she also avoided confronting the question of integrity.

In contrast to Copps, John Nunziata, the Liberal MP for York South-Weston, was dismayed that his government broke its promise to replace the GST. In protest, he voted against the budget in April 1996. His explanatory letter to Prime Minister Jean Chrétien said that the Liberal party's promise was "clear and unequivocal and I truly believe that we as a government are now in danger of breaching a fundamental trust ... Lack of honesty and integrity was one of the factors which contributed to the demise of the previous governments. ... I believe we will have to fight the next election with our own integrity in question."[33] For taking this stand, Nunziata was removed from the Liberal caucus.

The integrity of election promises is an important and difficult ethical problem. Two things lessen the likelihood of parties and candidates landing in hot water. First, parties should not make promises unless the implications of those promises are thoroughly researched. Promising to do one's best to promote particular goals is both more honest and more realistic. Second, the integrity of election promises should be addressed in a party's code of ethics.

We argue that the political institutions and practices in a democracy need to focus on the standard of mutual respect. Mutual respect implies social equality, deference to the majority, concern for minority rights, respect for freedom, and the pursuit of integrity in public life. These general principles mean that democracy cannot function without representative institutions that protect and promote both human rights and ethical political practices.

An ethical approach to democratic politics is one where political actors are expected to make principled decisions based on mutual respect. If they put personal gain or the interests of political friends ahead of the public interest, they have acted unethically by abusing the trust placed in them. Even if they behave dishonestly while believing their behaviour is in the public interest, there is an ethical lapse, at least in peace-time.

In the next chapter we show how mutual respect and the general principles of democracy are related to more specific ethical duties and the legal principles applicable to public administration.

2

Ethical Duties

The five key principles of democracy stemming from mutual respect — social equality, deference to the majority, minority rights, freedom, and integrity — imply certain ethical duties on the part of public officials. First, they have a responsibility to act as impartially as possible when carrying out a program established by law. Second, they are acting as trustees for the entire citizenry, and therefore they have a fiduciary responsibility not to abuse that trust. Third, they have a duty to account for their activities and decisions.

Impartiality

For our purposes, impartiality means a lack of bias in the decision-making process in a public organization. An impartial procedure is one where all parties to an issue have an opportunity to present their perspectives fully and where their views are considered in a fashion that is as free from bias as possible. Impartiality is a corollary of the basic principle of mutual respect, and it is implied by each of the five principles of democracy. Clearly, social equality demands the impartial treatment of everyone; deference to the majority combined with minority rights suggests that laws should be administered impartially; freedom means that public officials cannot interfere with the private lives of citizens except when authorized by laws applied impartially; and integrity denotes that public officials need to make an honest effort to act impartially. The right of those charged with offences to impartial treatment is essentially what the legal rights sections of the Charter are about — but the Charter represents the "entitlement" side of democracy. On the responsibility side, citizens, and in particular those entrusted with public office, have ethical duties to treat others impartially or fairly.

In 1993, Ontario Provincial Court Judge Walter Hryciuk made rude remarks about several women. A subsequent inquiry by Madam Justice Jean MacFarland recommended the judge's removal because Hryciuk's comments and behaviour made it impossible for him to be considered impartial toward women litigants or witnesses.[1] Similarly, in 1996 an investigating committee of the Canadian Judicial Council recommended that Quebec Superior Court Judge Jean Bienvenue be removed because during a sentencing procedure he remarked that women could "sink to depths to which even the vilest man could not" and that the Nazis killed Jews "in the gas chambers, without suffering."[2] The committee concluded that Bienvenue had failed to uphold the standards of impartiality expected of him. Bienvenue subsequently resigned, but Hryciuk did not and has won at the first stage of a judicial review of the recommendations of the MacFarland inquiry.

Although impartiality is a duty often associated with judging, it also applies more broadly to public officials as a result of the principles of democracy, but in different ways. Clearly, politicians do not have a duty to be impartial when arguing on behalf of their party platforms (although they have a responsibility to argue honestly); however, cabinet ministers have a duty to act impartially when administering the law, and MPs have a duty to represent their constituency impartially, rather than to act with bias in promoting the interests of just a few select constituents. In the Pearson Airport affair of 1993–96, members of both sides of the Senate violated the duty of impartiality when each side produced a biased report, which they tried to pass off as impartial.

Perhaps the greatest threat to the impartiality principle is patronage, the practice by some governments of providing special favours to their partisan supporters when making appointments or awarding contracts. Patronage became rampant in the United Kingdom and Canada after the introduction of cabinet government two centuries ago, and concurrently in the United States after the War of Independence. It provided an opportunity for those who had been powerless for years to take advantage of the potential spoils of office, but at the expense of those outside the party in power. Patronage was routed out of most parts of the public service in these countries during the last two decades of the nineteenth century and the first two decades of the twentieth century, although the habit is dying a slow death in parts of Atlantic Canada. Patronage remains a factor in provincial judicial appointments in the three maritime provinces and was an important component in federal judicial appointments at the trial-court level during the Mulroney period.[3]

At the upper levels of politics, patronage still plays an important role in all Canadian jurisdictions. One of the worst abuses concerns lucrative government advertising and public-relations contracts, which often go to firms with the appropriate political connections. In addition, there are the thousands of "order-in-council" appointments to supposedly independent boards and commissions. According to cherished Canadian political tradition, party supporters often end up filling these positions regardless of their qualifications both at the federal and provincial levels.

Patronage is so ingrained in the culture of Canada's political parties that it will take extraordinarily strong political will and careful planning to eliminate it altogether. But patronage, with very few exceptions, should yield to the criterion of impartiality. Patronage is simply a bad habit left over from the pre-democratic era.

Fiduciary Trust

Because public officials always act on behalf of the public, they are trustees of the public interest. A fiduciary relationship with the public is not a form of paternalism — we know what's best for you and it's too bad if you don't understand our superior wisdom — but rather a responsibility to protect and promote the public's best interests in ways the public is fully informed of and approves.

The Saskatchewan MLAs who participated in the expense-fund fraud abused the trust placed in them by the electorate. Mr. Justice Isadore Grotsky remarked in September 1995 in a judgement about one of the former members, "A Legislative Assembly comprised of members committed to the principles of honesty and integrity is fundamental to a democratic society as Canadians understand that term."[4] When public officials behave so as to undermine any of the fundamental principles of democracy, they abuse the standards of the trust relationship that is expected of them.

Accountability and Responsibility

The duty to be accountable means being able to demonstrate that the expectations of public office are being met. The most appropriate methods of accountability will vary from one situation to another, as Philip Stenning's book *Accountability for Criminal Justice* illustrates. For example, in a police force, line accountability up through a chain of command is quite effective. For judges, however, line accountability would violate judicial independence, and so accountability is achieved through such mechanisms as procedures for appointment and promotion, the moral suasion of the chief judges, judicial councils, courts advisory committees, continuing education, annual reports, and, of course, the delivery of reasoned public judgements.

Elected officials are accountable to their constituents at election time. In the parliamentary system the principles of responsible government provide a mechanism for continuous accountability. Responsible government is a convention, or a tradition that has attained the status of being part of the "unwritten" constitution. (Canada's constitution, or fundamental rules of government, is composed of written parts like the Charter of Rights and Freedoms, judicial decisions about constitutional interpretation, and conventions.) Responsible government has three aspects: ministerial responsibility, cabinet solidarity, and the rule that the cabinet can exercise power only so long as it maintains majority support in the legislature.

All three aspects of responsible government have ethical overtones. If a cabinet loses the support of the legislature in a vote of confidence and does not resign, it has behaved both unconstitutionally and unethically. It faces dismissal by the governor general or lieutenant-governor, as well as the likelihood of electoral defeat.

Ministerial responsibility means that cabinet ministers must take public responsibility for explaining the actions of officials in their departments (especially during question period), and they must resign if a serious administrative error has occurred in their department that they could have and should have prevented. Because the focus of accountability is on ministers, public servants can remain anonymous, meaning that they are not singled out for public blame. The purpose of public service anonymity is to encourage impartiality in public administration, as well as loyalty to the minister. If ministers avoid responsibility, as the federal solicitors general avoided responsibility for the RCMP's dirty tricks campaign in the 1970s and 1980s, or if ministers blame public servants instead of shouldering responsibility themselves, they have failed to act with integrity.

Cabinet solidarity means that the cabinet is collectively responsible for policy decisions. A minister who disagrees with any policy position adopted by the cabinet must resign, as did former Ontario cabinet minister Karen Haslam, who decided that she could not support the social-contract policy of the Bob Rae cabinet. Cabinet solidarity is intended to ensure that ministers will thoroughly debate all cabinet policies before they are agreed upon, because they realize that their personal political futures are intimately connected with the cabinet's collective position. To act with integrity, ministers must either do their best to explain cabinet policies to the public or resign.

Legal Principles

For the principle of mutual respect to inform the political process, ethics supports must be developed to facilitate its practice. These supports can take different forms — for example, constitutional conventions and traditions, rules of debate, legislation, or non-legislated codes of ethics. In the next chapter we'll consider ways to prevent three common types of unethical behaviour: patronage, conflicts of interest, and undue influence.

The specific supports that evolve to promote ethical politics are reflections of the general principles considered in Chapter 1 and the duties noted above. However, two important legal principles — the rule of law and the doctrine of fairness — help us to apply the general principles and duties. These legal principles help bring the general principles down to earth but are not enough by themselves to promote ethical politics. They must be buttressed and supplemented by ethics supports like conflict-of-interest rules.

The Rule of Law

The rule of law in Canada is a principle that reinforces the practice of mutual respect throughout society. In 1985, the Supreme Court of Canada described two aspects of the rule of law: a civilized community is governed by law rather than by the arbitrary decisions of public officials, and laws apply to public officials and institutions no differently than they apply to private individuals.[5] The rule of law means that a legal framework is provided for social co-operation, and everyone's conduct is subject to non-arbitrary regulation.[6] Public officials may exercise only the authority given to them by laws approved by representative legislatures and applied even-handedly to everyone. The rule of law emphasizes equality, in that everyone has the opportunity to participate in law making by voting or running for office. Furthermore, the equal application of the law helps protect minority rights.

Important as this principle has been to the unwritten part of Canada's constitution since 1867, it wasn't until the proclamation of the Charter of Rights and Freedoms in 1982 that our constitution effectively associated the rule of law with democracy. The preamble to the Charter recognizes the rule of law as a founding principle of Canada. Furthermore, the Charter itself makes it clear that any deviations from the equal-application principle, such as restricting the right to vote to those over eighteen, or prohibiting those without driver's licences from operating motor vehicles, must not only be clearly spelled out in law, but also be justifiable as reasonable in a free and democratic society.[7]

John Locke, the most prominent of the early supporters of liberalism, argued in 1690 that a reasonable government would exercise power not through

> extemporary arbitrary decrees, but ... by promulgated standing laws, and known authorized judges ... [The laws are] not to be varied in particular cases, but [there should be] one rule for rich and poor, for the favorite at court, and the countryman at plough.[8]

Locke argued that the rule of law is meaningless unless the law is applied impartially. The executive branch of government — the cabinet and the public service — is responsible for carrying out programs approved by the legislature, and the judicial branch is responsible for settling disputes over how the law is to be applied and interpreted. Locke stressed the importance of an impartial application of the law by the executive and judicial branches in order to protect the supremacy of laws approved by elected legislatures. He wrote that any activity involving the application of law requires impartiality. Thus, society needs unbiased judges and administrators.

Three hundred years later, some progress has been made toward the achievement of Locke's prescription for impartiality in liberal societies, but more so in the judiciary than in the executive branch of government. Ironically, the slower progress in the latter area can be attributed, in part, to the advent of responsible government in countries such as Canada, which have adopted parliamentary institutions. Responsible government means that the cabinet must be selected from the party with the greatest number of seats in the legislature and must continue to have majority support from the legislature in order to stay in power.

Responsible government came about in the United Kingdom around the middle of the eighteenth century. In a sense, it represented a step backwards for the impartiality principle, because it established the notion that the cabinet would necessarily be partisan. David Smith claims that through responsible government political parties gained more opportunities to reward their supporters and to provide them opportunities to use public office to achieve personal goals.[9]

At the same time, however, the judiciary was becoming more independent from the rest of government, and the principle of judicial impartiality was becoming more entrenched. The eighteenth-century French political scientist, Baron de Montesquieu, noted these developments and described the United Kingdom somewhat misleadingly as having three distinct branches of government — legislative, executive, and judiciary — each acting as a check on the other.

Montesquieu's observations were influential insofar as impartiality came to be associated primarily with the judicial branch of government. But the common-law doctrine of fairness serves as a reminder that, according to the rule of law, the executive branch also has an ethical responsibility to generate impartial decisions about how the law is to be applied and implemented.

The Doctrine of Fairness

The doctrine of fairness is a common-law rule that assigns all public officials, including cabinet ministers, the duty to act impartially when making administrative decisions. It was developed by the Supreme Court of Canada beginning in 1979 as an elaboration of the principle of the rule of law.

The doctrine of fairness is based on the older common-law principle of natural justice. Natural justice is derived from the rule of law; it holds that those coming before a judicial or administrative tribunal must be given a fair hearing, which means that the judge or tribunal must be impartial and must provide opposing litigants with the opportunity to explain their views fully. Natural justice is sometimes referred to as fundamental justice. Section 7 of the Canadian Charter of Rights and Freedoms states that the rights of Canadians to life, liberty, and security of the person cannot be interfered with "except in accordance with the principles of fundamental justice."

According to the common law, judges and members of administrative tribunals must fulfil the following three criteria in order to be considered impartial:

- they cannot be in a position to gain financially from one of their decisions;

- they cannot be in a position to favour people who are or were closely associated with them;

- if they have previously expressed views that indicate that they cannot reasonably be expected to apply a particular law even-handedly, they should disqualify themselves.

David P. Jones and Anne de Villars describe these three criteria as the "rule against bias." At one time or another, most Canadian judges have disqualified themselves from hearing a particular case because they feared that they might appear biased from the perspective of one of the litigants before them.[10]

According to the Supreme Court doctrine of fairness, all public officials who make decisions about the application of the law must be impartial, and the three aspects of the rule against bias that apply to judges also apply to administrators to whatever extent is reasonable. Reasonableness is determined by the judiciary on a case-by-case basis. The doctrine of fairness applies to cabinet ministers when they act as administrators of the law, but not when they act as legislators and policy makers.[11]

The courts have applied the doctrine of fairness to decision making by public officials in a number of cases since 1979, but very few cases have involved cabinet decisions, since cabinet decisions are rarely challenged in court. One of the few cases involving ministers of the crown was a 1981 decision in which the Supreme Court of British Columbia reviewed a cabinet decision that had overturned the decision of a provincial licensing commission.[12]

It is useful to consider how the doctrine of fairness applies, in theory, to public officials. The first aspect of the rule against bias — not being in a position to gain financially from a public-office decision — is clearly relevant to all administrative decision making by cabinet ministers and other public officials. This principle is reflected in the conflict-of-interest rules covering cabinet ministers, other elected officials, and public servants in general. For example, Sinclair Stevens, the federal industry minister in 1986, and Bill Vander Zalm, the premier of British Columbia in 1990, were found by independent investigations to have been in situations where they could have used their public office for personal financial gain; this meant that they were guilty of violating conflict-of-interest rules. Both paid the ultimate political penalty and resigned from office in disgrace.

The second aspect of the rule against bias is the prohibition against providing favours to friends and former associates. According to J.O. Wilson, the rule against bias means that judges must disqualify themselves from making decisions in cases that involve family members, friends and former business associates.[13] In the case of cabinet ministers and public servants, this second rule implies that they should refrain from making any administrative decisions that could result in special privileges for their family members, business and professional associates, and friends. For example, Richard Le Hir, who was a Quebec cabinet minister in 1995, was forced by political circumstances to resign because the process he had approved for hiring persons to conduct studies on sovereignty was not impartial and resulted in many of the contracts being handed out to friends and business associates of the top bureaucrats in Le Hir's office.

Because many of a cabinet minister's friends and allies are members of the minister's political party, it makes sense that a minister should refrain from making administrative decisions that might benefit them. Unfortunately, many cabinet ministers don't see it this way, although the most principled of the ministers do try to avoid favouring friends and party members.

The third aspect of the rule against bias — disqualification for making biased statements — applies straightforwardly to non-elected public officials, but presents some difficulties for cabinet ministers. Cabinet ministers in the parliamentary system wear two hats: they are legislators when working on changes to laws and regulations, and they are administrators of the law when supervising their departments and making administrative decisions under the law. They are elected as legislators in part because of their positions on various issues, which are anything but impartial. It requires great skill for cabinet ministers to respect the rule of law when undertaking their ministerial duties and at the same time to be actively involved in changing the law as legislators.

The cabinet has a dual purpose: to administer existing programs established by law, and to attempt, through amending the law, to change these programs or to create new ones that reflect the party's platform. This dual role — and the failure of our political system to clearly establish how to resolve the conflicting expectations it creates — has left cabinet ministers unsure of how impartial they ought to be. This lack of clarity helps to explain why patronage, conflicts of interest, undue influence, and dishonesty are problems in a country that supposedly respects the rule of law.

The Arguments against an Ethics-based Approach

To some readers, our suggested theoretical approach to ethical politics may seem so straightforward as to be self-evident. But this is likely the case only with readers for whom the principle of mutual respect is important. Not everyone is so sanguine about this principle. Whenever an ethics-based approach to politics is discussed, certain familiar arguments criticizing or dismissing it inevitably come up.

The argument we hear most frequently goes something like this: "Most politicians are corrupt" or, more sympathetically, "are forced by the system to act in corrupt ways even if they begin with honest intentions." This view, which derives from modern cynicism, suggests that power by its nature corrupts those in public life, and it provides a rationale for dirty-handed politics.[14]

From our perspective, this view is insupportable. When clear ethical standards are in place, the evidence suggests that the majority of elected officials in Canada do behave ethically. The British Columbia ethics commissioner, Ted Hughes, remarked, "My experience with the seventy-five current members of the B.C. Legislature ... is that today we don't have a rogue amongst them. If that's so, I think that augurs well for the future because I'm satisfied that they all want to do the right thing and they've now got, with [the B.C. ethics] legislation, the assistance to make that possible."[15] The major problems up to now have been standards for ethical behaviour that are either non-existent or unclear, and a paucity of institutionalized mechanisms providing scrutiny of unethical conduct. Prior to the 1990 enactment of conflict-of-interest legislation in B.C. and Hughes's appointment as ethics commissioner, there had been seven major conflict-of-interest scandals in five years.

Another argument dismissing an ethics-based approach goes like this: because there is no absolute proof, scientific or otherwise, that mutual respect is better than any other basic value, politics is really just a game of wits. (This outlook is supported by some of the more radical theories of scepticism and, to some extent, by contemporary post-modernism.) It is true that in both science and philosophy there are no absolute proofs of anything, including our own existence; we simply make the most careful judgements possible given the best evidence available. But we believe there is overwhelming evidence that democratic government based on mutual respect is more satisfactory than any other form of government.

John Rawls has argued that if we could imagine a group of reasonable persons suddenly cut off from the rest of society, such
persons would invent a government based on mutual respect because
this principle would result in all of the individuals involved being
better off than in any other possible system where equality, liberty,
and justice are valued.[16] Another way of defending the primacy of
the principle of mutual respect can be called the "individual rights"
approach. From this perspective, individual rights are treated as
"natural" in the sense that persons have certain entitlements by virtue
of their humanity that are independent of any political agreements or
historical arrangements. The right to be treated as an equal, the right
to have one's autonomy respected, and the right to develop one's
uniquely human attributes in association with others are entitlements
fundamental to any moral order.

And for those who find comparative evidence more convincing
than theory, since 1989 the United Nations has rated all countries in
the world according to a "human development index," which takes
into account indicators of quality of life such as health, education,
and income. The democracies that value mutual respect are consistently at the top of the index (Canada has been ranked first four times
out of seven), while the corrupt dictatorships tend to be near the
bottom.[17]

In our experience, most politicians who engage in unethical behaviour are opportunists who see a chance for personal gain or an
occasion to help their political friends or their family. They simply
take advantage of the situation without thinking about it very much.
Sometimes they fall into what they consider to be the normal game
of politics, and at other times the temptation for personal enrichment
is just too overpowering. George Hees, a member of parliament for
thirty-seven years, a former president of the Progressive Conservative party, head of the Montreal Stock Exchange, and a cabinet
minister in both the Diefenbaker and Mulroney governments, admitted to a reporter:

> You ask any member why they're here and they'll tell you it's
> to serve the people. That's bull! ... They're here because of
> why we're all here. Because we're arrogant and full of our-
> selves, vain and ambitious ... I'll at least admit it.[18]

What is problematic and disconcerting about opportunists is that they
often believe that what they do is acceptable because competitive

politics is about ego gratification, the reach for personal advantage, and the dispensing of favours. From their perspective undue influence and conflicts of interest are pseudo-problems. Everyone is entitled to as much influence and advantage as he or she can grasp. Ayn Rand's ideology of objectivism, which glorifies self-centredness well beyond the limits of classical liberalism and neo-conservatism, is an attempt to provide a philosophical rationale for opportunism.

The trouble with opportunism and egoism is that in a world filled with egoists and opportunists, eventually everyone is victimized by someone else. Philosophers from Plato to Locke to Rawls have demonstrated that such a world would not be a pleasant place to live in except for a few, and even these few would have difficulty sleeping at night out of fear that their turn as a victim was coming. Like juvenile gang members, most opportunists haven't thought very much about consequences.

Making Ethical Judgements

When a public official is faced with an ethical dilemma, he or she should first consider whether it is a situation covered by the law. The law is a reflection of the public will and should be considered binding in nearly every case.

There are two exceptions. The first occurs when a law might violate the Charter of Rights or another part of the constitution, and in such a case the advice of the department's legal counsel should be sought. The second exception is a situation where the public official feels strongly that the law itself violates a higher moral principle. These circumstances are often exceedingly complex, as Kernaghan and Langford demonstrate, and public officials should be very cautious about substituting their own judgement for that of the legislature.[19] However, situations do occasionally arise where there is a legitimate conflict between a public official's ethical principles and a law. Fortunately, some government agencies now have ethics counsellors who can advise in such a situation. For example, a police officer opposed to abortion may object to an assignment to protect an abortion clinic. In that case, an ethics counsellor may be able to support the officer's request for a reassignment. Ordinary elected members very seldom face such dilemmas as they are more concerned with law making than law implementation.

Cabinet ministers, however, might sometimes have ethical qualms about the laws they are supposed to administer and when they do they have an ethical duty to raise the issue with their cabinet colleagues. For example, in 1972 ministers in the newly elected Lougheed government in Alberta realized that there was a fundamental conflict between their new human-rights legislation and the Communal Property Act of the previous Social Credit government that restricted land purchases by Hutterites. (The Hutterites are a communal religious sect that was unpopular among some rural Albertans, and the Social Credit government had enacted the restrictive legislation to appease these interests.) Faced with a law that breached the ethical principle of equality, the Lougheed government quickly moved to suspend the operation of the discriminatory legislation and then to repeal it.

The most common ethical dilemmas that elected officials face, however, are ones on which the law is silent. For example, until the 1980s and 1990s, Canadian law was almost entirely mute in regard to how elected officials should deal with conflicts of interest or potential undue influence from lobbyists.[20] There are still big gaps in the federal legislation concerning conflicts of interests and in provincial legislation concerning lobbyists. There are also weaknesses in laws regulating party contributions at all levels, and it is difficult to enforce integrity through the law alone. In cases that fall into these legal lacunae, public officials must go through a process of ethical reasoning to reach a satisfactory ethical solution.

On the surface, reasoning out an ethical dilemma appears quite simple. You take the situation in question and apply to it the principle of mutual respect and each of the five principles of democracy that follow from it. For example, we know of a candidate who contested the leadership of a provincial political party during the 1970s. He withdrew from the race prior to the convention — even when all indications were that he would win — because he objected to the conditions set by those funding his bid. We do not know the details of these conditions, but for the purposes of this example let us speculate that the prominent political family that funded the leadership bid expected the candidate, if he became premier, to appoint some members of the family and their friends to patronage positions and to arrange for some hefty provincial advertising contracts to be awarded to family businesses. An ethical reasoning process about whether to agree to these terms might run as follows:

- The conditions of the deal will not allow me to make decisions based on equal concern and respect, but will force me to show special consideration to the funders.

- The deal violates the principle of social equality because it will result in increased wealth and privilege for a family already considerably privileged.

- The family is not seeking to advance the welfare of the majority, but its own special interests, and it certainly does not form part of a disadvantaged minority.

- The principle of freedom in this instance does not seem to be directly relevant to the decision.

- It would be difficult for me to act with integrity were I to become premier and reward my funders as anticipated because I would not be able to announce the real reason behind the patronage appointments or the contracts.

- For all these reasons, it would be unethical to accept funding for my leadership bid with these particular conditions attached, and so unless other funding with no strings attached becomes available, I must withdraw from the leadership race.

In this case, the reasoning process led to a clear solution. But there are other situations where an ethical decision would be far more difficult. What if, in the above example, the wealthy family did not demand favours for itself, but rather a commitment to cut taxes and to support bilingualism? The reasoning process would be the same, but the result might be different depending on the candidate's evaluation of the impact of each relevant principle.

Let us take another example. Suppose a federal MP is deciding whether to support in a free vote special legislation to enable the construction of a toxic waste disposal plant in an adjacent constituency. The majority in the adjacent riding support the plan because of the economic benefits it will bring to the region, but a substantial minority — those living in close proximity to the proposed construction site — oppose the idea even though scientific studies indicate that the risk to health, at least in the short run, would be minimal. Those in the MP's own riding do not have opinions as strong as those in the adjacent riding, but a slight majority favours the plan because toxic waste now being stored in the riding could be eliminated. The ethical policy choice is not clear. None of the principles of democracy provide direct guidance, and the dilemma may well boil down to a choice between deference to the majority and minority rights.

In this case, reference to more elaborate theories of ethics might be helpful. The academic study of practical ethics has resulted in two main streams of thought: consequentialism and intentionalism. Consequentialist theorists, such as utilitarians, stress results over process. Utilitarianism is a variant of liberalism that was popularized and given a philosophical defence 140 years ago by the English philosopher, John Stuart Mill. It adopts a goal-oriented approach to ethical propriety whose chief aim and rationale for moral behaviour is the principle that individuals and institutions ought to contribute to the greatest happiness for the greatest number. A utilitarian "holds that actions are right in proportion as they tend to promote happiness, wrong as they tend to produce the reverse of happiness."[21] So the object of public policy is to increase the net benefits that are accruable to the greatest number of people.

Intentionalist theories consider that the individual worth of every human being is so important that commitments to beneficence and fair process are key to the duty of respecting each individual's moral autonomy. The will to do one's duty takes priority over a consideration of the results of one's actions or decisions. Both approaches are consistent with the principle of mutual respect, and in most day-to-day situations a consequentialist and an intentionalist would agree on what constitutes an ethical course of action in politics. There are some difficult and, fortunately, relatively rare situations where they would disagree, as the case of the proposed toxic waste plant illustrates. A consequentialist MP would likely support the plant, thinking of the overall benefits to the community, while an intentionalist would probably oppose it, placing a greater emphasis on the welfare of those living close to the plant. It should be stated here that where the two approaches conflict, our own preference is toward intentionalism, though we are acutely aware of the wisdom in the old adage that the road to hell is paved with good intentions. Nevertheless, we prefer intentionalism because its stress on the individual worth of all people seems more in accord with mutual respect than consequentialism.

We could make our example even more difficult by hypothesizing that the MP's sister-in-law had a financial stake in the proposed toxic waste plant. Would this relationship affect the MP's impartiality seriously enough to disqualify him or her from voting? (More details would be needed to answer that question properly.) Moreover, does the duty of fiduciary trust vested in the MP apply more strongly with regard to the MP's own constituents, or does the trusteeship relationship also extend to other Canadians? The MP's answer to that question would depend on his or her own thinking about the nature of mutual respect. What is important from an ethics perspective is that the MP has applied the relevant ethical principles to the best of his or her ability in deciding what to do. If the MP's party had a code of ethics, it might be helpful in resolving such dilemmas.

In the case studies mentioned in this book, we will apply the kind of ethical analysis described above. In some cases, ethical judgements seem straightforward and we do not hesitate to present our conclusions. In other cases, the ethical course of action is not so clear-cut, and we defer to the judgements of our readers.

Ethics Supports

A number of mechanisms have already been developed in Canada to promote ethics in politics. These ethics supports include conflict-of-interest legislation and codes of conduct, lobbyists registration legislation, party financing laws, and ethics commissioners. Contemporary ethical problems are reviewed in Chapter 3, and excerpts from legislation and codes in effect in British Columbia and Ottawa are included in Appendix II. Because so much attention has been focused on conflicts of interest in politics during the past decade, Chapter 4 is devoted to case studies of some high-profile conflicts of interest. The federal lobbyists registration legislation and party financing laws are covered in Chapter 5, and the emerging role of ethics commissioners is the topic of Chapter 6. In Chapter 7, we show that integrity is hard to legislate, and its abuse in the form of dirty-handed politics is difficult to detect. Therefore, a strengthening of ethics supports is required to promote integrity. In Chapter 8 we review and discuss the supports that need to be strengthened and added.

Figure 1
Principles and Duties in a Democracy

Fundamental Principle:	Mutual Respect		
General Principles:	Social Equality	Deference to the Majority	Minority Rights
		Freedom Integrity	
Ethical Duties:	Impartiality	Fiduciary Trust	Accountability and Responsibility
Legal Principles:	Rule of Law		Doctrine of Fairness
Ethics Supports:	Codes of ethics, ethics commissioners, ethics audits, official inquiries		Rules controlling patronage, conflicts of interest, lobbyists and party finances, whistleblowing, recall, referendums

Ethical Problems in Public Life

There are three main ethical problem areas in the public sector that are amenable to control through better legislation and enforcement procedures. These areas of concern are patronage, conflict of interest, and undue influence.

Patronage

Patronage — or the tendency of political parties to reward their friends and supporters, particularly those making large financial contributions to the party — became an established part of parliamentary systems as a result of responsible government. The obvious conflict between patronage and the rule of law was simply accepted as one of the many ways in which people paid lip service to a particular ethical principle, but in practice did something entirely different.

"Reinventing government" has become the catchword of public-sector reformers in the 1990s. These people would like to reform government bureaucracies, which they believe are expensive and inefficient. In this context, some may be surprised to learn that the first wave of "reinventing government," which occurred in the early part of this century, was a reaction to patronage, the class system, and the abuse of power in the public service. The new, reinvented organization was called a "bureaucracy."

In the early 1900s, the German social scientist, Max Weber, adapted the term "bureaucracy" to describe an ideal organization that maximizes efficiency, effectiveness, and fairness. The "bureaucratic revolution" that occurred in Canada beginning in the 1920s was the process of reforming a bloated and inefficient public service. This revolution was a response to several forces — the need for a more effective public service to deliver post-war programs, public pressure to spend tax dollars more efficiently, and the extension of the democratic franchise to include the poor and women. Grass-roots political movements, such as farmers' organizations, promoted the merit system for public service hirings because they believed the traditional patronage system worked primarily for the benefit of the rich. Reg Whitaker claims that big business also endorsed the merit system at this time out of fear that the newly enfranchised lower classes would use the patronage lever to hire and promote their friends.[1] For a few decades after these major reforms, bureaucracies proved their worth as bureaucratic organization greatly improved the efficiency and fairness of the public service, and the bureaucratic model was widely copied in the private sector. But in the second half of the twentieth century, many bureaucracies themselves became stale and inefficient, leading to the current move to "reinvent government" again.

It is important to understand the tremendous impact of the original bureaucratic revolution because it led to higher ethical standards in the public sector. According to Weber, the two basic principles of a bureaucracy are:

- hiring according to merit, instead of patronage or social-class privilege. This principle led to the establishment of federal and provincial public-service commissions to replace the patronage system for hiring public servants with a system based on merit;

- legally defined relationships between managers and their employees — job descriptions — to ensure managers would not abuse their power, to fairly measure the performance of employees, and to promote or demote employees according to objective criteria.[2]

Public-sector bureaucracies therefore emphasize the importance of the rule of law. Ideally, hiring and promotion in bureaucracies are conducted according to merit. Services are provided impersonally and equitably according to rules applicable to both "the favorite at court, and the countryman at plough," and not according to privileges stemming from patronage or social class.

When the bureaucratic reforms began, they affected primarily the lower echelons of the public service. At the cabinet level, ministers resisted giving up all the perks of public office. Federal and provincial cabinets maintained partisan control over the distribution of benefits from economic development programs, over contracts for some lawyers and other professionals, and the remaining discretionary appointments such as judgeships and positions on agency boards.

According to Whitaker, this meant that the benefits of patronage remained available "almost exclusively to people with professional or business qualifications."[3] This is still true in the 1990s.

Because of the uneven application of bureaucratic principles in the public service, public servants in permanent positions are expected to apply the law impartially and to provide equally good services to all members of the public. However, Canadian cabinet ministers have inherited a confusing array of expectations regarding impartiality. With respect to their responsibilities in the day-to-day activities of their departments, they clearly have a duty to act impartially pursuant to the rule of law and the doctrine of fairness. Yet with regard to the discretionary areas that escaped the reforms of the bureaucratic revolution and that are still open to patronage considerations, partisanship is not only accepted, but expected.

For example, one of the major issues during the 1984 federal election campaign was the hundreds of patronage appointments either made by Pierre Trudeau just prior to his leaving office or agreed to by the new Liberal leader, John Turner. According to Ross Howard, Trudeau made 172 appointments during his last month as prime minister. And on the day the election was called, Turner announced the appointment of seventeen Liberal MPs to patronage positions — the Senate, judgeships, and diplomatic posts.[4] During the 1984 election campaign Brian Mulroney loudly criticized the Liberals for this "shocking vulgarity," and he promised to clean things up. He promised to "bring in a brand-new dimension ... of objectivity and representation and fairness for all Canadians ... Our appointments shall be of the highest order ... and shall bring honour to our country."[5] But immediately after becoming prime minister, Mulroney established the most efficient system yet devised for filling the order-in-council positions with his own loyal party supporters. Many were cemented into their positions for up to ten years with a no-cut contract. One of the most widely noted appointments was that of Rinaldo Canonico, Mila Mulroney's hairdresser, to the board of the Federal Business Development Bank.[6]

At the federal level, there are over 2,500 order-in-council positions. These include appointments to the boards of Canadian National Railways, Petro-Canada, the Bank of Canada, and the CBC; as well as the Immigration and Refugee Board, various port commissions, the Canada Pension Commission, the RCMP Review Board, the Environmental Assessment Board, the National Parole Board, the provincial lieutenant-governorships, provincial superior and appel-

late court judgeships, the Federal Court, and the Supreme Court of
Canada. There is a thirty-year tradition of making non-partisan appointments to the Supreme Court of Canada, and two different kinds
of advisory systems have been in effect since the beginning of Pierre
Trudeau's prime ministership to help ensure better-quality appointments to the other courts, but these latter reforms have controlled
rather than eliminated patronage.

In an effort to distance herself from the organized patronage of
the Mulroney government, so thoroughly documented by both Jeffrey Simpson and Stevie Cameron,[7] Prime Minister Kim Campbell
advertised in the *Canada Gazette* for qualified applicants for many
of the order-in-council positions. Campbell lost the 1993 general
election before it was possible to make appointments under the new
system, but the Chrétien government used the Campbell system to
make its first batch of appointments in 1993 and 1994. The government received widespread praise — and took credit — for beginning
the hard process of replacing patronage at upper levels with merit-
based appointments. However, not much time passed before the
Liberal government seemed to be dabbling in patronage nearly as
much as its predecessor.

While a number of merit-based appointments were made as a
result of the *Canada Gazette* advertising, a parallel system of patronage appointments still operated, although Penny Collenette, the
prime minister's appointments secretary, has tried to ensure that
friends of the Liberal party who receive appointments are at least
qualified for their jobs. A well-publicized example of how the patronage system can trump the *Canada Gazette* system is the December 1993 appointment of Marian Robson, a loyal Liberal worker in
Vancouver, as the Pacific member of the National Transportation
Agency. The job had been advertised in the *Canada Gazette*, and at
least four applicants were short-listed and interviewed by members
of the National Transportation Agency. According to Edward Greenspon, Robson was never interviewed for the job, although she did
have a solid background in the transportation industry.

Brian Mulroney's appointments secretary has admitted that "in
some cases it was reward over competence" for Mulroney's patronage appointments.[8] A poignant example was the use of the Convention Refugee Determination Division (CRDD) of the Immigration
and Refugee Board by Brian Mulroney to reward faithful party
supporters. A 1991 study by the Law Reform Commission of Canada
said of the Mulroney appointments that "Most members [of the

CRDD] came to the job with little or no training in law or procedure. This was observed to have a negative effect on the conduct of hearings, for example, where lack of control contributes to unnecessary prolongation; or where disregard of basic hearings etiquette, such as talking during testimony, results in intimidation of the claimant."[9] Commission research staff interviewed counsel in Toronto who represented refugee claimants before CRDD panels. According to the report,

> Again in Toronto, counsel criticized [CRDD] members for their ignorance of the rules of evidence or procedure, of how to apply the refugee definition, or of how to conduct themselves as decision-makers ... [From counsel's perspective], members did not need all to be lawyers, but compassion and knowledge of international affairs were needed ... Members generally should be tested for knowledge and merit, just like adjudicators. Present selection criteria were too superficial, often bringing in the functionally illiterate.[10]

The CRDD was not infrequently called on to make life-and-death decisions regarding refugee claimants; the presence of "functionally illiterate" friends of Brian Mulroney's certainly did not portend enlightened decision making. Under Chrétien, the system of advertising in the *Canada Gazette* has led to a higher quality of appointees to the CRDD, although a disproportionate number of appointees have Liberal party connections.

Members of administrative tribunals do not have unlimited security of tenure. At both the federal and provincial levels, they are appointed for term positions, usually ranging from one to five years. (But in 1996 Ontario's Mike Harris government began to appoint members of the Ontario Labour Relations Board "at pleasure" — in other words, the government can fire them at any time for any reason. This is a shocking attack on the impartiality principle.) Not only can patronage interfere with the quality of appointments, it can also have an effect on the members' impartiality toward the end of their terms. When the party in power changes at either the federal or provincial level, often some of the former government's appointees are kept on at the tribunals to provide continuity. Members no doubt feel pressure to please their new political masters in order to get reappointed. So much for the democratic principles of impartiality and the rule of law.

In addition to order-in-council appointments, another abuse of the rule of law through patronage is the time-honoured tradition of rewarding lawyers who are party loyalists by appointing them as federal "legal agents." Many of these agents end up acting as federal crown attorneys in narcotics prosecutions. Whenever the federal party in power changes, nearly all of the legal agents appointed by the previous government are fired and replaced by legal agents loyal to the new party. According to Tu Tranh Ha, during the 1994–95 fiscal year, "Ottawa handed out nearly $45 million to 600 legal agents."[11]

In 1980, Ian Greene interviewed a representative sample of 134 judges, lawyers, provincial crown attorneys, and court administrators in Ontario about sources of inefficiency in the court system. The patronage system of appointing the federal legal agents figured prominently on the list. There were complaints from judges, crown attorneys, and court administrators that very few of these legal agents had any background in what they were hired to do and were overpaid for being underqualified. This led to delays and botched prosecutions. There was nearly unanimous agreement that the narcotics prosecutions should be handled by provincial crown attorneys. Yet many of the lawyers in private practice in Greene's sample saw little harm in this patronage system. To them, it was simply a natural part of Canadian politics and harmless since few non-lawyers knew what was going on. And many of those without a current contract as a federal legal agent expected that they'd get their turn when the party they supported won the federal election.

Justice Minister Allan Rock tried to reform the system of appointing federal legal agents when he entered the cabinet in the fall of 1993, but Tu reports that he was faced with a wall of resistance from Liberal lawyers who had been expecting their rewards, especially in small-town Canada. The best he could do was reduce the overall number of federal legal agents by replacing some of them with Department of Justice lawyers and ensure that the Liberal lawyers who got the plum appointments were at least minimally qualified. As well, instead of firing all of the Tory-appointed agents, some of the better-qualified lawyers from the previous regime were kept on.

Our political system has not yet worked out an acceptable dividing line between positions that can justifiably be held by loyal party supporters and those which should be awarded on the basis of an impartial assessment. Very few would object to ministers hiring loyal party supporters to work as ministerial assistants, although some ministers, federal and provincial, disregard party affiliation even in these hirings. And clearly there is no justification for patronage in judicial appointments or appointments to administrative tribunals, although a background in party politics should not be considered a liability, and in some situations the policy orientation of candidates is a relevant criterion for selection. But what about appointments to the boards of Canadian National Railways or the CBC, the Immigration and Refugee Board, the Environmental Assessment Board, the National Parole Board, or a lieutenant-governorship?

Our view is that merit should be the sole criterion for all of these appointments. But what about the argument that no one will work for political parties unless there are potential rewards? Surely there are plenty of Canadians who will work for a party out of a sense of public duty rather than for a reward. Moreover, eliminating the reward-oriented supporters would make political parties much more attractive organizations to join. Besides, it takes tens of thousands more loyal party workers to get a party elected than there are patronage positions available. Why should only a select few receive political pay-offs?

However, making appointments according to merit is not a simple procedure. Criteria for a particular position need to be set out clearly, and a system needs to be established for matching candidates' qualifications to the criteria as objectively as possible. It is difficult for those who rate the candidates not to let their own biases affect the evaluation process. Even if the direction of a candidate's political leanings is ruled out as a relevant consideration, other equally objectionable biases might become factors in a supposedly merit-based system. For example, some ostensibly impartial methods of appointing judges have been criticized for placing too much emphasis on candidates' records of service to the bar association or the law society, and not enough stress on non-legal community service. Perhaps as the professional administrative training of public policy advisors improves, better ways will be found to minimize the influence of these biases.

The original bureaucratic revolution did not succeed in eliminating patronage at the upper levels of our political system. Yet perhaps patronage will breathe its last as a result of the current or next wave of "reinventing government" reforms. The practice of patronage clearly violates the rule of law and the principle of social equality.

Conflicts of Interest

There are two meanings of conflict of interest in the literature on politics, business, and law. One concerns conflicts between public and private interests, and this is the meaning we focus on in our ethics analysis. The other, more general notion of conflict of interest refers to disagreements about what the public interest is and how it should be served. This more general concept is also referred to as a conflict of values, which is the term we will use here.

The term conflict of values, which describes a crucial dynamic of any large-scale organization or political system, refers to conflicts about principles and beliefs. For example, a conflict of values can occur between ordinary working people and wealthy shareholders over a company's occupational health and safety policy, between homosexuals and conservative defenders of "traditional" family values over family-benefit policies, between capitalists and socialists over the regulation of business, and between smokers and non-smokers over the regulation of smoking in public places. Conflicts of values should be resolved in a fair and orderly manner. The democratic methods of dealing with these conflicts become corrupted when one side unfairly advances its own cause or subverts the legitimate activities of its opponents.

A conflict of interest between public and private interests occurs when a public official is in a position to use his or her public office to gain personal benefits or benefits for his or her family or party that are not available to the general public. Conflicts of interest are unacceptable in a society that values the rule of law: the law is to be applied equally to everyone except in the case of justifiable exceptions written into the law. Moreover, public officials who use their positions to provide special benefits to themselves, their families, or their political friends undermine the principle of social equality. We expect public officials — whether they are permanent or contracted public servants, elected representatives or senators — to serve the public interest. Where there is a conflict between the public interest and private, family, or party interests, the public interest should always prevail.

But these are general principles, and studies have shown that there is little consensus about exactly how these principles should apply to difficult cases. That is where the rules of ethical politics come into play. The various ethics rules represent the political system's current efforts to reconcile general principles with society's expectations about the appropriate behaviour of public officials.

Rules Governing Conflicts of Interest

There is a four-tier hierarchy of conflict-of-interest violations in Canada. At the top of the ladder are conflicts of interest that involve a financial benefit. Rules in the Criminal Code prescribe prison terms, but few public officials are prosecuted under the Code for benefitting from a conflict of interest. The explanation likely lies in a combination of two factors: the relatively high ethical standards of most public officials and the difficulty of obtaining sufficient evidence against the few who commit such a violation.

On the next rung of the ladder are conflicts without financial benefits. Public officials may find themselves in a conflict of interest, according to the conflict-of-interest code they are subject to, without actually benefitting from it. If someone could benefit unfairly from their public office (for example, by being in a position to influence the awarding of a contract to a company they have an interest in or to a family member or to a political crony), then that person has a duty to remove himself or herself from that situation. This official could sell certain assets, for example, or delegate decision making to someone who would not have a conflict of interest. If public officials fail to remove themselves from a potential conflict of interest, then they are guilty of what is known as a *real* conflict of interest, even if they do not receive any benefits.

On the third rung of the ladder are situations in which conflict-of-interest codes are violated without a real conflict of interest having occurred. For example, most conflict-of-interest codes require public officials to make confidential or public disclosures of non-personal assets and liabilities. These disclosures enable ethics counsellors to provide specific advice about how to avoid conflicts of interest. Failure to make a full disclosure is a breach of the rules, even if the assets and liabilities themselves would not result in a conflict of interest.

On the bottom rung of the ladder are apparent conflicts of interest. Even if all the rules are complied with, most conflict-of-interest codes state that public officials have a responsibility to show publicly that they are attempting to act impartially, in addition to actually acting as impartially as possible. For example, the federal conflict-of-interest code, which covers cabinet ministers and some other public officials, states that "public office holders have an obligation to [act in a manner] that will bear the closest public scrutiny, an obligation that is not fully discharged by simply acting within the law."[12] In other words, public officials have a duty to avoid apparent conflicts of interest — situations in which a well-informed observer might reasonably believe a public official to be in a conflict of interest, even if in fact this is not the case.

Consistent with the above analysis, Mr. Justice William Parker, who presided at the inquiry into the allegations of conflict of interest against Sinclair Stevens, defined a "real conflict of interest" as "a situation in which a minister of the Crown has knowledge of a private economic interest that is sufficient to influence the exercise of his or her public duties and responsibilities." A *potential* conflict of interest exists when a minister "finds himself or herself in a situation in which the existence of some private economic interest could influence the exercise of his or her public duties or responsibilities ... provided that he or she has not yet exercised such duty or responsibility."[13] A potential conflict becomes a real conflict unless a minister takes action to avoid the situation by disposing of relevant assets or withdrawing from certain public duties or decisions.

Unwritten Conflict-of-Interest Rules

Until the 1960s, there was little enthusiasm for written conflict-of-interest codes for elected officials in Canada. Federal and provincial governments followed the British approach of "reliance on unwritten rules and customs to avoid conflict of interest" by cabinet ministers.[14] This is not to say that no written rules whatsoever existed. The Criminal Code has always contained provisions that prohibit the bribery of public officials and the granting of benefits by ministers in return for explicit favours. In addition, the statutes governing Parliament and the provincial legislatures, the standing orders of the House of Commons and provincial legislatures, and the federal and provincial elections acts all deal with conflict of interest.

However, most of these provisions are designed to provide penalties if a private profit from public office has actually occurred (the highest tier of conflict-of-interest "wrongs"); they prohibit only some of the situations in which ministers could potentially make a personal profit from public office (the second tier). It has only been during the past thirty years, and especially the past ten, that unwritten codes of conduct have been replaced by written rules that prohibit ministers from being in situations in which they could potentially derive a personal benefit from public office.

It is curious that the shift to written rules did not occur earlier. Kenneth Kernaghan suggests three reasons for the break from tradition: the media began to pay greater attention to conflict-of-interest stories; the fall-out from the U.S. Watergate affair forced debate and action; and "a gradual but substantial modification [occurred] in the public's view of what standards of conduct are appropriate for government officials ... Certain kinds of official conduct that used to be tolerated or mildly disapproved are now considered unacceptable and punishable, especially in the area of conflicts of interest."[15] Public standards may have changed because of an increased public demand for social equality. Conflicts of interest are frowned upon not only because MPs and ministers might take advantage of their office for personal financial gain, but also because they might receive advantages, or distribute advantages to their friends and party colleagues on a basis not equally available to all citizens.

Federal Conflict-of-Interest Rules

In the federal sphere, written guidelines for cabinet ministers first appeared in 1964. As of 1996 there are no written guidelines for ordinary MPs and senators, although since 1988 various committees of the House of Commons and Senate have been debating, without result, whether such rules are needed.

In 1964, Prime Minister Lester B. Pearson distributed a letter to his ministers regarding cabinet ethics in response to public concern about political corruption. The letter stressed that formal adherence to the law is not enough; ministers "must act in a manner so scrupulous that it will bear the closest public scrutiny."[16] It warned in general terms against having a financial interest that might appear to interfere with official duties and the use of privileged information for personal gain. The ambiguity of the letter illustrates how little thought had previously been given by Canadian ministers about the nature of cabinet conflicts of interest.

No major changes were made to Pearson's guidelines until early 1973, when public concern was aroused by several allegations of conflicts of interest involving cabinet ministers. As a result, Allan MacEachen, president of the privy council, produced a green paper containing draft legislation designed to prevent conflicts of interest among MPs and senators, including cabinet ministers. According to MacEachen, all public office holders are trustees of the public interest, and if they allow their private interests to take precedence over the public interest, a conflict of interest has occurred. The recommendations focused on preventing situations in which members could derive a personal financial gain from public office.[17]

The legislation that MacEachen recommended never materialized. Instead, Prime Minister Pierre Trudeau sent a letter to all ministers, which contained more specific conflict-of-interest guidelines reflecting some of MacEachen's recommendations. The guidelines provided for the disclosure of non-personal assets and the choice of either selling assets that could possibly lead to a conflict of interest or placing them in a blind trust. In 1974, the office of assistant deputy registrar general (ADRG) was created to process the compliance documentation for ministers and other public officials covered by the guidelines. When Joe Clark became prime minister in 1979, he broadened the guidelines to apply to spouses and dependent children of ministers, thus closing some potential loopholes. In addition, he made the guidelines public for the first time. The application of the guidelines to spouses proved to be controversial. Some felt that this provision violated the principle of equality of spouses. Once back in office in 1980, Trudeau removed the applicability of the guidelines to spouses, thus unwittingly setting the stage for the Sinclair Stevens affair of 1986.

In 1983, Allistair Gillespie, a former federal cabinet minister, was accused of having profitable business dealings with his old department soon after leaving public life. The scandal precipitated the creation of a task force on ethical conduct co-chaired by Michael Starr and Mitchell Sharp, former cabinet ministers from Conservative and Liberal governments respectively. The task force presented the most thorough analysis of the conflict-of-interest problem that had ever taken place in Canada. Their report stated clearly that conflict-of-interest rules are intended to promote impartial decision making and equality of treatment. The task force envisioned a legislated code of ethical conduct that would apply to practically all public-office holders. The statute would also create an Office of Public Sector Ethics to aid in enforcing and interpreting the code. The Mulroney government chose not to implement these recommendations. Instead, as a response to widespread criticism that the government was prone to corruption, Mulroney produced a non-legislated conflict-of-interest code, which was somewhat more detailed than the Trudeau code.

The Trudeau and Mulroney guidelines both contained detailed rules concerning the handling of assets in order to prevent personal profit from public office and the granting of special favours to friends and associates. Neither document, however, contained a definition of conflict of interest. This omission illustrates that conflict-of-interest rules for ministers have been instituted more as a response to public concern in the aftermath of scandals, than as conscious efforts to promote principles such as the rule of law, social equality, and ministerial impartiality. Both sets of guidelines, however, at least acknowledge the impartiality principle. The covering letter that Trudeau attached to his guidelines in 1980 pointed to the goal of "fulfilling one's official responsibilities in an objective and disinterested manner." The Mulroney guidelines contained nine guiding "principles," the first of which was the need for "objectivity and impartiality of government."[18]

During the two-year period after the new federal guidelines came into effect in January 1986, the federal government suffered through no less than fourteen conflict-of-interest incidents involving ministers or their aides. The most publicized of these was the Sinclair Stevens affair. Stevens had been accused of numerous violations of the conflict code, in particular of continuing to be involved in the management of his companies, which had been placed in a blind trust and for which his wife continued to act as solicitor. These allegations resulted in a judicial inquiry conducted by Mr. Justice William Parker, Chief Justice of the High Court of Ontario. After finding that Stevens had been in violation of the federal conflict code on at least fourteen occasions, Parker recommended federal conflict-of-interest legislation, which would apply to spouses as well as to ministers. Like the Starr-Sharp report, Parker recommended the establishment of an independent ethics office to advise individual ministers and their families.

In an attempt to regain public confidence, in 1987 the Mulroney government tightened up the rules surrounding blind trusts and required ministers' spouses and dependants to disclose their assets in confidence to the ADRG. And in February 1988 the Mulroney government introduced conflict-of-interest legislation that would have covered the cabinet, members of Parliament, and the Senate. It would have established an independent ethics commission. However, the bill would have set lower standards for conflicts of interest involving party patronage. Gifts and loans from political parties would not have to be reported to the commission. The exemption of gifts and loans from political parties was probably intended to reflect the position that cabinet ministers cannot be considered in a conflict situation for showing favouritism to party supporters. However, the exemption left open the possibility that favours could be granted in return for party donations, and such situations would be outside of the powers of the commission to review.

Because of criticism from within the Conservative party that the proposed conflict-of-interest legislation was too strict, and from without that it contained too many loopholes, the bill was put on the back burner and was never enacted. It was reintroduced in substantially the same form during Mulroney's second mandate, and suffered the same fate. According to Stevie Cameron, the prevention of conflicts of interest involving the government was not a priority for the Mulroney regime.[19] The Conservative government's reputation for alleged unethical practices was a major factor in its overwhelming defeat in the 1993 general election.

The Liberal party's platform for the 1993 election, contained in the well-publicized "red book," devoted one of eight chapters to "governing with integrity." The book promised the appointment of an independent ethics counsellor primarily to oversee the activities of lobbyists, but it left open the possibility that this official might play a broader role, including supervising the prevention of conflicts of interest. The book also promised the development of a code of conduct for cabinet ministers, MPs and senators.

The Liberal government appears to be moving slowly toward these goals. In 1994, the title of the ADRG was changed to Ethics Counsellor, and Howard Wilson became the first to hold this office. Wilson helped to develop a revised conflict-of-interest code covering cabinet ministers and other public officials, which became effective in June 1994. It is similar to the Mulroney code, but clearer. The ethics counsellor has a higher status than the ADRG, but still lacks the independence promised by the Liberals in 1993. A Special Joint Committee of the House and the Senate began meeting in September 1995 to develop the promised new code of conduct, but as of October 1996 the committee had not reported.

Provincial Conflict-of-Interest Rules

The provincial experience runs parallel to that at the federal level. The provincial premiers began to draft guidelines for their ministers in the early 1970s in response to public concern about conflicts of interest, often in reaction to scandals. These documents frequently evolved into legislation, which usually applied to cabinet ministers as well as to other members of provincial legislative assemblies. Nine provinces — all except Quebec — now rely primarily on legislation to prevent ministerial conflicts of interest.

Newfoundland was the first province to enact conflict-of-interest legislation applicable to MLAs and cabinet ministers that was enforceable by an independent official. The legislation passed in 1973, and enforcement duties were given to the provincial auditor general; in 1993 this responsibility was transferred to the province's chief electoral officer. In two provinces — New Brunswick (1978) and Nova Scotia (1987) — conflict-of-interest legislation was enacted and became enforceable by a designated judge. In two other provinces — Manitoba (1983) and Prince Edward Island (1986) — the clerk of the legislative assembly is responsible for enforcement. Conflict-of-interest legislation was also enacted in Ontario (1987), British Columbia (1990), Alberta (1991), and Saskatchewan (1994) and is enforced by an independent conflict-of-interest commissioner, or ethics commissioner.

The Ontario experience is typical of developments in the provinces. In 1972, conflict-of-interest scandals involving cabinet members led to the issuance of conflict-of-interest guidelines by Premier William Davis later that year. The guidelines contained no definition of conflict of interest and no statement of purpose. They prohibited ministers from buying real estate except for personal use and required them either to sell their stocks or to place them in a blind trust.

The translation of an unwritten code of conduct into a written code of ethics was a controversial issue in the cabinet. According to a confidential interview with a former Ontario cabinet minister, some members of cabinet thought that a written code would open the door for less scrupulous ministers to take advantage of the loopholes inevitable in any written document. The result would be that the letter of the law might be followed, but not necessarily its spirit. A written code, which had the status of neither legislation nor a cabinet order, was considered a compromise between the perceived need for a legally binding regime and the fear that a written regime might actually lead to lower ethical standards.

The Davis guidelines remained essentially unchanged until the Peterson government was shaken by the Fontaine and Caplan affairs in 1986. In response to these events, Premier David Peterson commissioned John Black Aird, former lieutenant-governor of the province, to investigate. Aird found the Davis guidelines too vague and too difficult to enforce. He recommended conflict-of-interest legislation based on the principle of ministerial objectivity. He also suggested the appointment of an independent ethics commissioner to help ensure compliance.[20] The government implemented these recommendations, and the resulting legislation applied to both cabinet ministers and members of the assembly. Aird became the interim ethics commissioner in 1987, and in 1988 Gregory Evans, the retired chief justice of the High Court, Supreme Court of Ontario, began his term as the first ethics commissioner in any Canadian jurisdiction.

At both the federal and provincial levels, it is clear that written guidelines were a response to various crises of confidence in government caused by public outrage at elected officials, and in particular cabinet ministers, appearing to drink from the public trough. At first, conflict-of-interest rules usually attempted simply to prevent personal financial gain from public office. Later on, the relation between the prohibition of conflicts of interest and the principle of impartiality became recognized as a result of the recommendations of various inquiries. Concurrently, the rules began to increase in scope, often prohibiting the granting of favours to friends and associates. In other words, the conflict-of-interest rules came to have more in common with the rule against bias in natural justice and the doctrine of fairness.

The most common response to continued conflict-of-interest scandals has been to make the rules ever more complex and to move from informal guidelines to legislation. When legislation was drafted, it inevitably applied to both ministers and other legislators, sometimes with little recognition that the appropriate standards of impartiality for cabinet ministers should be higher. Moreover, although most of today's conflict-of-interest rules at least pay homage to the principle of "ministerial impartiality," not one attempts to define it. In short, conflict-of-interest rules for Canadian ministers and elected members have come about more as incremental adjustments to political crises than as carefully reasoned responses to basic principles of the political system.

Undue Influence

Undue influence is an attempt, whether successful or not, to influence a policy decision by taking advantage of privileges or connections not available to the general public. In other words, it is the attempt to manipulate public policy in violation of the principle that all citizens have a right to be treated as equals in the design and implementation of that policy. Undue influence is unacceptable in a democratic society for the same reasons that conflicts of interest are: it disregards the principle of equality and allows the policy process to be used for personal gain.

Both the electoral process and lobbying are particularly vulnerable to undue influence. Elections are corrupted if someone donates money to a candidate or a party in return for a public-office favour, such as a contract, job, or change in public policy that provides an advantage to a particular economic interest. As British Columbia's ethics commissioner mentioned in his 1993–94 Annual Report, "campaign contributions and assistance, whether financial or otherwise," can, in some circumstances, lead to a conflict of interest if an elected member makes a public-office decision affecting the contributor.[21] Although lobbyists can serve a useful public function through providing valuable policy information in a timely manner, they can also corrupt the policy process by arranging for political donations in return for public-office favours, or by offering unfair incentives to policy officials, such as lucrative job prospects in the private sector, exotic vacations, or even numbered bank accounts in Switzerland.

Election Financing

The first attempt to control undue influence associated with election financing in Canada dates from 1874. Prior to that time, only an act that could clearly be established as a bribe in a court of law, such as giving money to a party explicitly in return for a public-office favour, or bribing an elector with a promise of alcohol, was considered illegal under the Criminal Code.

Legislation specifically regulating party financing first came about toward the end of the nineteenth century as a result of the Pacific scandal, according to W.T. Stanbury.[22] Prime Minister John A. Macdonald had accepted very generous campaign contributions from the financial backers of the Canadian Pacific Railway. At the same time, the railway received generous contracts and subsidies from Macdonald's Conservative government. What appeared to be an obvious connection between campaign contributions and public-office favours was an important factor in the defeat of Macdonald's government in the 1874 election.

One of the first actions taken by Alexander Mackenzie's Liberal government in 1874 was to have Parliament enact the Dominion Elections Act. It provided for the registration of political parties, required candidates to appoint official agents to receive campaign contributions and pay campaign expenses, and required statements of the candidates' finances to be published within two months after an election.

There were no major changes made to this legislation until it was replaced by the Election Expenses Act of 1974. The changes were brought about by the realization that the cost of fighting elections was continuing to escalate, and without reasonable limits placed on campaign expenditures, elections would be determined primarily by which party could raise the most money.

The 1974 legislation continued the registration and agency system for parties and candidates established in 1874, but tightened up some loopholes that had made it possible for candidates to avoid the rules. As well, it limited campaign expenditures on media advertising to ten cents per elector and, in order to ensure compliance, required "third parties" (public-interest groups) to advertise under the umbrella of a registered party. Spending limits by candidates were set at one dollar per elector for the first 15,000 registered voters, plus fifty cents for the next 10,000 and twenty-five cents for each elector over 25,000. Candidates who received at least 15 per cent of the votes cast would receive reimbursement for some of their election expenses. Radio and television stations were required to accept up to 6.5 hours of prime-time paid advertising from registered parties according to a formula deemed to be fair to each registered party, and they were required to apply the same rules to all candidates wanting to buy advertising time. Registered parties were required to disclose all their revenues and expenditures on an annual basis; the public disclosure would include the names of all donors giving more than $100. Donations and expenditures during election periods had to be reported separately by both candidates and parties. Tax credits were provided for individuals and corporations making donations to parties and candidates; the maximum tax credit that could be claimed was $500 for a donation of $1,150. However, no limits were set on the total amounts of individual donations.[23]

During the 1984 election campaign, a right-wing lobby group, the National Citizens' Coalition, challenged the restrictions on third-party advertising under the Charter of Rights and won. The eventual result was the establishment of the Royal Commission on Electoral Reform and Party Financing in 1989 to review the entire field of election financing. The commission's twenty volumes of studies provided the most in-depth review of the electoral system in Canada's history. In 1991, the commission recommended changes that would make the system more transparent, but there were no major changes suggested in terms of the direction of the Election Finances Act. A relaxation of the restrictions on third-party advertising was recommended so that this provision would comply with the Charter, and these changes were accepted by Parliament. However, the National Citizens' Coalition contested these provisions and again succeeded in a court challenge under the Charter in 1996. This decision is under appeal at the time of writing. This is an important case, because if the restrictions on third-party advertising do not stand up under the Charter, election spending limits cannot be effectively enforced. The results of elections would then be open to manipulation by large financiers even more so than they already are, and this would have serious implications for the democratic principle of equal concern and respect.

One of the more controversial issues dealt with by the royal commission was the question of limits on individual campaign contributions. The purpose of setting limits is to keep individual contributions low enough to be ineffective as bribes, making the exchange of public-office favours for campaign contributions unlikely. Ontario and Quebec have set limits on annual contributions from single sources at both the provincial and the municipal levels. In non-election years, these limits are $750 in Ontario and $3,000 in Quebec; allowable amounts double during a campaign period. As well, Quebec prohibits donations from corporations and unions; only individual donations are allowed.

Unfortunately, the royal commission did not recommend limits to campaign contributions at the federal level, and so this remains an unresolved issue in ethics and politics. Making contributions to political parties in return for public-office favours is a long-established practice among the more unsavoury elements of party politics in Canada.

Without limits on campaign contributions, benefits that donors receive through discretionary government decisions become suspect. The following cases are examples from a study that Ian Greene conducted for the 1991 Royal Commission on Electoral Reform and Party Financing. It should be kept in mind that "there is no proven relation between the favour and the donation — the problem is that the close proximity of the two events raises the question of whether there might be a connection."[24]

- David Lam and his wife gave $17,000 to the PC Canada Fund in 1988; Mr. Lam was appointed lieutenant governor of British Columbia by the Conservative prime minister.

- Fraser River Dredge and Pile Driving gave $2,500 each to four federal Conservative candidates, $250 to another candidate, and $1,000 to the PC Canada Fund in 1988; it won a $13-million dredging contract.[25]

- Two companies that donated $33,000 to the Ontario Liberal party received a $5-million paving contract from the Liberal government. According to NDP Leader Bob Rae, companies that did not donate to the Liberal party either did not get contracts or received only small ones.[26]

- Peter Pocklington's Gainers meat-packing company gave $3,550 to the Alberta Conservative party; it also received $71 million from the government for various expansions. Another Pocklington company, Palm Dairies, gave $4,600 to the provincial Conservatives; it received a multi-million-dollar line of credit from the Alberta Treasury. A third Pocklington company, the Edmonton Oilers, gave $4,050 to the provincial Conservatives.[27]

- Don Cormie, head of the Principal Group, gave $20,000 to Don Getty's campaign fund when he ran for the leadership of the provincial Conservative party in 1985. The Code inquiry was eventually established to investigate the failure of the Principal Group and losses to investors. Alberta's Conservative government was criticized by the inquiry for failing to take appropriate action earlier against the subsidiaries of the Principal Group prior to their bankruptcy.[28]

- The Swiss arms manufacturer Oerlikon contributed $3,000 to the federal Conservatives in 1986; it received $678 million in federal contracts. Diedra Clayton of Oerlikon said that the company was led to believe that firms receiving government contracts in Canada were expected to make donations to the political party in office. She said that the company was approached by the Conservative party and that she said to the party spokesperson, "If others do it, then we will do it too."[29]

• *Le Devoir* discovered that fifty-four companies hired by a federal crown corporation responsible for the Old Port project in Quebec City donated more than $140,000 to the Liberal party, which controlled the federal government until 1984. The federal funding for the project amounted to $155 million over five years; $90 million was spent without any control by Parliament. Each of the companies donated an average of just over $1,000 during each of three years.[30]

These kinds of stories do little to assure Canadians that there is no relation between campaign donations and public-office favours. And now that the sources and amounts of political donations must be disclosed publicly in most Canadian jurisdictions on an annual basis, an analysis comparing donations with public-office favours is a yearly media event. Companies and individuals who donate less than $3,000 on an annual basis are rarely singled out for scrutiny; those making less than $500 in aggregate donations never are.

The solution to undue influence in party financing is simple: annual donations from single sources should be limited to somewhere between $500 and $3,000, as is the case now in Ontario and Quebec. Some party bagmen will undoubtedly complain that such a rule would hamstring party finances. But this has not been the case in Ontario and Quebec, and at the federal level, a contribution limit of $3,000 would leave the Conservatives, the Liberals, and the NDP with at least 80 per cent of their usual funding sources intact, as all parties rely heavily on small individual donations.[31] If a party cannot attract a large number of small individual donors, especially given the very generous tax credits for donations, it cannot claim to be representative of any significant group in society.

But limits to campaign contributions will resolve only part of the problem. Even in a jurisdiction with strict individual contribution limits, those intent on circumventing the rules will find a way to do so, although not always with impunity. In addition, the basic principles of political ethics need a firm foundation in the political parties and candidates. The development of codes of ethics by political parties, as well as extensive public education programs offered by electoral commissions or ethics commissioners, would help in this regard.

AUGUSTANA UNIVERSITY COLLEGE
LIBRARY

Lobbyists

In contrast to the rules governing elections and party financing, the regulation of lobbyists only began in 1988 at the federal level, and such regulations are only now being contemplated in some provinces.

Since the 1970s, the proliferation of professional lobbying firms in Ottawa, or "hired guns," has caused concern, especially among opposition MPs of every political stripe. Although the lobbying of elected members has always been an important part of democratic politics, the advent of significant numbers of paid lobbyists was something new. In September 1985, Brian Mulroney announced a consultation process to establish a new policy to register lobbyists. Some claim that he was forced into this position because the activities of lobbyist Frank Moores, who was Mulroney's friend, had raised so many concerns about undue influence.[32]

The Department of Consumer and Corporate Affairs released a discussion paper on the registration of lobbyists, and the House of Commons Standing Committee on Elections, Privileges and Procedures conducted extensive public hearings on this proposal. The committee reported in 1987, and in 1988 the Lobbyists Registration Act passed through Parliament. It came into force on September 30, 1989.[33]

The original Act did not require professional lobbyists to disclose how much they had been paid by the firms that employed them, and this provision was criticized by the opposition Liberals prior to the 1993 election. The Chrétien government introduced amendments to the Act in 1995 to require lobbyists to reveal whether they were being paid on a contingency fee basis, but lobbyists are still not required to disclose their fees. As well, the federal ethics counsellor is currently spearheading the creation of a Lobbyists Code of Conduct.

The amended Act, which was proclaimed in 1996, requires all those who are paid or professional lobbyists (the "hired guns") to register; they are labelled "consultant" lobbyists. They are required to disclose their clients and the subjects of their lobbying efforts. The Act also requires the registration of employees of corporations, unions, and umbrella groups (chambers of commerce, professional associations, labour and business federations) who spend a significant amount of their time communicating with federal public officials to influence policy. They are known as "in-house" lobbyists. The in-house lobbyists are divided into two sub-groups — "corporate" and "organization" — and they are required to provide a general description of the business or association that they work for. The lobbyists registration function is in the office of the federal Ethics Counsellor in Ottawa.

As of March 31, 1995, there were 1,006 consultant lobbyists who were employed by 552 different firms, three-fourths of which were corporations. The number of consultant lobbyists has been increasing by about 10 per cent each year. Consultant lobbyists must file a separate registration for each different lobbying assignment, and about 1,000 registrations are processed each year. As of March 31, 1995, 3,510 registrations were active.

The increase in the number of registrations and a glance at the interests the hired guns represent indicate how profitable professional lobbying is. The most common subjects of professional lobbying are industry, taxation, international trade, government procurement and contracts, science and technology, and economic development. (The least common issues include human rights, multiculturalism, criminal law, and women's issues.) The most common actions of lobbyists are meeting with a public official (elected or non-elected), attempting to influence a policy, attempting to influence the award of a government contract, and attempting to influence the award of a grant or another financial benefit.[34]

As of March 31, 1995, there were 1,744 in-house lobbyists, but their numbers have been decreasing by 3 or 4 per cent annually — an indication of recessionary times. The in-house lobbyists represented 821 different employers; two-fifths were corporations and the remainder were other kinds of organizations. In-house lobbyists are not required to provide the same detailed information about their lobbying activities as consultant lobbyists, because it is considered that the interests of the corporations and organizations that employ in-house lobbyists are well known.

The communications revolution has had a significant impact on the operation of the system for registering lobbyists, as the amended Act allows for electronic registration. More importantly, the public registry is now available on the Internet, which makes public and media access to information about the activities of professional lobbyists much more convenient than before. This new transparency ought to make an important contribution toward reducing undue influence.

We are clearly in the early stages of promoting ethical politics at the federal level through the regulation of lobbyists. In the provinces and municipalities, however, there are currently no regulations specifically governing the activities of lobbyists. In their 1994–95 annual reports, the ethics commissioners in British Columbia and

Ontario have recommended provincial legislation to regulate lobbyists, and an ethics review panel in Alberta made a similar recommendation in 1996. There is no doubt that the regulation of lobbyists will continue to be an important issue in Canada in the years to come.

Conclusion

Rules to ensure ethical behaviour are intended to promote the basic principle of mutual respect, as embodied in the intermediate legal principles of the rule of law and the doctrine of fairness. Both of these legal principles demand impartiality in applying the law. In government programs that have adopted the principles of bureaucracy (clear rules for management-employee relations, the merit principle, equality and fairness in providing services), ministers, if called upon to make administrative decisions, are expected to act impartially. But the upper levels of government escaped the original "bureaucratic revolution," and thus political patronage remains an important ethics problem.

Fair procedures in government are essential to ensure that everyone is treated as an equal. Such treatment is expected because of the ethical principle of mutual respect. Yet the media are full of stories about high-profile politicians involved in conflicts of interest, influence peddling by lobbyists, and financial contributions to political parties that appear to be rewarded by favours to the donor. If fair procedures are so important in a democracy, why are there so many lapses?

There is no single answer to this question. Undoubtedly, one of the contributing factors is a lack of understanding of the importance of fair procedures. Until recently, practical ethics received almost no attention in the school system and fared only slightly better in colleges and universities. Furthermore, past bad habits create a "hangover effect," and the current negative perception of politicians discourages honest people from running for elected office, while encouraging those who seek primarily personal enrichment. Yet compared with the situation in Canada one hundred or even thirty years ago, there has been a net gain. It takes centuries to build a good society, and the modern concern with fairness developed relatively recently along with the political theory of liberalism during the seventeenth century in England.

The successes and failures of the current rules governing conflicts of interest and undue influence can be assessed through an analysis of some prominent recent cases. Conflict-of-interest scandals are the subject of the next chapter, while Chapter 5 focuses on undue influence.

Conflict-of-Interest Cases

The need for rules to prevent conflicts of interest becomes painfully clear when we take a closer look at some of the widely publicized conflict-of-interest scandals over the past decade. These cases will be organized according to the hierarchy of conflict-of-interest wrongs presented in Chapter 3. The most serious wrong is the Criminal Code Offence of receiving a financial benefit in return for a public-office favour; the case of Michel Gravel provides an illustration. The next level of conflict is what Mr. Justice William Parker, in the Sinclair Stevens Inquiry Report, calls a *real* conflict of interest — knowingly being in a position to make a private profit from public office and continuing in that situation. The Sinclair Stevens and Bill Vander Zalm cases provide examples of this conflict.

The third level of conflict is being in violation of a conflict-of-interest code, although not in a real conflict of interest. There is nothing inherently wrong with being in a *potential* conflict-of-interest situation. But a potential conflict may become a real conflict of interest — which is unacceptable — unless the decision maker takes appropriate action. A conflict-of-interest code can be thought of as a tool to prevent potential conflicts of interest from becoming real ones. Michel Côté and Richard Hatfield provide our case studies here.

Finally, on the fourth level is an *apparent conflict of interest.* In this situation, a reasonable perception exists that the performance of a public official's official duties are affected by his or her private interest. We will consider the case of Robin Blencoe, the B.C. Minister of Municipal Affairs in 1993. As well, Ralph Klein and the Multi-Corp affair is reviewed as an example of the difficulty in determining whether a public official has broken the rules in some situations.

Finally, we examine a case that illustrates how conflicts of interest can extend beyond merely financial transactions. In the case of the ill-fated sovereignty studies commissioned by Premier Jacques Parizeau's minister for restructuring, Richard Le Hir, the minister received no personal financial benefits, but failed to stop the use of his office to provide favours to friends of the Parti Québécois and associates of an official in his office.

Fraud

The Gravel Affair

When it became increasingly likely that the Progressive Conservative party was going to win the 1984 general election, Michel Gravel left his Liberal roots and obtained the PC nomination for the Montreal east-end riding of Montreal-Gamelin and was elected. Gravel's campaign was financed by his former boss, millionaire Henri Paquin, who according to Stevie Cameron, spent more than $200,000 on the campaign, in the hope that Gravel's influence in government would prove useful to Paquin's business ventures.[1] The lack of contribution limits for individuals, corporations, or unions in federal elections makes the electoral system vulnerable to such corruption.

Mulroney's public works minister, Roch LaSalle, set up a system whereby Conservative members of Parliament were assigned responsibility for recommending government contracts in their own riding, as well as in a riding represented by an opposition member. Gravel was designated to look after these contract interests in Hull, which was represented by a Liberal. Hull presented a number of lucrative opportunities for landlords to lease office space to the federal government. Gravel somehow obtained a confidential list of all the federal government's leases of office space, and he used this information to promise important federal government leases to certain landlords — in return for kickbacks. The kickbacks took various forms: an agreement by the landlord to give a percentage of the proceeds to the PC party, buy a $5,000 ticket to a PC fundraising event, provide free renovation work on Gravel's office or residence, or offer personal bribes to Gravel.

However, because of some honest public officials in the Public Works Ministry, Gravel could not deliver on all his promises, and some people who had already paid their dues to Gravel began to complain publicly. The RCMP raided Gravel's office and residence in March 1986, and Gravel was charged with bribery and corruption in May. Gravel's lawyer managed to keep the case out of court until after the 1988 federal election. Just three weeks after the Conservatives won the election, Gravel pleaded guilty to the charges and admitted receiving $97,000 in bribes and kickbacks from business persons and contractors. He was fined $50,000 and sentenced to a year's jail term, of which he served two months prior to parole. According to Stevie Cameron, Gravel admitted to her that he was persuaded to plead guilty by an official in the Prime Minister's Office. The RCMP had subpoenaed twenty-seven witnesses, and the police hoped their testimony would reveal whether other kickback schemes existed.[2] However, thanks to Gravel's guilty plea, their testimony never took place.

There are only a handful of other examples in recent Canadian history of politicians having been convicted for fraud or influence peddling related to conflicts of interest. In 1986, a Conservative party organizer, Pierre Blouin, pleaded guilty to influence peddling in awarding a contract. He had arranged for a Drummondville business-man to give $50,000 to the PC party in return for a $1-million contract, but in the end the contract was given to another business-man with connections to the party. The businessman who had been promised the contract by Blouin blew the whistle.[3]

In 1982 and 1983, three fund-raisers for the Nova Scotia Liberal party, J.G. Simpson, Charles MacFadden, and Senator Irvine Barrow, were convicted of influence peddling. They claimed to have influence with the government and promised contracts in return for donations. They had raised nearly $600,000 for the Liberal party through this approach. The scheme included getting liquor compa-nies to contribute a percentage of their annual sales to the party in power (testimony indicated that both the Liberal and Conservative parties received funds in this manner), ostensibly in return for having their brands listed in the provincial liquor stores. A heavy-equipment contractor testified that in 1971 he had agreed to pay the Liberal party 3 per cent of his government contracts in return for getting those contracts.[4]

The dearth of examples of fraud resulting from conflicts of interest suggests three points. First, fraud may not be as widespread a prob-lem in our political system as real conflicts of interest. Second, it is sometimes difficult to obtain a criminal standard of proof about an actual fraud. How does a prosecutor prove the connection between a donation to a political party and a government contract unless the agreement is written down — which rarely happens — or unless a contractor is willing to risk a tarnished reputation by testifying? Political contributions and government contracts may not necessarily be directly related. Third, according to Stevie Cameron, the police and prosecutors are reluctant to investigate political corruption and to carry the investigations through to prosecution. These investigations are extremely expensive and time-consuming, and they may backfire on the investigating authorities. Cameron's study of corruption in the Mulroney government, *On the Take*, contains a number of examples of police investigations that were eventually abandoned either because of budgetary constraints, or from fear of the fall-out from a successful prosecution.

Real Conflicts of Interest

Sinclair Stevens and York Centre

In April 1986, *The Globe and Mail* published articles alleging that the federal industry minister, Sinclair Stevens, had used his public office to further his personal business interests. These allegations were echoed in the House of Commons. During much of the period when the accusations were being made, Prime Minister Brian Mulroney was out of the country on official business, and Deputy Prime Minister Erik Neilsen had to take the heat in the House. Neilsen's memoirs reveal that he had been worried about Stevens getting into conflict-of-interest situations for some time, but his fears were not shared by the Prime Minister's Office. Neilsen had orders to sit tight and reiterate that Stevens had complied with the prime minister's conflict-of-interest code until the story went away. But the story wouldn't disappear.

The media and the opposition alleged that Stevens had mixed his private business affairs with his public duties so as to advance his personal interests in ways that would not be open to him as a private citizen. For example, critics claimed that Stevens's wife, Noreen Stevens, had obtained a $2.6-million loan for the family business thanks to the intervention of Magna International Inc., a large auto-parts manufacturer that relied on Stevens's ministerial support for loans and grants worth millions of dollars. It was alleged that several other large corporations, which also stood to benefit from Stevens's ministerial discretion, had also been approached to assist the Stevens family business.

Finally, prior to Mulroney's return to Canada, the allegations of conflict of interest became too damaging and seemed too likely to ignore any longer, and Neilsen had to arrange for Stevens's resignation on May 12. On May 15, following Mulroney's return to Canada, the cabinet appointed Mr. Justice William Parker, Chief Justice of the High Court of Ontario, to inquire into the alleged conflicts of interest. Parker conducted much of his inquiry in public, and the hearings on cable television attracted one of the biggest audiences that the parliamentary channel had ever experienced. The hearings, which lasted from June 1986 to February 1987 and which called on ninety-three witnesses, produced eighty-three volumes of transcripts.

Parker released his report in early December 1987. He found that Stevens had been in a real conflict-of-interest position on at least fourteen occasions. This was the most thorough investigation of conflict-of-interest allegations ever undertaken in Canada and the most important catalyst of the current movement for ethics in government.

Background

Sinclair Stevens practised law for nine years before he turned to business full-time. He incorporated a trust company that eventually became part of National Trust and started or purchased several other businesses, including the York Centre group of companies. He was first elected to the House of Commons in 1972 and was re-elected in the riding of York Peel in 1979, 1980, and 1984. During the Clark government, he was president of the Treasury Board, and he became the minister of regional industrial expansion in the Mulroney government in 1984.[5]

Stevens was sworn into the cabinet on September 17, 1984, and on that day the federal official responsible for the conflict-of-interest paperwork, the ADRG, requested Stevens to submit information about his non-personal assets in order to comply with the prime minister's conflict-of-interest guidelines. In accordance with the guidelines, Stevens resigned from his management positions in the York Centre group of companies, and he placed his assets in these companies into a blind trust administered by National Victoria and Grey Trust Company. The managerial functions that he had previously handled were officially taken over by his wife, Noreen Stevens.

The prime minister's conflict-of-interest guidelines were superseded by a new conflict-of-interest code in 1986, and Stevens was required to fill out a new set of documents to show his compliance. Neither the prime minister's guidelines nor the new code permitted him to continue to manage his businesses while in the cabinet, and Stevens confirmed that he had complied with the rules. Although the ADRG requested to meet with Stevens to discuss his situation in person, Stevens claimed that he was too busy and delegated that responsibility to his ministerial staff and his lawyers.

The York Centre group of companies, in which Stevens had a controlling interest, faced a serious cash-flow problem while Stevens was in the Mulroney cabinet. The group had invested heavily in exploration in the Beaufort Sea, a venture that would not produce profits for some years. In 1984, York Centre lost nearly $600,000, and in 1985 their losses amounted to $1.13 million.[6] The group was unable to meet interest payments on loans, and the company's managers faced three choices: selling assets, refinancing through new loans, or investing in new business ventures that would turn a quick profit.

Stevens had enormous power as the minister responsible for the Department of Regional Industrial Expansion (DRIE). He chaired two cabinet committees that reviewed applications from businesses for assistance, worth millions of dollars. He was in charge of the government's privatization program, which involved arranging for the sale of the federal government's interest in corporations such as Canadair, de Havilland Aircraft, Eldorado Nuclear, Kidd Creek Mines Polysar, Massey-Ferguson and Falconbridge. Stevens was also responsible for the Canada Development Investment Corporation (CDIC), Investment Canada, the Federal Business Development Bank, crown corporations such as the Cape Breton Development Corporation and Teleglobe Canada, and the federal shares in the Canada Development Corporation, in addition to his responsibilities for DRIE.[7]

Clearly Stevens would have endless opportunities to use his ministerial powers and contacts to assist his private business interests, which is why Stevens and other cabinet ministers are required to sever their management ties with their private interests upon assuming their ministerial duties. What Parker discovered is that Stevens did not, in fact, cease to be involved in the management of the York Centre group of companies. He remained actively involved in searching for solutions to York Centre's financial troubles, and he did not shy away from using contacts made as minister to promote the interests of the York Centre group.

The Findings
Parker found that Stevens had been in a real conflict-of-interest situation on at least fourteen occasions. As noted above, a real conflict of interest is a situation in which a public official stands to make

personal financial gains from the exercise of public responsibilities and does not take appropriate steps to alleviate the situation. These conflict-of-interest situations are complex, but they are worth summarizing because they illustrate how a cabinet minister with personal business interests can potentially use a public office for personal ends. The fact that Stevens remained unrepentant indicates how little attention at least one high-ranking politician may have given to the ethics required for democratic government.

Crucial to Parker's conclusions were the findings that Stevens kept himself informed of the financial situation of the York Centre group of companies throughout his term as minister, and that the blind trust that held Stevens's share of the York Centre companies did not prevent Stevens from carrying on his private business interests while serving in the cabinet. Stevens cannot be assigned total blame for the failure of the blind-trust arrangement; prior to the Stevens affair, public officials had spent little time considering whether blind trusts were effective instruments for preventing conflicts of interest involving a family business. A blind trust is a device that enables a cabinet minister to transfer the control of shares to a trustee, such as a trust company. The minister receives annual reports about the income from the blind trust, but no details. In theory, the trustee could sell the assets in the blind trust and reinvest the proceeds in another company, and the minister would have no knowledge of this transaction until stepping down as minister and reassuming control of the assets placed in the trust. But Parker noted that the blind-trust device is simply not appropriate for a family business because no trustee would be willing to take active responsibility for managing a family business or selling the minister's share in it. Moreover, in a family business, it is unlikely that the minister could avoid learning about the company's situation from other members of the family.

During the hearings, Sinclair Stevens denied discussing the family business with his wife or other officers of the York Centre companies except in the most general terms. However, this evidence was contradicted by other testimony that Parker found more persuasive. Parker concluded that Sinclair Stevens not only kept himself informed of the financial situation of the York Centre group but also took part in some critical management decisions about how to deal with York Centre's cash-flow problems and used his contacts as a minister to further York Centre's interests.

Parker also found that Stevens had been in a conflict-of-interest situation on at least five occasions relating to Magna International Inc., a major Canadian auto-parts manufacturer. In the fall of 1984 and during the early part of 1985, Noreen Stevens and other officials of the York Centre companies approached Frank Stronach, chairman of Magna, to suggest that Magna become involved in two of York Centre's business ventures. Stronach declined, both because of the business risks involved and because of concerns about conflicts of interest. However, on April 4, 1985, Stronach introduced Noreen Stevens to Anton Czapka, and by the end of the month Noreen Stevens had negotiated a $2.62-million loan from Czapka to York Centre's real-estate arm. Czapka obtained the funds for the loan from the Bank of Nova Scotia, which lent the funds partly on the basis of a comfort letter from Magna. Czapka had been one of the key officials in Magna for a number of years and was about to retire from the company and turn his attention to his personal real-estate investments. The $2.62-million loan was interest-free for the first year, thus providing "significant cash relief to the York Centre group of companies." The collateral for the loan consisted of a number of properties owned by the York Centre group, and Czapka was to be involved in a participating mortgage, which gave him a "supervisory relationship over the timing of any sale of the mortgaged properties. In such circumstances, a need to maintain a positive relationship with the lender is obvious."[8]

During the negotiation of the loan and afterwards, Stevens was personally involved in five ministerial decisions about whether to assist Magna. His knowledge of the circumstances of the $2.6-million loan created the potential that Stevens might be biased in Magna's favour, since Czapka was still associated with the company.

First of all, Stevens personally approved applications for federal assistance of over $5 million to three Magna-related companies on April 17, 1985. Second, on the same day he approved an application by Magna for another $10 million in assistance for a Magna Class A Stamping plant, subject to approval by the cabinet's Treasury Board and to participation by the province of Ontario. (Three months earlier, Stevens had persuaded the cabinet's Economic Development Board to approve the project in spite of the recommendation of departmental officials to reject it.) Third, Stevens then pressed for the Treasury Board to consider the proposal in June, at which point it was accepted. Fourth, in July and August, Stevens promoted cabinet approval of the cancellation of a stock option that the federal

Enterprise Development Board had with Polyrim, a Magna subsidiary, which had the effect of allowing Magna and Polyrim to enter into a more advantageous business arrangement. Finally, Stevens promoted the approval in April 1985 of $64.2 million in federal assistance to Magna for projects in Cape Breton.[9]

Mr. Justice Parker was careful to point out that there was no hard evidence that Magna received preferential treatment or that Stevens would have acted any differently toward Magna's proposals had the York Centre group not received the $2.62-million loan. But whether such a bias exists is practically impossible to test because the issue at stake is a psychological state of mind. This difficulty in obtaining hard evidence about a minister's state of mind necessitates preventive action through conflict-of-interest rules.

In addition to the situations involving Magna, Stevens was in a real conflict of interest on three other occasions. In October 1994, he appointed Trevor Eyton as a director of the CDIC, while at the same time Eyton was working hard "in marshalling the resources of the Bay Street financial community, and particularly those of Brascan, Hees, Burns Fry, Dominion Securities, and Gordon Capital" to develop a rescue package for the York Centre group. Furthermore, in March 1985, Stevens approved financial advisory contracts by Burns Fry and Dominion Securities to CDIC. And in April or May 1985, he appointed Gordon Capital as the federal government's financial advisor regarding the sale of shares in the Canada Development Corporation.[10] Again, there is no hard evidence of preferential treatment, but Stevens was in a situation where his impartiality might have been compromised by his personal business interests.

But the story does not end there. Parker found that Stevens had "mingled his private interest with his public duties," resulting in a conflict of interest on at least five other occasions.[11] First, he met with officials of the Chase Manhattan Bank in New York in January 1986 and discussed some consulting work that Chase Manhattan was interested in doing for the Canadian government, as well as the possibility that Chase Manhattan might co-operate with the York Centre group in marketing a proposed "Christ coin" to mark the 2000-year anniversary of the birth of Christ. Parker's description of these events is instructive in that it illustrates the relation between a conflict of interest and the more serious Criminal Code offence of fraud:

I am prepared to accept Mr. Stevens' evidence that the discussions of the Christ coin proposal on the one hand, and the government consulting projects that Chase Manhattan was pursuing on the other, were not on a quid pro quo basis. Indeed, had this been so, both Mr. Stevens as minister and the Chase Manhattan officials as applicants for government-related work would have been in violation of the criminal law of Canada. However, the fact that Chase Manhattan's involvement in the private Christ coin project was not explicitly conditioned on the award of the government consulting contracts does not alter the fact that Mr. Stevens' mingling of his private interests and his public duties was a conflict of interest.[12]

Second, Stevens met with an official of the Morgan Grenfell merchant banking company while on a government business trip to Singapore in March 1985. During the meeting, he discussed a possible role for Morgan Grenfell in the government's privatization program; he also asked the official for advice on finding investors for one of the York Centre companies with offshore oil rights.[13]

Third, Stevens met or telephoned Tom Kierans of McLeod Young Weir in July and August 1985 to discuss the possible involvement of McLeod Young Weir in the government's privatization program. During this period, he asked for Kierans's advice about the handling of a strip-bond portfolio owned by one of the York Centre companies. As well, Noreen Stevens met with Kierans about the strip-bond situation. There was no firm evidence of a possible quid pro quo, but Parker found that "Mr. Stevens' private interest at this time was sufficient to influence the exercise of his public duties and responsibilities ..."[14]

Fourth, Stevens telephoned a senior vice-president of Olympia & York to ask for advice about the strip-bond portfolio in August 1985 and arranged for the vice-president to meet with Noreen Stevens on this matter. At the same time, Stevens, was involved as a cabinet minister in negotiations with Olympia & York with regard to their interest in taking over Gulf Canada. "By requesting private help from a senior officer of a corporation with which he was dealing as a public office holder, Mr. Stevens was in a real conflict of interest position."[15]

Finally, while on an official government visit to Seoul, South Korea, in August 1985, Stevens paid a courtesy call on senior officials of the Hanil Bank with his wife in attendance. Gill Construction, part of what Parker referred to as the York Centre group (and Stevens's private company in the blind trust), had a loan with the Hanil Bank for $900,000 and was behind in its repayment schedule. Parker found "that Mr. Stevens, knowing that the credit facility with the Hanil Bank was approved and directed from Seoul, chose to visit the Hanil Bank to impress upon the executives of the bank his own importance as a government figure ... in order to ensure that the Gill loan would not be placed under serious pressure ... [This] was another instance of Mr. Stevens mingling private interests with the performance of his public duties and responsibilities [which placed him] in a position of real conflict of interest."[16]

The Recommendations

The evidence against Sinclair Stevens was overwhelming. He ended up in real conflict-of-interest situations on a regular basis in part because of the pressure he must have felt to rescue his family business from its creditors and in part because he apparently saw nothing wrong with building on his ministerial contacts to further his family business. We suspect that Sinclair Stevens is not the only business person in politics with this view.

In his report, Parker made major recommendations to help prevent future conflict-of-interest situations. First, he recommended that cabinet ministers fully disclose their financial situation to the ADRG in confidence, and that public disclosure of the ministers' non-personal financial assets be complete. To protect members' privacy, Parker said that there was no need for elected members to disclose personal assets "such as place of residence, household goods and personal effects, automobiles, cash and saving deposits, RRSPs, and so forth." However, "All other financial interests — all sources of income, assets, liabilities, holdings and transactions in real or personal property — would have to be disclosed in a financial disclosure statement that would be filed in the Public Registry and made available to the media and other interested citizens."[17]

Second, Parker recommended the abolition of the blind-trust device as a means of preventing conflicts of interest involving family assets. Third, he recommended that the conflict-of-interest code be clarified and simplified, and most importantly that it contain a clear definition of a real conflict of interest: "a situation in which a minister of the Crown has knowledge of a private economic interest that is sufficient to influence the exercise of his or her public duties and responsibilities."[18] Fourth, he recommended that the conflict-of-interest guidelines apply to ministers' spouses. Fifth, he advised that the office of the ADRG should be redesigned to "have a clearer mandate, broader powers, and a higher profile so that it can have greater impact in ensuring that the new conflict of interest system will be understood, implemented, and enforced."[19] In particular, he said that the redesigned office should be able to make rulings and have the power and resources to investigate possible conflicts and to hold independent inquiries when necessary. Parker may have been hinting at the establishment of an independent ethics commissioner similar to the one then being put into place in the province of Ontario.

Parker reviewed the three conventional ways to avoid a real conflict of interest: divestment, disclosure, and recusal. Divestment was the most common method used from the 1950s to the 1970s, prior to the time of formal conflict-of-interest guidelines. Both in the federal and provincial realms, the first minister required cabinet ministers to sell, or to place into blind trusts, assets that might cause conflict-of-interest problems, such as shares in companies that could secure specific benefits from cabinet decisions. But in Parker's view, because blind trusts frequently fail and because forcing members to sell non-personal assets is often unfair and might discourage people from running for elected office, the emphasis should shift to broad public disclosure as the cornerstone of modern conflict-of-interest rules. The premise is that a "healthy measure of public vigilance," made possible through public disclosure, will eventually result in greater confidence in the integrity of elected officials, as long as they stay away from conflicts of interest.[20] From this perspective, ministers should be required to sell assets only when these assets would be likely to result in a potential conflict of interest so frequently as to seriously interfere with a minister's ability to perform public duties (for example, a minister of transportation with a heavy investment in a bus company). Whether such divestment is required would be determined by an independent ethics counsellor.

With emphasis on disclosure rather than divestment, however, cabinet ministers would in some instances find themselves in potential conflict-of-interest situations, and in these cases they would need to "recuse," or withdraw, from the situation creating the conflict.[21] For example, a minister whose husband owned an advertising agency might be called upon to approve an advertising campaign that involved contracting with private-sector advertising agencies. In this situation, she ought to recuse herself from this particular program and arrange for another cabinet colleague to handle all activities regarding the advertising campaign. The ethics counsellor would be available to provide advice concerning whether a specific situation required recusal.

While Parker was investigating the Stevens situation, the federal government was hit with another conflict-of-interest scandal. André Bissonnette, minister of state for transport, and his campaign chairman were accused of using insider information to profit from land flips involving the site of a new Oerlikon Aerospace Inc. defence plant in Quebec in January 1987. Bissonnette was fired from the cabinet. Later Bissonnette was acquitted of fraud charges in a jury trial, although the campaign chairman was convicted. Allegations that Bissonnette had violated the conflict-of-interest code were never independently investigated.

As a result of the Parker report, and the Bissonnette scandal, Mulroney promised to take tough action to protect the "political integrity of the nation." All the trusts set up under the conflict-of-interest code were reviewed, and frozen trusts were no longer permitted. Ministers' spouses and dependants were required to make confidential disclosures to the ADRG. But nothing more than this happened until February 1988, when Supply and Services Minister Michel Côté left the cabinet because he had failed to report a $250,000 loan he had received from a Progressive Conservative party organizer, as he should have under the conflict-of-interest guidelines, and Mulroney himself became embroiled in a conflict-of-interest dispute. In late February, the government tabled ethics legislation, Bill C-114, which would have created conflict-of-interest legislation along the lines recommended by Parker, as well as an independent ethics commission. The legislation would have covered ministers, MPs, senators, and parliamentary spouses.

The legislation was attacked both by those who felt it did not go far enough and by those who felt it was too tough. On the one hand, the legislation exempted elected officials from reporting payments they had received from a political party. In other words, a minister would be free to make discretionary decisions about a corporation or individual who had donated hundreds of thousands of dollars to the minister's party, some of which the party might pass on to cover the personal expenses of the minister, and there would be no "official" conflict of interest, according to the legislation. On the other hand, some business interests claimed that the proposed legislation was too strict. Conrad Black called it "Draconian," and others claimed that the disclosure requirements would prevent good candidates from running for public office. [22] Some spouses of MPs from all parties claimed that the legislation represented not only an unnecessary invasion of their privacy, but discrimination against women, since most parliamentary spouses were women.

Parker disagreed with speculations that stricter disclosure requirements would deter people from public life. With reference to the rigid disclosure requirements governing members of the United States Congress since 1978, Parker said that he "was particularly interested to learn that the disclosure requirements have not discouraged 'good people' from entering politics or running for public office." He noted that in a 1985 study, the "vast majority of senators and representatives interviewed said that they knew no one who declined to seek public office because of the disclosure requirements. The disclosure obligation is seen as a reasonable requirement that quite properly attaches to the privilege of holding public office."[23]

With regard to the impact of spousal disclosure, Parker noted that nine provinces already require the spouses of ministers to disclose at least some of their assets, and that spouses were covered by the federal cabinet's conflict guidelines in the 1979 Clark government. The removal of spouses from compliance procedures by Pierre Trudeau in 1980, a practice continued by Mulroney in 1984, was triggered by the belief that "their inclusion is inconsistent with recognizing that independent spouses have separate professional, economic, social, and political interests."[24] But Parker argued that it is precisely because the spouses of elected officials do have independent business and professional lives that public disclosure of their non-personal assets is critical. Most marriage laws now recognize a marriage as a partnership of equals, so spouses definitely have an interest in each others' assets. Parker said that he could find no evidence that the disclosure requirements for spouses in the nine provinces that have them or in the United States had caused hardship to the affected spouses. He hinted that part of the opposition to spousal disclosure might be coming from male elected members who are uneasy about being overshadowed by their wives' "public profile."[25] Parker concluded that the public perception that too many elected officials "lack integrity" cannot be successfully reversed unless spouses are covered by conflict-of-interest disclosure requirements.

The controversy over Bill C-114 gave the Mulroney cabinet a convenient excuse to put the legislation on the back burner of parliamentary business, and it was not passed prior to the 1988 federal election. The Conservatives promised to reintroduce the legislation if they returned to power, and they did introduce almost identical legislation during their second term in office. It suffered the same fate as Bill C-114, languishing at the bottom of the government's order of business until it died with the calling of the 1993 election.

The Liberal party's "red book," the platform for their successful election campaign, contained a section on "governing with integrity," which focused on reforming the regulation of lobbyists. It promised the development of a code of conduct governing the relations between lobbyists and elected members, senators, political staff, and public servants, and the appointment of an independent ethics counsellor to provide advice and enforce the code. In 1995, the Liberal government created a Special Joint Committee of the Senate and House of Commons on a Code of Conduct to follow up this election promise, and at the time of publication the committee was considering whether such a code of conduct ought to cover conflicts of interest as well as relations with lobbyists.

There are indications, however, that the same problems that prevented the Mulroney government from creating an independent ethics office and legislating a conflict-of-interest code are at play in the Parliament elected in 1993. There is a tendency, perhaps reflective of the times in which we live, for MPs and senators to focus on their personal rights and interests, and not to devote as much energy to considering the implications of the public interest in a democratic society.

In spite of this resistance to reform, it will be difficult for any federal government to postpone indefinitely conflict-of-interest legislation covering cabinet ministers, MPs, and senators and establishing an independent ethics commissioner. The arguments in favour of such an approach are too compelling, and the results of this approach in the provinces that have adopted it are encouraging (see Chapter 6). Ironically, when these changes do come, we can consider Sinclair Stevens as their unwitting designer.

Bill Vander Zalm and the Fantasy Gardens Affair

In 1991, a conflict-of-interest scandal involving Bill Vander Zalm, premier of British Columbia, resulted not only in the premier's resignation, but in the beginning of the once-mighty Social Credit party's decline in that province.

This episode resulted from the confluence of two factors: a political culture in the governing Social Credit party that condoned mixing business and politics and the recent appointment of a competent conflict-of-interest commissioner who took his job seriously.

Background
During the 1980s, British Columbia had the highest incidence of conflict-of-interest scandals of any Canadian jurisdiction, next to Brian Mulroney's scandal-prone cabinet. There were five separate conflict-of-interest incidents involving Social Credit cabinet ministers in B.C. (compared with ten involving ministers in the federal Conservative cabinet). In reaction to some of these events, Vander Zalm, who succeeded Bill Bennett as premier in 1986, issued a two-page set of conflict-of-interest guidelines for ministers and parliamentary secretaries. These guidelines, announced in January 1987, failed to stem the tide of ethics scandals, and so in the fall of 1990 the government spearheaded the passage of the province's first Members' Conflict of Interest Act. This Act was proclaimed in December 1990 and included a provision for the appointment of an independent commissioner on conflict of interest. The Honourable E.N. (Ted) Hughes, a retired superior court judge from Saskatchewan, became the interim commissioner.

Bill Vander Zalm served in Bill Bennett's cabinet from 1975 to 1983 and then stayed out of politics until he was elected leader of the Social Credit party, becoming premier in 1986. In 1984, Vander Zalm and his wife, Lillian, bought a property in a suburb of Vancouver. The property was developed into a theme park called Fantasy Garden World. After Vander Zalm re-entered politics, Lillian Vander Zalm took over the management of Fantasy Gardens. After 1986, the theme park began to lose money, and by 1989 the Vander Zalms were seeking potential purchasers for it.

In September 1990, Fantasy Garden World was sold to Tan Yu, a wealthy businessman from Taiwan. Tan Yu had been fêted in the premier's office and the lieutenant-governor's residence, and he was considering making other investments in British Columbia, such as opening a trust company. The opposition charged that Vander Zalm had violated his own conflict-of-interest guidelines by mixing business and politics. In spite of the government's action in promoting conflict-of-interest legislation, the allegations would not go away, and on Valentine's Day, 1991, both the premier and the leader of the opposition requested Ted Hughes to investigate the matter. Hughes agreed, although he emphasized that he was not accepting the assignment pursuant to his role as interim commissioner on conflict of interest because the events in question had occurred prior to the passage of the new conflict-of-interest legislation. Hughes offered to conduct the investigation as a public inquiry under the auspices of the province's Inquiry Act, but the Vander Zalms did not want a public inquiry.

Hughes was asked to determine what role the premier had played in the sale of Fantasy Gardens, and whether the premier, through such a role, had violated his conflict-of-interest guidelines.

The Inquiry

On April 2, Hughes released a sixty-page report in which he showed that the premier had committed several obvious violations of the conflict-of-interest code. Although he resigned as premier, Vander Zalm has repeatedly claimed since that time that he did nothing wrong.

According to Hughes's Report, the Vander Zalms met Tan Yu through Faye Leung, a real estate agent who had her own financial problems. In October of 1990, the B.C. Supreme Court had issued an injunction freezing Leung's assets pending determination of an action by her creditors; Leung was subsequently convicted of contempt of court. According to Mr. Justice McColl of the B.C. Supreme Court, Leung "... does not hesitate to resort to duplicity, deceit, obfuscation, convenient loss of memory and finally mendacity when the facts would disadvantage her."[26]

Faye Leung informed the Vander Zalms in July 1990 that Tan Yu, for whom she was acting, might be interested not only in purchasing Fantasy Gardens, but also in making other investments in the province. To start the negotiation process on a positive note, Leung persuaded the premier to send an official congratulatory certificate with the B.C. coat of arms to Tan Yu's son on the occasion of his wedding in the Philippines. She also suggested giving Tan Yu the "red carpet" treatment during Tan Yu's intended visit to B.C. in August.

The premier complied. On August 1, Vander Zalm met Tan Yu for dinner and personally provided him with information from the minister of finance on starting a trust company. On September 6, the premier and his wife arranged for Tan Yu and Faye Leung to meet Mel Couvelier, B.C.'s minister of finance, in the premier's office. (This was the only time that the premier's wife had attended an official business meeting in the premier's office.) This meeting was followed by a luncheon for Tan Yu hosted by the lieutenant-governor, an event requested by the premier. On September 7, the sale of Fantasy Garden World to Tan Yu was made public.

Tan Yu's purchase of Fantasy Garden World for $14.5 million had been negotiated between August 2 and 4. Of this amount, $11.5 million consisted of a mortgage granted by the Vander Zalms. Bill Vander Zalm also agreed to make his best efforts to persuade the owners of some properties adjacent to Fantasy Gardens, in particular a vacant Petro-Canada lot, to sell to Tan Yu. On August 20, Vander Zalm telephoned Bill Hopper, chairman of the board of Petro-Canada, and obtained an indication that Petro-Canada would sell the lot in question, without tender, for $1,050,000. After Tan Yu bought Fantasy Gardens, his company negotiated directly with Petro-Canada, and the sale of the land was finalized on November 8.

While examining Faye Leung, Hughes discovered, almost by accident, that Tan Yu had given the Vander Zalms $20,000 in cash early on the morning of August 4. Vander Zalm had not mentioned this fact during his examination under oath but later confirmed the transaction. No receipts were ever issued. Hughes was never able to ascertain the exact purpose of this mysterious transaction, although it appeared to Hughes that it may have been an acknowledgement of the premier's promise to assist with the purchase of the Petro-Canada property.

The premier's conflict-of-interest guidelines in effect during the negotiated sale of Fantasy Gardens read, in part, as follows:

1. Ministers ... shall ensure that their ability to exercise their duties and responsibilities objectively is not affected, and does not appear to be affected, by either financial interests of their own or members of their immediate family unit.

2. Ministers shall not be involved in day-to-day activities of a business or a professional nature where such activity is likely to conflict with their public duties.

4. Ministers ... shall not use information obtained in the performance of official duties, and which is not available to the general public, for personal gain or for the gain of any other person.

5. Ministers ... shall withdraw from participating in all decisions, whether in Cabinet or any other situation relating to the duties and responsibilities of a Minister ... in which either they or members of their immediate family unit have a financial interest, other than interests shared in common with members of the general public. ...[27]

Hughes found that first, Premier Vander Zalm had violated paragraphs 1 and 2 of the guidelines because "From the very beginning of the negotiations through to the date of closing, the Premier mixed his public role as chief citizen of this province entrusted with the leadership of the Government of British Columbia with his private business interest."[28] Because Vander Zalm wished to sell Fantasy Gardens, he took advantage of his public office to do special favours for Tan Yu, such as

- requesting and delivering to Tan Yu a special briefing about trust companies from the minister of finance,
- discussing the sale of Fantasy Gardens and the establishment of a trust company with Tan Yu at the same meeting,
- arranging for Tan Yu to meet the minister of finance in the premier's office, with the premier's wife present, and
- arranging a special luncheon for Tan Yu hosted by the lieutenant-governor.[29]

According to Hughes,

> by providing the "red carpet" treatment to Tan Yu who is also proposing to purchase the Premier's property, the Premier may appear to have been creating in Tan Yu the expectation that the "red carpet" treatment would only continue if Tan Yu purchased the Premier's property ... It matters not whether it would be good or otherwise for the Province if Tan Yu invests in British Columbia. As Commissioner [William] Parker stated with which I concur, "It is clear that a conflict of interest can exist even where private interests and public duties coincide."[30]

Second, Hughes found that Vander Zalm breached the guidelines by accepting $20,000 in cash from Tan Yu. According to Hughes, "... reasonably well-informed persons could properly conclude that the Premier's ability to exercise his duties and responsibilities objectively in the future might appear to be compromised given the bizarre circumstances in which the money was given to the Premier and the lack of any reasonable explanation."[31]

Finally, Hughes found that Vander Zalm breached paragraphs 1 and 4 of the guidelines by using his position to persuade Petro-Canada to sell the lot adjacent to Fantasy Gardens. Because he was influenced by the desire to sell Fantasy Gardens, the premier was not acting as an objective representative of the people of British Columbia, as required by paragraph 1 of the guidelines, when he telephoned the CEO of Petro-Canada. Furthermore, "If, as I find is most likely, the

Premier received information from Petro-Canada that the site could be purchased for about $1,000,000.00 without a public tender and that such information was probably not available to the general public, I find that the Premier is in breach of paragraph 4 of the Guideline." Bill Hopper testified that "a premier of a province demands some attention," and that the premier's telephone call "helped open the door for [the purchasers]."[32]

The Aftermath

Scandals involving political corruption have always had a major impact on the fortunes of political parties in Canada, but rarely has a scandal led to the actual demise of a powerful political machine. Hughes's report was followed by Vander Zalm's resignation as premier and the resounding defeat of the governing Social Credit party in the 1991 provincial election. The party is now all but irrelevant on the provincial political scene.

In the final pages of his report, Ted Hughes posed a question that is certainly on the minds of anyone familiar with the Fantasy Gardens saga: "If the Premier's breach of the Guidelines was so obvious, how could the Premier have allowed this series of events to occur?"[33]

Hughes offered two explanations. First, Vander Zalm was reluctant to keep his advisors informed about potential conflict-of-interest situations, and when he did inform them, he was unwilling to take their advice. Second, the Premier demonstrated an "apparently sincere belief that no conflict existed so long as the public wasn't aware of what was going on."[34]

Like Sinclair Stevens, Bill Vander Zalm denied that he had done anything wrong. He apparently had no grasp of why it is imperative in a liberal democratic system of government for public officials to both act and appear to act in an objective and impartial fashion, and why it is not acceptable for public officials to bestow special favours on themselves, their family, and their business associates. It would appear that B.C. voters have a somewhat deeper understanding of the fundamentals of democracy.

Violations of Conflict-of-Interest Codes

Michel Côté and Richard Hatfield

Conflict-of-interest rules ordinarily require elected officials to disclose their sources of income, their assets, and their liabilities. This disclosure is usually confidential, and its purpose is to enable an ethics counsellor to advise as to whether each particular source of income, asset or liability might result in a conflict between the private interests of the official and his or her public duties. In some jurisdictions, the ethics counsellor has the power to disclose publicly the sources of income, assets, and liabilities that might, in some situations, lead to a conflict of interest unless the member takes appropriate action.

The failure to disclose all relevant income, assets, or liabilities results in a third-level conflict-of-interest violation, even if a conflict of interest would not have occurred had they been properly disclosed.

In February 1988, the media revealed that Michel Côté, minister of supply and services, had failed to disclose to the ADRG (the federal official responsible for ensuring the public disclosures required by the prime minister's conflict-of-interest guidelines) loans of about $250,000, which he had received in 1985 and 1986 from a friend and PC party organizer. Loans are "liabilities" that must be disclosed to the ADRG to ensure that a potential conflict of interest does not develop whereby a cabinet minister is in a position to do a public office favour to the person who holds his loan. By this time, Mulroney was sensitive to the damage that conflict-of-interest scandals could cause, and he was quick to fire Côté.

Just three days later, on February 5, 1988, Mulroney found himself in a similar situation. Jean-Pierre Kingsley, the ADRG, confirmed in response to opposition inquiries that Brian Mulroney had failed to disclose a loan of $324,000, which the PC Canada Fund had provided to him for decorating his residences. When questioned about this loan, Mulroney claimed that the $324,000 was really just an "advance," and therefore did not have to be disclosed. But when Kingsley was asked whether an advance was a liability that had to be reported under the guidelines, he replied, "Yes, I consider a liability something whereby a person owes another person money." (As every accountant knows, an advance is a kind of liability.) However, three days later, Kingsley changed his mind. On October 8, Mulroney read a statement from Kingsley in the House of Commons maintaining that at no time had the "arrangement" between Mulroney and the PC Canada Fund been considered to fall under the conflict-of-interest guidelines.[35]

Kingsley's change of heart was not credible, however, because he had no independence. As William Parker's report on Sinclair Stevens pointed out, Kingsley's office "is not constituted as an independent policing and investigative authority ... Responsibility for ... approval of compliance measures rests with the prime minister as first minister."[36] We might say that Brian Mulroney had in the end investigated the matter and found himself to be in compliance with his guidelines.

It is curious that Mulroney was not pressured to accept the same fate as Michel Côté — leaving the cabinet. It is worth reflection to consider whether our country's political situation would be as precarious as it is now, had this happened. On February 12, 1988, the matter was raised forcefully in the House of Commons by Liberal Brian Tobin, now premier of Newfoundland, but after that it died. There are at least two explanations for this lack of action. First, it was well known that some prominent opposition politicians had received supplementary payments from their parties, and there is no doubt that these payments would have become an issue if the opposition had pressed Mulroney. Moreover, these "salary supplements" are so entrenched in Canadian party politics that to question their legitimacy seems absurd to some party loyalists. (On February 12, *The Globe and Mail* published an article by Ian Greene in which he called for Mulroney's resignation over this incident; several days later, Greene was told by a senior official in the Privy Counsel Office that "payments from political parties have never been considered subject to conflict-of-interest rules in Canada.")

Second, many members of the opposition considered that they had a better chance of doing well in the upcoming general election with Brian Mulroney as head of the PC party, rather than a newcomer who might be able to overcome Mulroney's reputation for mishandling issues of corruption.

Perhaps as a result of this episode, the conflict-of-interest legislation introduced into the House in late February 1988 included a clause that exempted elected officials from disclosing payments they received from political parties. This clause was dubbed the "Mulroney clause" by the opposition, and it is unique in proposed or actual conflict-of-interest rules in Canada, with the exception of New Brunswick.

A situation parallel to Mulroney's problems with his guidelines occurred in New Brunswick in 1980. The New Brunswick conflict-of-interest legislation, enacted in 1978, required ministers to disclose benefits received from any source to a judge, who would rule on whether they placed the minister in a conflict of interest. Premier Richard Hatfield disclosed that he was receiving a supplement to his salary from the provincial Progressive Conservative party. The judge who had been assigned to deal with the conflict-of-interest legislation, Mr. Justice J. Paul Barry, found Hatfield to be in a conflict of interest for accepting the salary supplements. (These payments might have interfered with Hatfield's ability to make impartial judgements in situations where he had discretion to provide benefits to the donors who supported the PC party's salary supplements.) Hatfield repaid the salary supplements, but in 1980 the government initiated an amendment to the legislation that exempted cabinet ministers from reporting payments from political parties.

Mr. Justice Barry resigned his position as the "designated judge" under the conflict-of-interest legislation in protest, stating that "The Act has been amended to legalize what I consider a conflict ... In my opinion, the Conflict of Interest Act is becoming a farce."[37] Barry had also found the natural resources minister, J.W. Bird, to have been in a real conflict-of-interest situation because he was a surety for companies that had substantial provincial government contracts. The 1980 amendment to the Conflict of Interest Act made it legal for a cabinet minister to act as a surety for companies contracting with the government, and Barry found this situation equally disturbing.[38]

Two lessons can be derived from these episodes: For conflict-of-interest rules to work effectively, disclosure of income must be full and complete, including income from political parties; and the official who rules on conflicts of interest must be independent.

Apparent Conflicts of Interest

The idea of an "apparent" conflict of interest was considered by Mr. Justice William Parker in his report on Sinclair Stevens. The federal conflict-of-interest guidelines that applied to Stevens required public-office holders to avoid apparent conflicts of interest, but this concept was not clearly defined. Parker concluded that "An apparent conflict of interest exists when there is a reasonable apprehension, which reasonably well-informed persons could properly have, that a conflict of interest exists."[39] In a *real* conflict-of-interest situation, a public official is quite aware of private interests that could be affected by how he or she conducts public business. But in an apparent conflict, "No such actual knowledge is necessary ... [although] the perception must be reasonable, fair, and objective ... [but not necessarily] based on a complete understanding of *all* the facts ..."[40] In other words, public office holders must not only avoid mixing their public duties with their private interests, they must also take the appropriate steps to prevent the *appearance* of such mixing.

Whether the concept of an apparent conflict of interest is sufficiently clear to be covered by conflict-of-interest legislation is an important issue. Ontario's ethics commissioner, Gregory Evans, considers the concept too vague to be useful, while the former B.C. ethics commissioner, Ted Hughes, thinks that public expectations require elected officials to avoid apparent conflicts. In 1992, an amendment to the conflict-of-interest legislation in British Columbia prohibited MLAs from engaging in official duties "if the Member has a conflict of interest or an apparent conflict of interest."[41] An apparent conflict of interest is defined in the legislation as follows:

> For the purposes of this Act, a Member has an apparent conflict of interest where there is a reasonable perception, which a reasonably well-informed person could properly have, that the Member's ability to exercise an official power or perform an official duty or function must have been affected by his or her private interest.[42]

In 1993, a B.C. citizen wrote to Mr. Hughes with an allegation that Robin Blencoe, the minister of municipal affairs, recreation and housing in the Harcourt government, was in an apparent conflict-of-interest situation because of his close political ties to developers who had applied to the minister for approval of their development project. Hughes concluded that an apparent conflict of interest did exist. As of mid-1996, the Blencoe situation is the only clear example of an apparent conflict of interest which was the subject of an investigation by an ethics commissioner.

Robin Blencoe and the Bamberton Project

The Bamberton Project was a major housing development proposed for Vancouver Island, which would turn 1,500 acres of forest land into a community housing up to 15,000 people. The project was owned by holding companies that managed pension funds for unions, and these holding companies contracted with the South Island Development Corporation (SIDC) to manage the development. Ed Tait, a political ally of Municipal Affairs Minister Robin Blencoe, had a 35 per cent ownership interest in SIDC. Another of Blencoe's political supporters, Robert Milne, was a lawyer for SIDC. Hughes found

that "Both Tait and Milne [stood] to gain in a very significant financial way," if the Bamberton project was approved.[43]

The project was conceived prior to the election of the NDP government in 1991, but the majority of official contacts between the
developer and the provincial government occurred after the election.
In order for the project to proceed, it had to be approved both by the
Cowichan Valley Regional District and by the minister of municipal
affairs.

In June 1993, one of the opponents of the Bamberton project wrote
to the ethics commissioner and suggested that Blencoe might be in
a real or apparent conflict of interest because of his political association with two of the chief proponents of Bamberton. Blencoe had not
yet officially approved the project, although he had sanctioned a
special planning grant of $35,000 to the Regional District to expedite
the approval process and had met with some opponents and supporters of the project, including Tait.

Key to Hughes's decision was his definition of "private interest,"
because the B.C. legislation defined an apparent conflict of interest
as a situation "where there is a reasonable perception ... that the
Member's ability to exercise an official power ... must have been
affected by his or her private interest." Hughes wrote that his definition would be based on current realities rather than on legal defi-
nitions that dated back for centuries. He noted that the 1992
amendment that prohibited apparent conflicts of interest was "necessary because of the low ebb to which ... public confidence [in
elected officials] has sunk in recent years." He said that the "heart
and soul" of the amendment was "the restoration of public confidence in the conduct of the people's business by politicians who have
achieved electoral success."[44] He observed that Colin Gabelmann,
B.C.'s attorney general, had said in 1992 that the government's
objective was "to have conflict of interest rules in British Columbia
which are second to none in terms of rigour and fairness."[45]

As a result, Hughes concluded that a "private interest" could
include something other than financial gain. "Where the Member's
decision can be perceived to create a scenario, perhaps usefully
described as a "quid pro quo" for past favours, that is also caught by
the Act ... Campaign contributions and assistance, whether financial
or otherwise, can, in my opinion, in some circumstances, be a private
interest.'" Therefore, elected members must take care to ensure that
they avoid situations where they can "confer an advantage or a

benefit" on those who made significant campaign contributions, "financial or otherwise."[46]

The evidence convinced Hughes that both Tait and Milne had made significant campaign contributions, both in terms of financial donations and other kinds of support. Tait had endorsed Blencoe on a campaign leaflet, had advised on fund-raising, and had personally raised nearly $400 for Blencoe's campaign. Milne had been Blencoe's official agent during four election campaigns, including the 1991 provincial election, had made "significant" financial contributions to Blencoe's constituency association, and had knocked on doors for him. Although Blencoe tried *not* to be informed about the sources of financial contributions so that those would not affect his judgement, he was certainly aware of the other kinds of campaign support provided by Tait and Milne.[47]

Hughes concluded that a "reasonably well-informed person" familiar with these facts would conclude that Blencoe would be guilty of an apparent conflict of interest if he were to make a ministerial decision about whether to approve the Bamberton project, because the favours done for him by Tait and Milne might affect his judgement about the project they were lobbying for. A reasonable observer might suspect a quid pro quo situation. Blencoe told Hughes that he had acted and would act with strict neutrality in considering the Bamberton issue, and Hughes wrote that he accepted Blencoe's sincerity. "But, that is beside the point. [The point is] the perception of a conflict of interest held by a reasonably well-informed person ..."[48] And from that perspective, Blencoe's ability to remain neutral was questionable.

According to the B.C. Conflict of Interest Act, a cabinet minister in a real or apparent conflict-of-interest situation must withdraw from that situation, and the cabinet can appoint another minister to handle the duties causing the conflict. Hughes concluded that Blencoe should remove himself from any official duties regarding the Bamberton project, and that the cabinet should appoint another minister to handle the Bamberton file in his place. As Blencoe had not made an official decision approving the project, he would avoid "significant consequences" by removing himself at this point.[49] Hughes also thought that Blencoe should have divested himself of the Bamberton file right from the start, and that by meeting with proponents and opponents of the project and by approving the special development grant he had been guilty of a minor breach of the Act. However, because this was the first case involving an apparent conflict of interest, the minister could not have been expected to understand all the implications of the concept. Therefore, Hughes did not recommend that Blencoe be penalized. However, Hughes wrote in his 1993–94 Annual Report that "members henceforth will know the standards [regarding apparent conflicts of interest], by which their conduct will be judged."[50]

Both the inclusion of apparent conflict of interest in the B.C. ethics legislation and Hughes's broad interpretation of this concept have significantly raised the standards of impartiality expected of elected members in British Columbia. If Hughes is correct in assuming that this new standard reflects public expectations, then there will be public pressure to hold elected officials in other parts of Canada to the same high standards. Such expectations may help to explain Alberta Premier Ralph Klein's difficulty in distancing himself from the 1995 Multi-Corp controversy, even though he was cleared of wrongdoing by Alberta's ethics commissioner.

Ralph Klein and the Multi-Corp Affair

Alberta's Conflicts of Interest Act was passed in 1991, replacing the informal guidelines in place prior to that time. Among other things, the Act provides for the appointment of an ethics commissioner and requires members of the legislative assembly to disclose their investments to him or her. The ethics commissioner must meet with members to discuss their disclosure statements and advise them how, given their assets, they should behave to avoid conflicts of interest. As well, members must inform the ethics commissioner of any gifts or benefits with a value of more than $200 so that the commissioner may determine whether the gift or benefit represents a conflict of interest and therefore must be returned.

The first ethics commissioner, appointed by the provincial cabinet in 1992, was Robert Clark. Clark had been a Social Credit MLA from 1960 to 1981 and had served in the cabinets of Premiers Ernest Manning and Harry Strom. In contrast to the ethics commissioners appointed in Ontario and British Columbia, Clark had a political rather than a legal or judicial background.

According to Charles Rusnell of *The Edmonton Journal*, on November 20, 1993, Ralph Klein attended the ribbon-cutting ceremony of the Hong Kong office of an Alberta company named Multi-Corp. Multi-Corp had recently acquired the rights to computer software that translated texts from certain Asian languages to English. Klein stayed for a meeting of company officials and a few potential investors, where the inventor of the software talked about the software package's potential.[51]

During the weeks that followed the return of Premier Klein and his wife from Hong Kong, Michael Lobsinger, president of Multi-Corp, heard that Colleen Klein wished to acquire some shares in Multi-Corp. On December 14, Lobsinger personally delivered 10,000 shares of Multi-Corp to Colleen Klein (the certificates were dated November 25) and told her that she didn't have to pay Multi-Corp for them until she sold them. She was told that at the time of sale she would only have to pay $1.00 a share for them plus 10 per cent interest, even though the shares were trading on the Alberta Stock Exchange for $1.62 on that day.

According to Alberta's Conflicts of Interest Act, members of the legislature must report changes to their investments or their spouse's investments within thirty days of the change. On January 25, 1994, Premier Klein reported the acquisition of the Multi-Corp shares to Robert Clark, the ethics commissioner. (The report was late, but that is a minor breach of the rules.) However, Mr. Klein did not report that the shares were acquired at below-market value and that they had not been paid for, and both of these facts should have been disclosed, according to the legislation. This is because the below-market-value transaction could be considered a "gift or benefit," and because the money owing for the shares was a liability that might affect the ability of the member to act impartially.

The Inquiry of the Ethics Commissioner

In October 1995, Alberta Liberal MLA Frank Bruseker became aware of the Kleins' transactions with Multi-Corp. By this time, shares of Multi-Corp were selling at more than $8 a share. Bruseker requested Ethics Commissioner Bob Clark to investigate and report back to the legislature. On October 31, Clark agreed to the request, and he reported to the legislature on November 10. On the day prior to the release of Clark's report, Klein made a public statement that he would resign if Clark's report indicated even a "hint" of wrongdoing.

Clark noted that in 1993, Colleen Klein did not reveal to him that the Multi-Corp shares had not been paid for, as she should have under the Act. However, he blamed himself for the breach because he said he had not specifically asked her whether she had paid for the shares. He concluded that because Colleen Klein was not a sophisticated investor, she had not realized that it was unusual not to have paid for them.[52]

The Aftermath

Unfortunately, Clark's report did not clear the air for the Kleins. For one thing, the Kleins' explanation as to why they did not report the money owing on the shares was unconvincing. For another, Clark did not deal with the fact that the receipt of the Multi-Corp shares at well below market value was clearly a "gift or benefit" under the Conflicts of Interest Act. Finally, Klein's statement, the day prior to the release of Clark's report, that he would resign if Clark found even a hint of wrongdoing, was ill-advised. It could be interpreted, for example, as an attempt to pressure an independent official, as the resignation of a provincial premier is a very serious matter that few public officials would be willing to take responsibility for. It is unacceptable for elected politicians to comment on an issue before a court prior to the judge's decision, since that comment could be interpreted as pressuring the judge contrary to the constitutional principle of judicial independence. Similarly, it is imprudent for the premier to comment on a case being considered by the ethics commissioner, especially when the case concerns the premier himself.

On November 20, the Kleins announced that Colleen Klein would sell her shares in Multi-Corp and donate the profit — about $51,000 — to charity. Ralph Klein's chief advisor, Rod Love, had also purchased shares in Multi-Corp along with his wife; Love and his wife announced that they would also sell their shares and donate the profits to charity. But after making this announcement, Klein said that he and his wife had "agonized" about what to do with the Multi-Corp shares because they represented a "nest egg" for their later years.

On November 29, at Klein's request Clark appointed a three-member panel chaired by University of Alberta political scientist Allan Tupper to review the Conflicts of Interest Act and to recommend improvements. The panel's report, released on January 11, 1996, made the following recommendations:

- the Act should be revised in order to be clearer and easier to comprehend;

- public officials should be required not only to meet the letter of the law, but to arrange their affairs so as to avoid even the *appearance* of a conflict of interest, as in British Columbia;

- the Act should be broadened to include a lobbyist registration process.

As of November 1996, the Alberta government had not implemented the recommendations, probably hoping that the Multi-Corp affair was behind them. But on November 4, 1996, Bruseker requested Clark to conduct another investigation of the Multi-Corp affair because an Access to Information request showed that the Kleins had dinner in Hong Kong in 1994 with Lobsinger — at government expense. As well, Klein met with Chinese government officials in Guangdong province and subsequently their government signed a $26-million contract with Multi-Corp. Clark agreed to investigate the new allegations. [53]

Discussion

Ralph Klein's handling of the Multi-Corp affair indicates that neither he nor Colleen Klein had thought very carefully about the purpose of conflict-of-interest rules prior to that time. The two major purposes of the conflict-of-interest rules are to promote impartial decision making by public officials and to ensure that public officials do not receive any special favours because of their public office.

It should have been clear to the Kleins that when Colleen Klein received 10,000 Multi-Corp shares at below-market value from the president of the company, without having to pay for the shares until sold, she accepted a special favour not available to members of the general public. They should have refused the offer. Ralph Klein's lament that he and his wife had to give up a legitimate "nest egg" indicates that the Kleins may still not understand that it is unacceptable in our system of government for public officials to receive special favours that are more than just tokens of appreciation.

Moreover, Ralph Klein should have realized that although the Multi-Corp ribbon-cutting ceremony in Hong Kong was open to the public, very few Albertans could afford to fly to Hong Kong to attend that meeting. Therefore, using the privileged knowledge obtained at that meeting might be considered at least an apparent conflict of interest — that is, the appearance of mixing public duties with private interests. Because Klein and his wife might have been privy to privileged information about Multi-Corp, they should have avoided any investments with the company after the 1993 trip to Hong Kong, which after all was made at public expense and for public, not personal, business.

It is possible that these errors in judgement could have resulted from a political culture in which building up a "nest egg" at the public's expense is seen as a legitimate *quid pro quo* of a life in politics — a life that is stressful, hard on one's family, and does not yield high financial rewards in and of itself. As well, Klein may be a victim of his own government's axing of MLA's pensions.

Bob Clark's failure to be as strict with the Kleins as, for example, Ted Hughes was with the Vander Zalms, or William Parker was with Sinclair Stevens, may be the result of his background as a politician rather than as a judge. If the political culture in Alberta condones the "nest egg" syndrome, then this culture is just as likely to have affected Clark as the Kleins. Moreover, no ethics counsellor can advise elected members about how to avoid conflicts of interest unless the members are completely open about their financial situations. Since the Kleins did not reveal to Clark that the shares were received without payment at a below-market value, it was impossible for Clark to give adequate advice. Clark was generous to accept the blame for this omission — from our perspective overly generous.

Clark's report cleared Ralph and Colleen Klein from real conflict-of-interest charges. Even those convinced that Clark's judgement was correct, however, would find it hard to deny that the Kleins were in an apparent conflict-of-interest situation. And although the Alberta legislation currently does not prohibit apparent conflicts of interest, the Tupper review panel recommended that apparent conflicts should be included in future improvements to the Act.

Broadening the Scope of Conflicts of Interest

Richard Le Hir and PQ Propaganda Contracts

Richard Le Hir is a Quebec lawyer and businessman who became a Parti Québécois member of the national assembly in 1994. Just prior to his election victory, he had been Chairman and CEO of the Quebec Manufacturers' Association and vice-chairman of the Canadian Manufacturers' Association. He was appointed to the Parizeau cabinet as minister for restructuring and was responsible for spending over $9 million on forty-four studies about the potential effect of Quebec independence, which were released during the 1995 referendum campaign.

In September 1995, at the beginning of the Quebec referendum campaign, the provincial Liberal opposition charged conflicts of interest in Le Hir's office had affected the process of awarding research contracts. Premier Jacques Parizeau asked the provincial auditor general to investigate, which effectively put the issue on ice until after the referendum. The day after the referendum, Le Hir resigned from the cabinet and later withdrew from the PQ caucus pending the investigation.

The auditor general, Guy Breton, released a preliminary report in December 1995. Breton's report showed that Pierre Campeau, Le Hir's deputy minister, hired his former private-sector boss, Claude Lafrance, to oversee the sovereignty studies. "Lafrance, in turn, awarded nine contracts worth $1.9 million to firms he personally owned in whole or in part — without seeking competing bids."[54]

Faced with proof of such a blatant conflict of interest, Parizeau asked the auditor general to expand his investigation. Breton's final report of March 1996 was even more devastating to the PQ. According to the Montreal *Gazette,* "Le Hir's department systematically flouted the government's rules on the awarding of contracts. Breton said more than a 100 invoices, totalling $360,000, are not accompanied by any proof that the goods or services were received ... In 77 other cases, representing $1.19 million, the work was already finished even before the signature of the contract or Treasury Board authorization was obtained. In addition, 39 mandates, totalling $465,000 were carried out without any contract being signed."[55]

Subsequently, an internal PQ investigation was critical of Le Hir, and on April 30, 1996, Le Hir left the PQ caucus permanently to sit as an independent member of the assembly. Le Hir blamed Jacques Parizeau for the conflicts of interest, claiming that Parizeau's office had orchestrated the contracts. "When you see a situation like this, you ask yourself serious questions about the quality of our democracy," Le Hir stated.[56]

The evidence uncovered so far indicates that Pierre Campeau, Le Hir's deputy minister, may have been in a conflict-of-interest situation for two reasons. First, he may have benefitted personally from the contracts that he approved. Second, even if no personal gain was involved, Campeau showed favouritism in singling out friends, associates, and PQ stalwarts for the contracts. He was certainly not impartial in awarding the contracts as ethical politics would have required. There is no evidence that Le Hir was in a position to make personal financial gains from the contracts, but he ought to have been aware that the process for awarding the contracts was not impartial. This case illustrates how conflicts of interest, the prohibition of which is based on the impartiality principle, can extend beyond a minister's personal financial considerations.

The Le Hir affair illustrates not only a conflict of interest, but one facet of the problem we call the "dirty hands" syndrome. Several of the studies commissioned by Le Hir on behalf of the Quebec government were clearly misleading. For example, one of the studies purported to survey the views of U.S. trade officials about Quebec independence and concluded that the U.S. officials preferred continuity of trade relations regardless of Quebec independence. Later, it was discovered that the survey didn't even mention the possibility of Quebec independence. Another report on federal transfer payments indicated in a summary that Quebec had lost $11 billion through the transfer-payment mechanism between 1983 and 1993, but the report itself actually stated that Quebec had gained through the transfer payments.

Another ethics problem that came to light through the Le Hir affair is the unfair treatment of minorities. When Le Hir resigned from the PQ on April 30, 1996, he said that his time out of the caucus had given him an opportunity to reflect on the costs of "the sovereignty dream." In their enthusiasm for this goal, Le Hir accused sovereignists of practising "exclusion and intolerance" toward ethnic and language minorities in Quebec, and he was disturbed by the actions of Quebec's language police, whom he referred to as "mean-spirited ... zealous bureaucrats."[57]

The Le Hir affair illustrates that the development of more effective means of preventing conflicts of interest is a necessary but not a sufficient mechanism for combatting ethical problems in politics. Politicians are unlikely to develop a reputation for integrity unless ethical deficiencies are addressed on all relevant fronts, including conflicts of interest, dirty-handed propaganda campaigns, and unfair treatment of minorities.

Conclusion

Infractions of the rules designed to prevent conflicts of interest vary in their degrees of seriousness. The Gravel affair is an example of the relatively rare case of a criminal conviction of a public official who took advantage of a conflict of interest. The Stevens and Vander Zalm case studies illustrate real conflict-of-interest situations, while the Côté and Hatfield examples show how the rules designed to prevent conflicts of interest can be broken even if real conflicts of interest have not occurred. Robin Blencoe's situation provides an example of an apparent conflict of interest and from our perspective lends support to those who favour the toughening-up of ethics legislation by prohibiting apparent conflicts. The Le Hir case shows that situations involving conflicts of interest might also have overtones of additional ethics problems.

The Stevens and Vander Zalm cases underline the importance of having an independent official conduct inquiries into allegations of conflict of interest. Without an independent official available to set the record straight, a cloud of suspicion may continue to hang over someone alleged to have broken the rules, as the Mulroney example illustrates. But in addition to independence, the person conducting the inquiry requires support of comprehensive ethics legislation, as the Klein case shows. Moreover, it is useful for the investigating official to have a background in law or investigative procedures. The legislative committees selecting ethics commissioners should give careful consideration to their background. A retired judge, in our view, is more likely to be effective than a former politician, who may still be too close to the political fray to be impartial.

It would be a mistake to fight corruption in politics by focusing exclusively on conflicts of interest. As Patrick Boyer has noted, those intent on being corrupt will exploit the weakest parts in the structure of the ship of state. In the next chapter, we consider the problem of undue influence — the regulation of lobbyists and party financing. Here are two compartments in the ship of state that are generally in worse shape than those designed to prevent conflicts of interest.

Undue Influence: Party Financing and Lobbyists

Undue influence, as noted earlier, is an attempt to influence a policy decision by taking advantage of privileges not available to the general public. Forms of undue influence range from individuals cultivating manipulative friendships with politicians in order to influence hirings or contract decisions to individuals offering bribes of hundreds of thousands of dollars to officials in order to achieve particular outcomes.

Since prior to the time of Confederation, the electoral process at all levels has been subjected to increasing regulation to make it more fair and to combat corruption. In contrast, the regulation of lobbyists began as late as 1988 at the federal level, and such regulations are only now being contemplated in some provinces.

In this chapter we will consider cases that illustrate some of the gaps in electoral and party-financing laws. We will examine the cases of Patti Starr and Michael Harris, as well as problems associated with party leadership campaigns and weaknesses in municipal election financing regulations that allow candidates to be captured by the development industry. Furthermore, we will consider two cases that show why the regulation of lobbyists is an important consideration in promoting ethical politics: the 1993 attempt to privatize Pearson Airport and the Airbus affair.

Undue Influence in Party Financing

The two most powerful methods of preventing corruption in party financing developed by our political system so far are public disclosure and limits on campaign contributions from single sources.

The federal government and the provinces require political parties to disclose the amounts and sources of all of their donations over certain minimum amounts — usually $100. The theory behind disclosure is that party members, whether in or out of government,

would not want to be seen to offer favours to their financial supporters because such actions would damage the party's reputation. In
addition, Ontario and Quebec limit annual contributions from single
sources at both the provincial and municipal levels. In non-election
years, these limits are $750 in Ontario, and $3,000 in Quebec.

Unfortunately, the exchange of party contributions for public-office favours has not been eradicated, and those intent on continuing
this practice are ingenious in finding ways to circumvent the rules.
The Patti Starr affair is a case in point.

The Patti Starr Case

In February 1989, *The Globe and Mail* discovered that the Toronto
section of the National Council of Jewish Women (NCJW), a charitable organization run by Patti Starr, had made substantial contributions to various federal and provincial politicians in the Liberal and
Conservative parties and to municipal politicians.[1] At that time, there
was a limit of $500 on single-source contributions to provincial
riding associations and municipal candidates in Ontario; this amount
could be doubled during an election period. Although there was no
limit on contributions to federal parties and candidates, federal law
prohibited charitable organizations from making political donations.

The allegations led to a provincial inquiry, which was discontin-
ued when a judge ruled that the inquiry's terms of reference exceeded
provincial jurisdiction and that the inquiry might jeopardize the
rights of persons investigated. However, a separate police investigation led to charges being laid against Starr, and in 1991 she was
convicted of eight violations of the Ontario Election Finances Act
and two breaches of the Canadian Criminal Code.[2]

The Globe and Mail and *The Toronto Star* reported that Starr's
organization had donated as much as $150,000 to candidates and
politicians either directly or through fund-raising dinners. At the
federal level, those receiving contributions included Prime Minister
Brian Mulroney, Immigration Minister Barbara McDougall, Opposition Leader John Turner, Conservative MP William Attewell, and
Liberal MP Robert Kaplan. Politicians who benefitted at the provincial level included Premier David Peterson; Liberal ministers Elinor
Caplan, Ed Fulton, Hugh O'Neil, Bernard Grandmaître, Alvin Curl-
ing, Chaviva Hosek, and Mavis Wilson; Conservative MPPs Susan
Fish, Dennis Timbrell, and Kenneth Keyes; and Liberal MPPs Joseph
Cordiano, Ron Kanter, and Claudio Poisinelli. Municipal politicians
who were favoured by Starr's largesse included Mayor Art Eggleton.

The money came from a Toronto development company, Tridel Corporation, which paid the charity for consulting services, and from provincial sales-tax rebates that were supposed to have been passed on to tenants in a housing project operated by the Toronto section of the NCJW.[3]

Starr had attempted to bypass Ontario's $500 annual contribution limit by giving a number of persons associated with the charity funds from the charity's political slush fund; these persons would in turn pass on the funds in $500 allotments to various provincial and municipal candidates. The donations were often made at strategic times to increase their impact — for example, when it appeared that candidates were running short of funds during a campaign. The politicians who received the illegal donations — which for the most part were returned after the scandal broke — were in positions (current or potential) to provide political assistance to the charity, to Tridel, or to Starr personally. (For example, the Toronto section of the NCJW needed support to maintain its charitable status, and Tridel was concerned with municipal zoning regulations. Furthermore, the Liberal cabinet appointed Starr as chair of Ontario Place in September 1987.) None of the politicians who received donations said that they had ever done any political favours for the charity, for Tridel, or for Starr in return for the campaign contributions.[4]

According to *The Globe and Mail*, NDP MP John Rodriguez accused Immigration Minister Barbara McDougall of intervening to help the housing project run by the Toronto section of the NCJW receive official charitable status from Revenue Canada.[5] Normally, a housing project must devote 100 per cent of its units to charitable purposes to receive charitable status, but only 60 per cent of the units in the NCJW project were reserved for charitable purposes. Nevertheless, the housing project did eventually receive charitable status after Revenue Canada received inquiries from staff in Barbara McDougall's office. Revenue Minister Otto Jelinek maintained that McDougall's staff had merely made routine inquiries about the status of the application and had not attempted to influence the position of Revenue Canada. But as Ontario Integrity Commissioner Gregory Evans has noted in his annual reports, routine inquiries from a minister's office, unless handled carefully, can often be interpreted as indications of a minister's preference, even if this is not the case.

Starr eventually admitted that she had illegally used provincial sales-tax rebates intended for the housing project for political contributions. However, she saw nothing wrong with what she had done.

"It wasn't sinister. It wasn't sleazy. It wasn't political."[6] Her conclusion is difficult to accept, however, given all the illegal activities that Starr was convicted of participating in.

The evidence that surfaced during the time of the Starr scandal indicated that few of the politicians who had received donations from Starr's charity realized that these donations had been made. If politicians do not pay much attention to where their funds come from, then what is the point of making strategic political donations in the first place?

There are several possible explanations for these kinds of donations. The connection between a campaign contribution and a public-office favour is rarely explicit. Donors may expect that their donations will result in favourable treatment in the future, but the candidate receiving the funds may not be aware of such an expectation. If elected, the candidate may attempt to provide excellent service to all constituents, regardless of whether they donated to the campaign fund. In such a situation, donors to the campaign might well assume that the service they receive is related to the campaign donation, even if there is no connection. Or a candidate may assume that a pay-off for a large donation is expected, although no discussion has taken place about what form it might take. And although favours may be expected and eventually provided, their exact form may never be explicitly discussed and may come as a surprise to the recipient.

There are very few politicians who would agree explicitly to taking a campaign donation of any size in return for a public-office favour. But the question is, do those who make campaign contributions sometimes receive special treatment because of those contributions? Clearly some do, and whenever it is perceived that a political favour is connected to a campaign contribution, the public suspicion that the political system is inherently corrupt is strengthened.

Both Stevie Cameron, in *On the Take*, and Jeffrey Simpson, in *Spoils of Power*, document how the PC Canada Fund had a well-orchestrated system for providing special favours to those who made generous contributions to the Conservative party under Brian Mulroney. According to Cameron, donors giving more than $1,000 to the party annually were invited to Ottawa once or twice a year (at their own expense) to spend a day enjoying exclusive policy briefings with cabinet ministers, including Brian Mulroney. In 1988, this scheme raised $6 million. Those giving several thousand dollars (personally or as the CEO of a corporate donor) were invited to a black-tie dinner at 24 Sussex Drive, the prime minister's residence. The guest list often included celebrities from the media world who were invited for the interest of the major Conservative funders. Only the best food and wine were served at these VIP dinners. The cost was borne by Canadian taxpayers.[7]

But most favours to campaign donors are much more subtle. When Ian Greene worked as executive assistant to an Alberta cabinet minister in the 1970s, it was not uncommon for a constituent to introduce himself or herself as someone who had made a contribution to the minister's last campaign or to the party. Clearly, some special treatment was expected. In fact, these constituents were treated no differently from others, but because minister's assistants can often help to cut through administrative red tape, the donors may well have concluded that they had received special treatment because of their financial contributions. There is no evidence that the kind of influence Patti Starr hoped to wield as a result of campaign contributions was different in nature from the expectations of those constituents met by Greene in his minister's office. However, it was magnified hundreds of times by the scope of the funding activity. But regardless of how minor the contribution and how small the favour sought, the expectation that campaign contributions will result in public-office favours is contrary to the ethical principles of democratic government.

Another lesson can be derived from the Starr affair. We may safely assume that, as Starr saw nothing wrong with what she had done, there are likely others involved in politics with similar views. In fact, in our political science classes, there are always a few students who think that Starr was simply playing the normal game of politics. "Why else would people donate?" they ask.

There are two remedies to this situation. First, the party-financing rules must be strict enough to prevent such abuses. As we will show below, a great deal of improvement is required in this area. Second, and more importantly, party workers need a better understanding of the ethical issues involved in party financing. If political parties were to develop and enforce their own codes of ethics, and if these codes of ethics were faithful to basic principles of democracy, we could anticipate a substantial improvement in the ethics of party financing.

Payments from Political Parties

The Complaints against Michael Harris

In April 1996, *The Globe and Mail* reported that Ontario Premier Mike Harris had received substantial payments from his riding association to cover personal expenses over the years. In 1994 alone, these expenses totalled at least $18,000, and included $7,000 for upgrading his Toronto residence, $2,000 for meals and entertaining, $1,000 for golf club dues and fees, and nearly $1,000 for dry cleaning. Those making the donations that covered these expenses received tax credits ranging from 44 per cent to 75 per cent. As a result of the tax credits, Harris's expenses for entertainment related to party activities are subsidized by Ontario taxpayers.

Lyn McLeod, leader of the opposition, and Dave Cooke, NDP house leader, complained to Ontario's integrity commissioner that Harris had violated the province's Integrity Act by receiving these payments. They claimed that the payments might have put him in a conflict of interest, in that he might feel obliged to provide public-office favours to those contributing to his riding association. As well, they suggested that those making the contributions intended for Harris might be seeking undue influence. Furthermore, McLeod suggested that Harris had accepted gifts contrary to the Act.

The integrity commissioner, Gregory Evans, investigated and reported in early May that Harris had not been in violation of the Act. Considering the claims of conflict of interest and undue influence, he examined the relation between the donations and possible public-office favours for the donors and could find no evidence of a connection. (Because in Ontario contributions are limited to $750 per source and because most of these contributions would have been used to conduct the election campaign, there is no clear connection between the amounts Harris received for his expenses and particular donors.) Moreover, Evans did not consider the money received from the riding association to be a gift that had to be disclosed under the Act, as the payments were connected with Harris's constituency work rather than his work as an MPP or as premier. Besides, Harris had already disclosed these payments to the elections commissioner pursuant to the Election Finances Act.

The tone of Evans's report implied that political parties need to exercise caution when making payments to elected members. He stated that if a gift or benefit were provided to a member, the "ap-

lobbying for the benefit or the donor," that gift would be unacceptable under the Act. From this perspective, he noted that although the disclosure of payments from political parties is currently not required under the Act, "Whether such disclosure would be prudent is another matter."[8]

Can payments from political parties to elected members ever be used as lobbying devices? Clearly, the answer is yes. We could imagine a hypothetical situation in which someone wanting a public-office favour knew that a member's riding association already had enough money to cover election expenses up to the limit set by law. (Any active member of the riding association would be aware of the state of the association's finances.) Let us suppose that surplus funds were traditionally used by the riding association to cover expenses peripherally related to the member's constituency activity (such as a golf club membership), or even as direct payments to the member as an income supplement. In Ontario, such a person could donate $1,500 to the riding association in an election year, knowing that this amount would end up as a direct benefit to the member. As well, that person could donate an additional $8,000 to the member's provincial party association. If the member knew of the details of these donations, this knowledge could well influence the member's thinking about the donor's lobbying agenda. In Ontario, the prospect for undue influence in these kinds of situations is minimized because of the legal limits to the amounts that can be donated. At the federal level, where individuals and corporations can donate as much as they want to party associations, it is easy to see how these donors might influence an MP. As the Gravel affair indicated, some donors gave money to the Conservative party because Gravel had promised federal contracts in return. And as Brian Mulroney was advanced nearly $400,000 from the PC Canada Fund in 1988, it is natural to wonder whether someone expected a favour in return.

To prevent such practices, Ontario's Integrity Act should be amended to require disclosure to the integrity commissioner of payments from political parties. Such disclosure would enable the commissioner to advise members about how to avoid conflicts of interest that might result from these payments and would give the commissioner the jurisdiction to investigate alleged conflicts of interest in this area (just as the ethics commissioner in B.C. investigated whether campaign support from a developer placed the minister of municipal affairs, Robin Blencoe, in an apparent conflict-of-interest situation). As Mr. Justice J. Paul Barry commented with regard to

Premier Richard Hatfield's breach of New Brunswick's conflict-of-interest rules in 1980 for accepting supplemental payments from the Conservative party, conflict-of-interest rules that exempt payments from political parties from scrutiny are "a farce."

But in addition to this potential conflict-of-interest problem, which is not covered by Ontario's Integrity Act, payments from political parties to members represent another type of ethical breach directly related to the general principle of equality. It is unfair that political parties can use tax-subsidized dollars to help their candidates and elected members in any manner they wish when other tax-subsidized organizations, such as charities, are not permitted to do so. There is no good public-policy reason for candidates to receive such privileged treatment; it simply exacerbates public cynicism about the political process. Moreover, it is dishonest for political parties to collect donations for the express purpose of fighting an election and then use some of these funds to subsidize the lifestyle of a candidate.

A similar point was made in 1996 by Tom Flanagan, a University of Calgary political scientist, in an analysis of the controversy surrounding payments made by the Reform party to party leader Preston Manning and his wife. "Since 1994, Reform has been spending more than $40,000 a year on Mr. Manning and his family — on clothing, personal travel, holidays and other items." Flanagan's primary criticism of the payments concerned the party's attempt to disguise them as "personal expenses," even though Revenue Canada treats them as a taxable salary supplement. He claims that the party's handling of the issue "illustrates a culture of concealment that is out of place in *any* democratic political organization, let alone Reform."[9]

Our view is that salary supplements to politicians from their parties are acceptable under the following conditions:

- these gifts are *not* tax-subsidized;

- persons receiving such gifts report them as taxable benefits on their income tax returns;

- donors are made aware that their contributions are going into a fund for the personal benefit of the candidate rather than to fight an election campaign;

• there are limits to the single-source amounts that can be donated to the party's special fund to safeguard against the possibility of undue influence. An absolute annual limit of $500 per source might be appropriate, because this amount is small enough that it would be unlikely to result in undue influence; and

• payment should be fully and publicly disclosed pursuant to conflict-of-interest rules.

At the present time, these conditions do not apply in Ontario. Therefore, although Mike Harris did not violate the Integrity Act, the process by which he accepted tax-subsidized gifts from his riding association was, from our perspective, unethical.

Party Leadership Campaigns

Next to the financing of election campaigns, the financing of party leadership campaigns represents the most significant potential for undue influence through party channels. Even with an extremely effective election financing regime, if party leadership contests are open to undue influence, then another avenue exists for corruption of the democratic process.

The financing of party leadership contests in Canada, where candidates now can spend millions of dollars in their bids to get elected, is currently unregulated by legislation. It is up to the parties themselves to develop their own regulations for spending limits and for disclosure of the sources and amounts of financial contributions to leadership candidates.

The usual practice of political parties in Canada is to delegate to a committee organizing a leadership convention the task of making rules about disclosure of contributions and overall spending limits for candidates. In the 1990s, it is common for spending limits to be set and for contributions over $100 to be disclosed within three months after the convention. Yet there are three problems: only the NDP has required that the *amounts* of the donations be disclosed; the names of the donors are not disclosed until *after* leadership conventions; and there are few restrictions on how surplus funds can be used.

Two federal leadership contests since 1980 have been surrounded by controversy because of leadership funding issues. The leadership campaign fund for John Turner, who was elected head of the federal Liberal party in 1984, exceeded campaign expenditures by nearly

$300,000. The excess was used to defray Turner's living expenses during the months after the leadership convention, and to finance the transition from the Trudeau to the Turner cabinets.[10] This amount of money seemed like a rather large supplement for someone receiving the salary of the leader of the opposition, especially since most transition expenses are normally absorbed by the Privy Council Office.

Brian Mulroney's bid for the leadership of the Conservative party was a second source of controversy. Twelve candidates ran for the Conservative leadership in 1976, and all agreed to reveal the sources of funding for their campaigns as well as the total amounts that they spent. All eventually complied, except for Mulroney. Joe Clark spent $168,000 to win the leadership, while costs for runner-up Claude Wagner amounted to $266,000. According to Cameron, Mulroney may have spent more than $500,000. In 1982, Joe Clark promised to call a leadership convention if he did not receive at least two-thirds support at the party's national convention in Winnipeg in January 1983. Questions were raised about the sources of the funding for anti-Clark forces; former Conservative party president Dalton Camp suggested a few days prior to the January convention that Montreal businessman Walter Wolf was one source of large amounts of "offshore" money for the battle against Clark.[11] Although Clark marginally achieved two-thirds support — 66.9 per cent — he called for a convention in June to settle the contentious leadership issue.

For the 1983 leadership convention, the Conservative party had not yet put limits on campaign spending and, unlike the 1976 leadership convention, did not require candidates to disclose their sources of funding. According to Cameron, Clark's total expenses for the June convention were about $3 million, but Mulroney spent much more. Someone apparently anxious to know the sources of Mulroney's leadership funds organized at least three illegal break-ins into homes or offices where these records might have been kept in March and September 1984. As to the motive behind the break-ins, one "... theory, the one most favoured today, is that someone in the Mulroney camp staged the robberies, with the real motivation being the destruction of the financial records, including all the details of donors and expenditures that Mulroney himself steadfastly refused to make public."[12]

Then, in 1985, a company owned by Walter Wolf, Wolf Sub-Ocean Ltd., received $363,000 from a joint development fund established by Newfoundland and Ottawa. No bids were sought from other companies. The opposition parties criticized the contract as a token of appreciation for Wolf's efforts to get Mulroney elected as Conservative leader. Although Wolf himself confirmed donating $25,000 to Mulroney's campaign, Montreal's *Gazette* reported that he may have spent as much as $250,000. In response to the criticism, Science Minister Tom Siddon denied that the contract and the donations were connected.[13]

Controversies over the funding of leadership conventions have not been limited to federal politics. For example, in 1985, the Ontario Progressive Conservative party held two leadership conventions, and the riding associations for candidates Dennis Timbrell and Larry Grossman were criticized for channelling funds collected for electioneering purposes to their candidates' leadership bids.[14]

Clearly, the funding of party leadership contests needs to be completely transparent if undue influence, as well as rumours about undue influence, are to be prevented. Without doubt, the best route would be for the parties themselves to develop their own rules for transparency and to compete with each other for the highest standards. To promote access to leadership positions, reasonable spending limits should be placed on the candidates; and to prevent candidates from being "captured" by individuals or businesses, limits as low as $500 should be placed on contributions from individual sources. In addition, the names of contributors and the amounts donated should be made public prior to the convention. If the parties themselves find taking these steps difficult, then Parliament and the provincial legislatures would be perfectly justified in regulating party leadership contests.

Undue Influence in Municipal Politics

It takes money to fight elections. If campaign funds come from a wide variety of sources, then it is unlikely that any single source could have an undue influence as a result of campaign financing. If the winners tend to receive a large proportion of their funds from specific interests, there is reason for concern.

According to James Lightbody, a common problem in many large Canadian cities is that the development industry has a tendency to fund municipal candidates in order to further their own interests. "At an early stage of Laurence Decore's victorious 1983 Edmonton mayoralty campaign, his senior policy adviser asked that he be cautious in his solicitation of developers' funds; the answer was, 'There are basically no other sources!' "[15]

Decore was advised to avoid development industry funding in part because of the infamous example of former mayor William Hawrelak, who was first elected in 1951. "By the standard of virtually any day or place, he was corrupt."[16] In the late 1950s, a judicial inquiry found that Hawrelak had used public-office knowledge for personal gain on a number of occasions. For example, Hawrelak purchased some land for his brother-in-law near a motel strip and then intervened as mayor to have it rezoned for development purposes, thus substantially increasing its worth. He used his public position to negotiate real estate deals for Dominion Stores and Loblaws and accepted retainer fees from the latter while mayor. Release of the judicial inquiry report forced Hawrelak to resign, and in 1962 Hawrelak paid the city $100,000 in an out-of-court settlement for damages in these incidents.

Then, incredibly, Hawrelak was re-elected as mayor in 1963, claiming that his transgressions had been the result of minor oversights. In 1964, he got into land-dealing problems again and was dismissed from the mayor's office by an Alberta court. But once again in 1974, Hawrelak ran for mayor and won, telling voters that his past problems were merely conflict-of-interest technicalities. One theory about why "Wild Bill" Hawrelak was re-elected in spite of a history of corrupt practices was that there was a public perception that nearly all Edmonton politicians at the time were in the pockets of the development industry. Hawrelak was the most appealing candidate among a limited set of choices. Lightbody argues that Hawrelak's two re-elections were in part a result of his success in persuading many voters that British standards of morality were simply there to prevent non-Anglo-Saxons from assuming their rightful place in government. Lightbody considers that similar strategies would unlikely be successful today because of higher ethical expectations among voters in the 1990s.[17]

Recent electoral incidents in Winnipeg illustrate these higher standards. Manitoba has had a municipal conflict-of-interest act since 1983. In addition, a 1990 Winnipeg city by-law limits campaign spending of registered candidates; the formula is based on the Consumer Price Index, and the result limits expenditures of candidates for mayor to about $200,000 and candidates for councillor to about $40,000. As well, the by-law limits single-source contributions ($750 for council candidates, and $1,500 for mayoral candidates) and requires the disclosure of all contributions of over $250. As a result of these laws, during the 1992 civic elections, ethical issues dogged

Dave Brown, who was dubbed by the media the "developer's candidate" for mayor. It became public knowledge that the development industry had established a $350,000 campaign war-chest for Brown, but he had to dissociate himself from the fund because it was $150,000 over the legal spending limit. As well, Brown had previously been involved in conflict-of-interest allegations surrounding his subcontracting firm. The firm had gained a city contract, which Brown had not only lobbied for when he was on city council, but had voted on. These ethical concerns, according to Kenneth Gibbons, led to his resounding defeat in the election.[18]

Despite advances elsewhere, development-industry involvement in municipal politics remains a troubling issue in the Toronto area. From the early 1980s, it was suspected that members of the development industry funded the campaigns of many municipal politicians in Toronto in the hope that if their candidates won, they would make decisions favourable to the developers. Pressure was put on municipal politicians to disclose voluntarily their campaign contributions, but many resisted. In 1987, legislation was passed in Ontario to limit municipal campaign contributions to $500 from a single source (since raised to $750) and to require donations of more than $100 per source to be disclosed.

The Globe and Mail examined campaign donations in the 1988 Toronto municipal elections and reported that three-quarters of the campaign contributions received by politicians elected in Toronto and the four surrounding regions were donated by developers, contractors, lawyers associated with the development industry, real-estate brokers, and construction-supply firms. These are all businesses that could potentially reap great benefits from the decisions of the municipal councils regarding zoning, planning, and contracts for the construction of water works, sewers, roads, and garbage collection. Moreover, the election law allowed candidates to pocket any contributions that were not spent on the campaign, and a number of candidates had surpluses.[19] In 1987 the newspaper noted a number of occasions in which councillors whose campaigns were funded primarily by the development industry voted routinely in favour of changes to zoning by-laws as proposed by their financial backers. In some cases, lawyers for developers would interrupt council meetings to lobby the councillors whose campaigns they had helped fund.[20]

Some members of the development industry were not content to seek influence through campaign contributions alone. As a result of *The Globe and Mail* stories and other allegations of corruption in

municipal politics in the Toronto area, in 1991 the police forces of
Metro Toronto and the surrounding regions launched an investigation
into municipal corruption. A number of persons were consequently
charged and convicted of municipal corruption and breach of trust
under the Criminal Code. Anthony Mandarano, the former deputy
mayor of the borough of York, was sentenced to fifteen months in
prison, and Jim Fera, a former York councillor, to eighteen months.
However, the best-known case is that of Mario Gentile. Gentile was
a Metro Toronto councillor who, between 1988 and 1992, accepted
$170,000 in bribes from a developer named Louis Charles for voting
in favour of by-laws that would advance Charles's development
projects and for trying to persuade other councillors to support the
projects. Gentile was sentenced to two years in jail and fined
$92,000, while Charles was sentenced to nine months in prison.[21]

At Gentile's trial, Charles testified that he spent $190,000 over
two and a half years on business-related entertaining, and about a
third of this amount was spent on municipal politicians. "A developer has to know somebody to get a project started, Mr. Charles
said. If you can address Mr. Tonks [Metro Toronto's Chairman] as
Alan, 'the ball game and the playing field changes.' " He also described his dining of politicians as "a reward for something that
might happen in the future ... He said he was not unique among
developers."[22]

It is interesting to note that when Gentile was being sentenced, a
number of character witnesses testified that he was a generous, com-
munity-spirited person. North York Mayor Mel Lastman said that
during the seventeen years he had known Gentile, he was a "conscientious, caring man whom the 'small people' turn to for help." And
several Roman Catholic priests testified that in spite of the conviction, Gentile was respected for his financial generosity to charitable
causes and his public service. One priest said that "the reputation of
Mario is very high in spite of this incident. The people still think that
Mario is a very honourable man."[23]

Of course, it is easy to be generous when one is wealthy, especially
if part of that wealth is derived from bribes. But the point is that
Gentile was not necessarily motivated in his crimes by evil intent.
He might have never questioned the assumption that politicians are
the natural financial intermediaries between persons needing public-
office favours and public officials. He might have fallen into that
mode of operation by observing the political world around him and
never have stopped to think about whether democracy required a

higher standard. According to John Barber, "in the aftermath of the Gentile affair ... Metro Council seems finally to have realized that 'the usual way' [of conducting municipal politics] stinks."[24]

Given the potential for conflict-of-interest troubles in Canadian municipalities, it is no wonder that in his 1995–96 Annual Report, the British Columbia ethics commissioner, Ted Hughes, recommended that ethics and conflict-of-interest legislation be extended to cover municipal governments. He suggested that the commissioner's role should become full-time instead of half-time, allowing the commissioner to establish an education program about municipal conflict-of-interest rules and receive inquiries from municipal officials and members of the public. (The additional annual cost would come to just over $100,000.) We heartily endorse Hughes's views in this regard, and recommend that a similar approach be adopted in every province and territory. As Gregory Evans, Ontario's integrity commissioner, has pointed out, extending the commissioner's role in Ontario to the municipalities would not be feasible because there are more than 8,000 municipalities in Canada's most populous province.[25] In this case, a separate municipal integrity office would be worth the additional cost. In fact, in December 1994 the Ontario legislature passed the Local Government Disclosure of Interest Act, which requires not only members of municipal councils, but also members of school boards and other public boards to disclose their assets, to withdraw from potential conflict-of-interest situations, and to refuse gifts that would lead to a conflict. The Act makes provision for a municipal ethics commissioner to investigate alleged violations of its rules and to bring applications to Ontario's superior court to determine whether the Act has been contravened. As of August 1996, the Harris government has not had the Act proclaimed.

Undue Influence and Lobbyists

The regulation of lobbyists is a recent innovation in Canada, dating from 1988. Since that time, two incidents have not only confirmed that regulations to promote ethics in lobbying are required, but have led to pressure for greater openness and public accountability for the lobbying industry. First, there is the controversy about the Mulroney and Campbell governments' attempts to privatize Toronto's Pearson International Airport during the 1990–93 period. Second, there is the scandal over the 1988 decision of the Mulroney-appointed board of Air Canada to purchase a fleet of aircraft from Airbus Industries, a European consortium, rather than the U.S. Boeing Corporation.

There have been serious allegations of undue influence in both situations which involve former prime minister Mulroney himself.

The Pearson Airport Deal

About three weeks prior to the October 25, 1993 election, it became known that Prime Minister Kim Campbell was about to order the final approval of an agreement to give a private company, Pearson Development Corporation (PDC), a fifty-seven-year lease on Terminals 1 and 2 at Pearson International Airport in Toronto. This was a major project, committing PDC to between $340 million and $700 million in investments, and holding out the possibility of tens of millions of dollars in profits over the life of the agreement. There were reports in the media that prominent Conservative party supporters and lobbyists could reap substantial financial benefits from this agreement, and the Liberals attacked it as the most extravagant example of Tory patronage that had yet materialized. Jean Chrétien stated publicly that Campbell ought not to approve the agreement so close to the election. If she did, Chrétien promised to have it reviewed if he was elected and to cancel it with legislation if necessary.

Campbell, maintaining that the contract was good public policy, approved it, and political analysts agree that this decision was one factor in the most harrowing defeat ever suffered by a ruling party in the history of western democracy. Three days after the October 25 election, Prime Minister-elect Jean Chrétien appointed Robert Nixon, a friend and the former Liberal treasurer of Ontario, to review the Pearson Airport agreement and report back by November 30. Nixon found that the contract was "inadequate" and that the process leading up to it was "flawed" and "under the shadow of possible political manipulation." He recommended its cancellation, and on December 3, Chrétien announced that the government would cancel the contract, even though the cost of cancellation might reach as much as $700 million.[26]

After failed negotiations with PDC over the cost of the cancellation, the government introduced legislation in April 1994 to limit compensation to out-of-pocket expenses (about $30–40 million). The Senate established a special committee to study the Pearson débâcle in May 1995, and the committee reported in December after hearing from sixty-five witnesses. The majority of the committee, reflecting the Conservative majority in the Senate, condemned the Chrétien government for every aspect of its handling of the Pearson Airport issue. The Liberal minority issued a separate report, which not only confirmed the conclusions of the Nixon report, but provided additional ammunition for the Liberal government's position. Meanwhile, the Senate forced some amendments to the April bill to permit more compensation and then eventually defeated the bill on June 19, 1996. During this period, PDC began a lawsuit against the government for about $660 million, and the government was in the process of handing authority for administration of the Pearson Airport over to a not-for-profit Local Development Corporation.

This complex web of events raises a number of ethical questions. Was the process leading to the PDC contract fair? Was there undue influence? Did Prime Minister Campbell behave ethically when ordering the agreement to proceed shortly before a general election? Was the cancellation process fair? Were the Senate committee's majority and minority reports written with integrity? Did the Senate behave ethically in defeating the compensation bill? To answer these questions, a closer look at the events is required. The following information is derived from the Senate committee's majority and minority reports, unless otherwise noted.

Background
Pearson is Canada's busiest airport, and the second-busiest in North America, processing one-third of all air traffic in the country. It is the only airport that consistently makes a profit for Transport Canada. In recent years, Terminals 1 and 2 at Pearson have earned as much as $40 million annually for the Canadian government.[27] A 1987 study showed that the airport had a $4-billion impact on Ontario's economy and on nearly 60,000 jobs.

In 1987, the Mulroney government announced a policy to delegate control of Transport Canada's airports to provincial or local airport authorities. The preferred route was to encourage the development of municipally supported, not-for-profit Local Airport Authorities (LAAs) to take on management or ownership functions, although private-sector involvement would also be considered. Prior to this policy, the government had already decided to let the private sector construct and operate the new Terminal 3 at Pearson, the terminal that handles flights for Canadian Airlines International.

According to most observers, the bidding process for the construction of Terminal 3 was handled fairly and efficiently. Requests for proposals were invited late in 1986, and in June 1987 Airport Development Corporation (owned by Toronto developers Huang and Danczkay) was selected through an evaluation process overseen by an auditing firm. In June 1989, Claridge Properties Ltd. purchased control of the Airport Development Corporation, and therefore of Terminal 3. Claridge is controlled by Montreal's Bronfman family, known not only for its substantial wealth but also for its traditional support of the Liberal party. Claridge invested in Terminal 3 in the hope that Terminals 1 and 2 would eventually be privatized, and that ownership of Terminal 3 would prove an advantage in a bid for control of the whole airport. Claridge anticipated that due to the huge expansions needed in Terminals 1 and 2 to meet the extraordinary air-traffic pressures of the late 1980s, a Toronto LAA would not be in a financial position to make the necessary investments, and so private-sector involvement would be inevitable. And with thirty-five municipalities in the greater Toronto area, organizing a Toronto LAA was proving slow and arduous.

One of the losers in the bidding process for Terminal 3 was Falcon Star, owned by the Matthews Group of companies. Donald Matthews had been co-chair for the Conservative party leadership bid of Brian Mulroney in 1983 and was a past president of the PC party. Like Claridge, Matthews anticipated that the government would privatize Terminals 1 and 2, and he was determined to win the contract even though his company had no previous experience with airports.

In March 1989, Claridge's Airport Development Corporation sent an unsolicited proposal to Transport Canada to develop Terminals 1 and 2. In the fall, Minister of Transport Doug Lewis publicized the need to expand air traffic capacity at Pearson Airport. Three more unsolicited development proposals were sent to him, including one from Paxport Inc., a company owned by the Matthews Group and the Toronto development firm, Bramalea Inc. Then, in October 1990, the minister announced the government's intention to release a request for proposals for the private-sector development of Terminals 1 and 2; however, the formal request was not made until February 1992. The delay was caused in part by requests from municipal officials in the greater Toronto area to wait for the establishment of a Local Area Authority in Toronto, for a proposal from Air Canada to develop Terminal 2, and for an environmental assessment of the expansion of the runways at Pearson.

By 1992, the serious recession that had begun in 1990 had altered the economic reality of the Pearson airport. Air traffic volumes had been drastically reduced, and therefore any pressing need to expand Pearson evaporated. Furthermore, Air Canada requested postponement of the redevelopment of its Terminal 2 building because the drop in air traffic meant that it could not afford the increased costs. Moreover, the thirty-five municipalities in the Toronto area had finally agreed on the general shape of an LAA that could operate Terminals 1 and 2. However, the federal government had reservations about three aspects of the Toronto LAA proposal: the presence of municipal councillors on the board; Mississauga's insistence that the LAA should control the Toronto Island Airport as well as Pearson; and provincial involvement in the LAA. The Senate majority saw these as legitimate reasons for not negotiating an agreement with the LAA. However, the Senate minority, citing similar difficulties with other LAAs that had nevertheless been given authority for airport management in other parts of the country, viewed these reasons as convenient excuses for rejecting the LAA option and proceeding with privatization.

On March 13, 1992, Don Blenkarn, the Conservative MP for Mississauga South, wrote to Jean Corbeil, the new minister of transport, to urge the government not to proceed with the privatization of Terminals 1 and 2. After pointing out that the recession had eliminated the need for airport expansion, he emphasized the potential harm that privatization could do to the Conservative party's political fortunes: "What comes through to all sorts of people critical of our government is some sort of a quick pay off to friends who want to develop airports and it doesn't taste well and it doesn't sound well and it leaves all sorts of suspicions ... I know the close relationships [of a] number of the proponents of airport reorganization and their relationship with our Party and how supportive they have been in the past ... Overwhelming interest is to make sure that our constituents, and the country generally, are well governed and the whole proposal at this point does not balance and our detractors clearly know that."[28]

Nevertheless, on March 16, 1992, Transport Canada released a Request For Proposals (RFP) for the redevelopment of Terminals 1 and 2. The deadline for submissions was very tight — ninety days — although requests for extensions would be considered. According to advice from Price Waterhouse, the firm the government had hired to assist with the proposal process, the ninety-day deadline might have created the impression that the government was "not committed to a fully open and competitive process."[29] In the end, only two proposals were received — one from Matthews's company, Paxport, and the other from the Bronfman's company, Claridge. Paxport had already begun preparing its proposal, so the ninety-day deadline was no obstacle. Claridge requested and was granted a thirty-day extension of the deadline for submitting its bid. The Greater Toronto Area Regional Airport Authority attempted to mount a proposal, but had to abandon the process both because it could not meet the ninety-day deadline and because federal government policy continued to exclude recognition of the Toronto LAA for the reasons mentioned above.[30] A proposal was also submitted by a private company, Morrison Hershfield, but the proposal could not be considered because it was not accompanied by the required $1-million deposit. According to Robert Nixon's testimony before the Senate, he had been told by Morrison Hershfield that they were under the "impression, under the realities of the situation, that their opportunity for success was remote."[31]

Transport Canada established an elaborate evaluation process for the bids under the chairmanship of Ron Lane, a career public servant. Five evaluation sub-committees and a main committee examined the two proposals intensively between July 13, when Claridge submitted its proposal, and the end of August. Six categories were rated, and Paxport was judged to be superior on four; overall, Paxport received 577 points and Claridge obtained 497. An auditing firm was hired to ensure that the evaluation criteria approved by the minister were properly applied.

According to the Senate minority report, 50.6 per cent of the evaluation points depended on the proposed return to the Crown. The Paxport proposal promised greater revenues to the Crown, but on what turned out to be the questionable assumption that most of its costs could be passed on to the airlines and their passengers. The financial ability of the companies to follow through on their proposals was weighted at only 5 per cent. Claridge came out ahead on this criterion, but because of the 5 per cent weighting it did not count for much.

One key weakness in the evaluation process was the absence of a comparative model. The minister had directed Transport Canada not to undertake a comparative study of the costs and benefits of Transport Canada continuing to operate Terminals 1 and 2. Without such a study, the department was not able to advise the government how much better or worse off it would be through privatizing the terminals. These three evaluation criteria — emphasis on return to the Crown, minimal concern about the companies' financial viability, and the absence of a comparative departmental development model — had all been urged on the transport minister by Paxport's lobbyists.[32]

In July, according to the Senate majority report, "political intervention" came from an unexpected source. Michael Wilson, the industry minister, was concerned about the financial ability of Paxport and Claridge to follow through with their proposals, and he arranged to have two of his officials review the bids. This review raised serious concerns about the financial health of the Matthews Group, which controlled Paxport, and also questioned the high level of its proposed management fees. In November, a report from an assistant deputy minister in Transport Canada affirmed that the Paxport proposal, if it could be implemented successfully, would likely generate more revenue for the Crown than under current Transport Canada management policies, "but only at a very high cost to the airlines and travelling public."[33]

Glen Shortliffe, clerk of the Privy Council and Canada's top public servant, testified that by early November 1992, he had informed Prime Minister Mulroney that Paxport had been recommended by the evaluation process. A few days later, Mulroney told Shortliffe that he had seen Charles Bronfman — who of course did not know about the result of the evaluation — at a social function, and that Bronfman had made "a pitch at the Prime Minister about the importance to Claridge of winning the bid for Pearson redevelopment. As a result of that discussion, the next morning when I met with the Prime Minister, the Prime Minister asked me whether or not there was any possibility that once the announcement was out that the two could be — would — could come together so that everybody could get a piece of the action."[34]

In response to this inquiry, on November 16, Shortliffe sent a memorandum to Mulroney, which concluded that "there are few incentives for the bidders to get together." The memo also informed Mulroney that Transport Canada saw no need for construction prior to 1996 in light of reduced air traffic during the recession, that Air Canada had requested postponement of the project because of the high costs it would have to absorb, and that there was pressure from the Toronto municipalities and Ontario to approve an LAA option.[35]

In spite of these concerns and those of the industry minister, on December 7, the minister of transport, Jean Corbeil, made a public announcement that Paxport had won the competition, contingent on proving that it could finance the proposal. The Senate majority report concluded that this announcement was good public policy because Paxport's proposal would have resulted in significantly higher revenues for the Crown (if, in fact, the airlines and the public could have absorbed the extra costs); the minority report suggested that the announcement was a move designed solely to ensure that Paxport got "a piece of the action" if the company had to withdraw its sole-source bid because of financial problems. As both the Paxport and the Claridge proposals were judged acceptable, if Paxport had to withdraw because of its financial situation, Claridge would get the contract. But with Paxport publicly declared the winner, Claridge would be motivated to negotiate a merger with Paxport rather than wait for Paxport's withdrawal and risk Paxport finding another financial partner.

At this point, a number of high-profile lobbyists became involved, including Fred Doucet and Bill Neville for Paxport, and Pat Mac-Adam and Bill Fox for Claridge. Many of these lobbyists had close connections with the Conservative party and Brian Mulroney and were well paid for their efforts. Fred Doucet, a former senior advisor to Mulroney, was given a ten-year, no-cut contract worth $2 million.[36] The potential fees for the lobbyists totalled over $10 million.[37]

In fact, in January 1993, Paxport and Claridge began to negotiate a joint-venture partnership, which eventually became known as the Pearson Development Corporation (PDC). The negotiations did not result in a 50-50 partnership agreement until May; in the meantime, Transport Canada continued the process of determining whether Paxport had the capability to finance what it had undertaken to do in its proposal. Paxport had to prove financial viability to keep its bid (and the chance for a joint venture with Claridge) alive, and this was proving difficult. The Matthews Group, which owned Paxport, was in financial trouble, and so Paxport had to look for partners to help back its bid. One of these was Agra Industries, a company with ties to the Conservative party and which controlled Allders International Canada. (Agra had donated more than $275,000 to the Conservative party between 1985 and 1992, according to Cameron.) In return for agreeing to loan Paxport $20 million, Allders would get a twenty-five-year exclusive contract for the duty-free shops in Terminals 1 and 2.[38] This deal raised alarm bells for the government's independent auditor because if Paxport defaulted, an airport tenant would end up taking over the whole airport. It was furthermore unclear whether Agra was controlled by Canadian interests, as required for bidders on Terminals 1 and 2. The failure of Paxport to find suitable partners jeopardized the continued viability of its bid, and the Senate majority report fails to provide an adequate explanation as to why

Paxport's proposal remained alive after Paxport failed to meet the deadline for proving financial viability.

The events that occurred between December 7, 1992 and June 25, 1993, when Kim Campbell succeeded Brian Mulroney as prime minister, are even more complicated than those that had transpired up to the December 7 announcement of Paxport's win. They are set out in detail in the Senate majority and minority reports. Suffice it to say that the difficulties encountered in the development of a Paxport-Claridge proposal acceptable to the government were so significant that there was heavy involvement by Glen Shortliffe, clerk of the Privy Council, and other officials in the Privy Council Office. The assistant deputy minister for airports, Victor Barbeau, was "sent home on 'gardening leave' " because Paxport considered that his concerns were slowing down negotiations. According to Senator Michael Kirby, who himself had been a deputy clerk of the Privy Council, this level of involvement of the Privy Council Office in a business transaction was unprecedented.[39]

Mulroney evidently wanted to ensure that a deal was signed with PDC prior to his leaving office in June, but in the end this proved impossible. By the end of August 1993 a deal was reached that was acceptable both to PDC and to the Treasury Board. (The Treasury Board later refused to provide documents connected with its approval to the Senate committee, claiming that they were cabinet confidences. However, Robert Nixon apparently obtained these documents in error and relied on them heavily to criticize the Paxport deal. As well, *The Ottawa Citizen* obtained at least some of these documents and published summaries showing that the Treasury Board had reservations about the deal.) It was October before all the documents were ready for signing.

Bill Neville, one of the lobbyists for Paxport, became head of the transition team for Kim Campbell when she became prime minister in June 1993. But Neville continued to invoice Paxport for his lobbying efforts right up to the end of August. On September 8, a general election was called for October 25. At the end of September, the media began to question the propriety of the Pearson deal, and it soon became a major election issue. Opposition Leader Jean Chrétien publicly asked Kim Campbell on October 5 "to stop that deal right now ... You don't make a deal like that three weeks before an election when hundreds of millions of dollars are at stake ... I'm proposing a very simple thing — put it in the fridge for three weeks and let the government that is there deal with it" after the election.

On October 6, Chrétien stated that if he became prime minister, the Pearson deal would "be reviewed, and if legislation is needed [to undo the agreement] we will pass legislation."[40]

According to Kim Campbell's memoirs, *Time and Chance*, Campbell's campaign team advised her to delay finalizing the Pearson deal until after the election. She received different advice from Glen Shortliffe, who had remained clerk of the Privy Council, and went to Conservative Senator Lowell Murray for further counsel; both assured her that the deal was perfectly transparent and proper, and Shortliffe warned her about the government's potential legal liability for failing to proceed with closing on the date previously agreed upon — October 7. As well, Campbell writes that she was convinced that the Pearson deal would create jobs and encourage investment. She admitted that she had not considered whether it would violate constitutional convention to sign the deal so close to the election. Constitutional convention holds that governments refrain from making major policy decisions during the "caretaker" period after a defeat at the polls; they are also to exercise caution in this regard between the calling of an election and election day. Campbell wrote that she expected officials in the Privy Council Office to alert her if there was a constitutional reason for delaying the Pearson agreement — she said she would have welcomed a good reason for taking the Pearson issue off the election agenda — but no one sounded the alarm bell. As a result, Campbell ordered the deal to proceed on schedule. She also ordered that all relevant documents be made public to prove the claim of transparency, but details were not released as quickly as she had hoped. Clearly, the public preference at the time was for a more cautious approach, and as a result Campbell's remaining hopes of winning the election were further diminished.

Three days after the election, and before becoming prime minister, Chrétien appointed Robert Nixon, a former treasurer in Ontario's Liberal government of the 1980s, to study the Pearson transactions and report back. Nixon was given only a month, and the assistance of a small research team, to complete this task. After a succinct review of the 1987–93 events that led to the Pearson Airport agreement, Nixon's fourteen-page report points to five major deficiencies in the process.

- There was no good policy reason for the government's decision to settle on the privatization of Terminals 1 and 2 instead of choosing the LAA route, which was implemented in 1992 in

Calgary, Edmonton, Vancouver, and Montreal. In fact, the special privileges granted to PDC and not to the four LAAs were likely to create friction with the LAAs.

• Even if the privatization route had been justified, other management and construction firms should have been "sought out and given reasonable time to participate" in the bidding process if the government had truly wanted to generate the highest quality proposals possible. The Request For Proposals stressed the desirability of competition between the owners of Terminal 3 and the new owners of Terminals 1 and 2, yet the October 7 agreement would have created a monopoly situation.

• It was "highly unusual and unwise" that "no financial prequalification was required in this competition." Why go to the trouble of evaluating proposals that have little or no chance of being financed?

• Prime Minister Kim Campbell's order to approve the Pearson agreements "in the midst of an election campaign where this issue was controversial ... flies in the face of normal and honourable democratic practice. It is a well known and carefully observed tradition that when governments dissolve Parliament they must accept a restricted power of decision during the election period."

• The lapses in good business and public-policy practices were likely the result of patronage and the undue influence of lobbyists. "When senior bureaucrats involved in the negotiations for the Government of Canada feel that their actions and decisions are being heavily affected by lobbyists, as occurred here, the role of the latter has, in my view, exceeded permissible norms."[41]

Nixon recommended the cancellation of the agreement with PDC, with reasonable compensation for the expenditures incurred by the company. But compensation for "lost opportunity or profits foregone" would be unreasonable because of "... the circumstances of this unhappy situation, and the very early stage of its life ..."[42]

In early December the Nixon report was released, and the government announced that the contract signed on October 7 would be cancelled. Negotiations over compensation took place until April

1994 and then broke down. PDC wanted about $200 million including foregone profits and fees for lobbyists; the government was willing to pay only for out-of-pocket expenses in the range of $30 to $40 million. Without any prospect of a negotiated settlement, the government introduced a bill into the House of Commons on April 13, 1994, which would have limited the government's liability to out-of-pocket expenses.

When the cancellation bill reached the Senate, it was vehemently opposed by Conservative senators, who were in the majority until 1996. The controversy eventually led to a decision to form a special committee to hold public hearings into "all matters concerning the policies and negotiations leading up to, and including, the agreements respecting the redevelopment and operation of Terminals 1 and 2 at Lester B. Pearson International Airport and the circumstances relating to the cancellation thereof."[43] The committee consisted of seven members (plus the government leader and the opposition leader as ex officio members) and was co-chaired by Finlay MacDonald, a Conservative, and Michael Kirby, a Liberal. The Conservatives had the majority of seats on the committee. The Conservative senators wrote a 170-page "majority" report, and the Liberal senators a 125-page "minority" report. The committee met thirty times during the summer and fall of 1995, and the report was released in December.

The majority report found the entire process leading up to the Pearson Airport agreement to have been faultless, while the minority report not only backed Nixon's conclusions, but found a number of additional problems with the process and the decision. When both reports are read together, it is hard to believe that the writers attended the same meetings and heard the same testimony. The reality of the situation is more likely to be gleaned from a combination of both reports than from either one. The evidence reveals that dedicated public servants did their best to ensure that whatever the political overtones of the Pearson negotiations, in the end the agreement was acceptable according to departmental standards. But this does not mean that the process was necessarily ethically sound throughout, or that the agreement would not have resulted in ongoing management difficulties at Pearson Airport had it been implemented. Neither report should be given more weight than the other; it should be kept in mind that the "minority" report would have been the "majority" report had it come out a few months later, after the Liberals gained control of the Senate.

In spite of a Liberal majority in the Senate, the bill to limit compensation was defeated by the Senate on June 19, 1996. The vote was tied at forty, which according to the rules meant that the motion to approve the bill was lost. Four Liberal senators were absent, and one, Herb Sparrow, voted against the bill. Although Senator Sparrow thought that the Pearson Airport agreement was properly cancelled, he also felt it was wrong to prevent the courts from determining fair compensation.

The Ethical Questions

Returning to the ethical questions posed earlier, was the process leading to the Pearson Airport agreement fair, meaning that prospective bids were judged impartially? The testimony at the Senate inquiry showed that in most respects it was fair, but in one critical area it was not: the criterion of the financial viability of firms submitting proposals. Financial viability did not have to be demonstrated in advance, and it was weighted at only 5 per cent in the evaluation process. This decision was made at the ministerial level, and it is no coincidence that it reflected the position of Paxport's lobbyists. Not having to demonstrate financial viability up-front is unusual for a project of this magnitude, and it had the effect of biasing the process in favour of Paxport. (The Senate majority report skirted this problem.) After it became apparent that Paxport did not have the financial resources to proceed with the project, it seems to us that it was unfair to retain the Paxport bid instead of awarding the contract to Claridge. At this point, Prime Minister Mulroney played an active part to ensure that both Paxport and Claridge "got a piece of the action" before he had to relinquish the prime ministership. Mulroney was clearly not in a position to be impartial regarding his relationship with Paxport's owner, Donald Matthews, who had been long associated with the Progressive Conservatives and had been instrumental in helping Mulroney to win the leadership of the party. In these important respects, the process was unfair and therefore unethical.

Second, was there undue influence? Did certain parties, deliberately or not, attempt to influence a policy decision by taking advantage of privileges not available to the general public? Clearly, there *was* undue influence. Many of the lobbyists for Paxport and Claridge were friends of Brian Mulroney and were well connected to the Conservative party. Because of these connections, they had access to political decision makers that others did not. The Senate majority report provided plenty of evidence that the lobbyists probably did not have a great deal of influence on professional public servants (although one wonders why Paxport and Claridge would commit to spend millions of dollars on lobbyists' contracts if this were really the case). Nevertheless, these lobbyists obtained interviews with the top political decision makers whereas others did not, and this is unfair and therefore unethical. Important questions about their influence at this top political level generally went unanswered during the Senate committee hearings.

Did Prime Minister Campbell behave ethically when ordering the agreement to proceed shortly before a general election? No. The Senate committee interviewed three political scientists who were experts on constitutional conventions. John Wilson, a political scientist at the University of Waterloo, said that Campbell had violated the "caretaker" convention. The other two, James Mallory, professor emeritus at McGill University, and Andrew Heard of Simon Fraser University, thought that the caretaker convention applied only *after* a general election, but nevertheless both considered Campbell to have acted imprudently by not exercising the caution traditionally expected after an election is called.[44] The principle of parliamentary sovereignty holds that current parliaments cannot bind future parliaments, in order to ensure continuing democratic accountability. But Campbell's decision was not even a reflection of the current Parliament's will; it cemented into place a decision of the previous Mulroney cabinet. Campbell did not consult with her own cabinet about whether to proceed, and there was no chance that the decision could have been reviewed by the new Parliament after the election without Parliament having to accept substantial liability. In addition, the Senate testimony proved that there was no pressing legal need for the documents to be signed prior to the election.

Campbell's decision is surprising, given her earlier step of advertising in the *Canada Gazette* for what had previously been purely patronage order-in-council positions. In advertising these positions, she had demonstrated more courage in ridding Canada of its patronage yoke than any recent prime minister. The problem may have been with the advice she received. It is ironic that Campbell chose to rely on Glen Shortliffe — the man who had devoted so much effort on behalf of Brian Mulroney to get the Pearson deal approved. Shortliffe was hardly in a position to provide dispassionate advice.

Was the cancellation process fair? No. First, Robert Nixon cannot be regarded as an impartial investigator. He is a friend of Jean Chrétien and the Liberal party. His report is not as inadequate as the

Senate majority report claims, but it clearly suffered from time constraints, and therefore neither side in the dispute received a fair
hearing.

Were the Senate committee's majority and minority reports written with integrity? Clearly not. Nearly all the senators are patronage
appointments from Conservative or Liberal governments, and the
Conservatives were in the majority until the report was released.
They are the least likely group imaginable to investigate a possible
patronage deal impartially. Both the majority and minority reports
are biased.

Did the Senate behave ethically in defeating the bill that would
have limited compensation to the parties involved? No. The House
of Commons represents Canadians, and by tradition the Senate ought
not to interfere with democracy except very occasionally to protect
disadvantaged minorities. Paxport and Claridge, which sought to
claim millions of dollars in unearned profits, do not comprise what
is generally considered to be a disadvantaged minority.

Nevertheless, the compensation issue should be settled in a fair
and impartial manner. The rules of statute and common law may not
adequately cover the unique circumstances of the Pearson agreement
débâcle, but compulsory arbitration before a truly independent tribunal would be infinitely more fair than legislation imposed by one side
in the dispute.

If there is one bright spot in this sad affair, it is the presence of so
many professional public servants who were determined to act with
integrity in spite of the standards of their political masters. But it is
truly disheartening that not a single politician involved in the matter
can claim a clean bill of ethical health. The Pearson Airport fiasco
clearly shows that even a toughened-up Lobbyists Registration Act is
not enough to prevent abuses of the system that can occur when elected
officials are in a position to reward their friends. In addition, codes of
ethics are needed not only for lobbyists, but for political parties, as well.

The Airbus Affair

The scandal over Air Canada's purchase of a fleet of thirty-four
passenger jets from Airbus Industries shortly before Air Canada's
privatization is potentially the most important story of political intrigue in Canadian history. It has embarrassed Canada internation-
ally. As this book is being written, the story is still incomplete and
will undoubtedly overshadow the Canadian political landscape for

years to come. Like the Pearson Airport deal, it does little to enhance the image of professional lobbyists.

In 1988, Airbus Industries was a European aircraft manufacturer composed of a consortium of French, German, British, and Spanish interests. Its major competitor was Boeing of Seattle, and Airbus was looking for a way to break Boeing's stranglehold on the international market for mid-range passenger jets. A big contract with Air Canada, which was planning to renew its fleet, would represent a major boost.

The chair of the supervisory board of Airbus Industries in 1988 was Franz Josef Strauss, who was also the leader of the Christian Social Party in Germany. Strauss had an ally in Canada: Karl-Heinz Schreiber, who managed Strauss's businesses in Alberta and who was friendly with Brian Mulroney. Schreiber arranged for Airbus to acquire the services of his friend, lobbyist Frank Moores. Moores, who had been premier of Newfoundland from 1972 to 1979, was embroiled in several ethics scandals during that time.[45]

Moores was a close friend of Brian Mulroney, having nominated him for the federal Conservative leadership in 1976. After Mulroney became prime minister in 1984, Moores started a lobby firm in Ottawa called Government Consultants International (GCI). "By 1986, it was the biggest lobby firm in Ottawa, with billings of close to $5 million a year." He became known as "Ottawa's most powerful and controversial lobbyist," someone who could take clients straight into ministers' offices. "Former Mulroney cabinet minister Erik Neilsen has said there is 'no question' that Moores' influence included the ability to have cabinet decisions undone."[46] After the Conservatives were annihilated in the 1993 election, Moores sold his interest in GCI.

In March 1985, Brian Mulroney fired the Liberal-appointed board of Air Canada and replaced it with his political friends, including Frank Moores. Shortly afterwards, Air Canada began to consider how it would replace thirty-four of its older Boeing 727 aircraft. According to Cheney and Brazao, GCI was a lobbyist for Airbus at the time and was also representing two of Air Canada's competitor airlines. By acting for both Air Canada and GCI, it appears to us that Moores was in a conflict of interest, but there were no rules in place at the time to control such conflicts. Although Moores claimed that there was no conflict of interest, nevertheless he was eventually forced to resign his Air Canada board seat.

The Mulroney-appointed Air Canada board made two major decisions in 1988. First, Airbus Industries was awarded the contract to replace Air Canada's fleet. Second, Air Canada was privatized shortly after the fleet-purchase decision.

In 1994, journalist Paul Palango claimed that Brian Mulroney pressured Air Canada, prior to its privatization, to pay $5 million in consulting fees to Frank Moores's consulting company, a charge that has been denied by both Moores and Mulroney. Then in March 1995, both CBC television and the German media suggested that Airbus may have paid bribes to Canadians to ensure the sale of the Airbus aircraft to Air Canada. (Such dealings are not uncommon in the very competitive international aircraft industry; in Europe bribes are sometimes considered a legitimate business expense.[47] But the allegation of the payment of bribes in a first-world country raised international eyebrows.) Possibly as a result of these reports, the RCMP revived an earlier investigation of the Airbus sale.

In September 1995, the federal Department of Justice asked Swiss authorities to assist in the RCMP investigation, requesting them to freeze a bank account the RCMP claimed may have been set up as a conduit for Brian Mulroney to receive payments resulting from the Airbus deal. Karl-Heinz Schreiber tipped off Mulroney that the two of them were being investigated and faxed Mulroney an unofficial translation of the Department of Justice letter to Swiss authorities. Somehow, this letter ended up in the hands of the *Financial Post*, which published its contents in November. Shortly afterwards, Mulroney launched a lawsuit against the federal government for $50 million. The federal government has attempted — so far unsuccessfully — to delay proceedings under the suit, claiming that evidence presented in the course of the lawsuit might jeopardize its investigation of Mulroney. As well, in July 1996 a Federal Court decision backed up Schreiber's argument that the Charter of Rights and Freedoms applies to the actions of Canadian government officials abroad. According to Charter decisions, officials who wish to examine private records must obtain a search warrant signed by a judge. Department of Justice officials had not obtained a search warrant for the Swiss bank accounts because they were outside Canada, and this could make evidence obtained from the search inadmissible.

Regardless of the outcome of the Mulroney lawsuit and the RCMP probe, the Airbus scandal has alerted Canadians once and for all not only to the potential for corruption in the lobbying industry, but also to the depth and breadth that such corruption might assume. From this perspective, it is surprising that the regulation of lobbyists did not begin at the federal level until just prior to 1990, and that there are no regulations at the provincial and municipal levels. However, Ontario's integrity commissioner, Gregory Evans, has recommended that "efforts should be made to control [lobbying] by bringing it into public view through registration and other restrictive measures. In so doing, it will help to eliminate the more corrupt practice of influence peddling in which political decision-makers solicit benefits in exchange for a favourable decision."[48] If the Bob Rae government did not heed this advice, it is unlikely that the Harris government will. Unfortunately, it may take the provincial equivalent of an Airbus incident to persuade the provinces to enact safeguards against potential abuses in the lobbying industry.

Ending Undue Influence

The government of Canada is by far Canada's largest business, followed closely by the governments of the larger provinces. And yet the regulation of business to prevent fraud and corruption — both internally and externally — is far more extensive.

Until now, undue influence, when it occurs in the fields of party financing and paid lobbying, has often been tolerated as an inevitable part of the political process. Yet these practices have no place in democratic politics. Annual limits to single-source political contributions in Ontario and Quebec, and federal lobbyist-registration legislation represent steps in the right direction. These examples need to be followed in other Canadian jurisdictions. But most essential is a solid consensus among elected officials at all levels that undue influence is unacceptable. The additional changes that are needed — appropriate legislation, codes of ethics for political parties, a higher proportion of honest Canadians entering public life, and the more widespread use of independent ethics commissioners — will follow. It is to the role of ethics commissioners that we turn our attention now.

Ethics Commissions

Prior to the era of ethics commissioners, the most common reasons that elected officials became embroiled in ethics scandals were a failure to appreciate the seriousness of ethical breaches and their consequences, a lack of understanding of the rules, or an inappropriate interpretation of them. An ethics commissioner is an independent official who provides advice to elected officials about how to comply with the government's ethics rules and investigates complaints about possible breaches. If an investigation determines that there has been a breach of the rules, the commissioner can sometimes recommend a particular sanction to the legislature, such as declaring a member's seat vacant.

As of mid-1996, there were five provinces with independent ethics commissioners — Ontario, British Columbia, Alberta, Newfoundland, and Saskatchewan. Nova Scotia and New Brunswick have delegated the power to undertake this role to specific superior court judges. Manitoba and Prince Edward Island have conflict-of-interest legislation, and the clerk of the assembly handles the compliance paperwork, but there is no ethics commissioner. Quebec is the only province without conflict-of-interest legislation. Conflict-of-interest legislation exists in the Northwest Territories and Yukon with an interesting twist. The clerk of the assembly handles compliance procedures and provides advice, but investigations are carried out by a commission that includes the ethics commissioners of Ontario, British Columbia, Alberta, and Newfoundland. In the federal sphere, the ethics counsellor is not currently independent, but an independent counsellor has been promised by the Chrétien government.

One of the strengths of Canadian federalism has always been its flexibility. The provinces and the federal government can experiment with public policies, and the other jurisdictions can evaluate these innovations and build on them. In 1988, Ontario became the first province to establish an independent ethics commissioner in an attempt to reduce conflict-of-interest problems, and each experiment since then has taken a slightly different direction.

Independent ethics commissioners are an essential feature of the ethics rules of any government that is serious about integrity; therefore it is worthwhile to compare the various experiments with ethics commissioners. At first, provincial ethics commissioners were expected to deal solely with the prevention and investigation of conflicts of interest, but recently their duties have broadened to cover other aspects of political integrity.

Our review of the experiences of ethics commissioners begins with Ontario, the first province to create an ethics commissioner, and then considers the experiences of the other provinces. We will examine the results of the commissioners' official investigations and consider the consequences of their advice to elected officials, in order to determine the impact of the commissioners' role.

Ontario

The first ethics commissioner in Canada was appointed in Ontario in 1988 as a result of a series of conflict-of-interest scandals faced by David Peterson's Liberal government in the previous two years.

In 1986, there was no law in Ontario specifically directed toward the prevention of conflicts of interest. However, the premier's conflict-of-interest guidelines required all members of the cabinet, their spouses, and minor children to disclose publicly their real estate holdings (other than their home or cottage) and their shares in private companies and partnerships. They were required to sell or put into trust all shares in public companies (no matter how few) and to withdraw from potential conflict-of-interest situations by delegating the duties that created the conflict to a cabinet colleague. Ministers and their spouses were prohibited from entering into contracts with the government, in person or through a business. In addition, the Legislative Assembly Act prohibited persons involved in businesses that contracted with the government from sitting as members of the assembly.

The guidelines seemed adequate until David Peterson's Liberal government ran into two major conflict-of-interest scandals in 1986. First, the Eleanor Caplan affair erupted in June. Caplan was chairman of the management board and one of Peterson's chief ministers. She was accused of a conflict of interest because her husband, Wilfred Caplan, was an officer of a company that had negotiated $3 million in provincial government financing, in spite of the premier's guidelines that prohibited spouses of cabinet ministers from having an interest in companies contracting with the government. The issue was referred by the legislature to its Standing Committee on Public Accounts.

The committee reported in September that the Caplans had clearly violated the conflict of interest guidelines. But in addition to having simply broken the rules intended to prevent conflicts of interest, the committee suggested that Wilfred Caplan's association with the $3 million financing application "may have been one of the factors that weighted upon" the departmental officials when they were considering the application.[1] The committee found no evidence that the Caplans had attempted to use their influence for personal benefit but expressed concern that public officials might have wanted to impress the cabinet by looking favourably upon the application that Wilfred Caplan was associated with. This factor put the Caplans into a real conflict-of-interest situation.

Both Eleanor Caplan and Premier Peterson admitted in testimony before the public accounts committee that they had not taken the conflict-of-interest guidelines seriously enough. The committee concluded that the best way to prevent these kinds of oversights in the future would be to create clear conflict-of-interest legislation that would be interpreted and enforced by a "non-partisan and independent advisor."[2] This recommendation might have gone unheeded after the political storm blew over, had it not been for a series of new conflict-of-interest problems that came to light even as the Caplan investigation continued.

The René Fontaine affair created more unsavoury publicity for the government just a few weeks after the Caplan investigation began. Fontaine, who was Peterson's minister of northern development and mines, was accused by the opposition of failing to disclose all his holdings in forest companies, as the premier's guidelines required. This matter was investigated by the Standing Committee on the Legislative Assembly, which reported around the same time as the release of the Caplan report. The committee concluded that Fontaine had breached the premier's guidelines "in three major respects [by neglecting to disclose all his holdings in three forest companies] and in many minor respects" by failing to withdraw from potential conflict-of-interest situations regarding government decisions about his companies.[3] The premier was also blamed for failing to ensure that his ministers complied with the guidelines.

In July, with two of his ministers under investigation and amid rumours of other allegations, Peterson was compelled to take action to limit further political damage. He requested John Black Aird, the former lieutenant-governor of Ontario, to review the compliance of all cabinet members with the guidelines and to recommend improvements to the rules. Aird reported back to the premier in the fall, and like the Caplan committee, recommended the establishment of conflict-of-interest legislation and an independent ethics commissioner. He found that fifteen of twenty-one members of the cabinet, including Peterson himself, had breached the premier's guidelines in one way or another because the guidelines were too vague or poorly worded.

Aird recommended legislation that emphasized full public disclosure of non-personal assets (which would include everything except the member's home, cottage, automobile, bank savings, and pension plans), combined with recusal from potential conflict situations, rather than the divestment or selling of assets. "My fundamental assumption has been that full public disclosure of all economic interests and relationships is the strongest weapon in the arsenal of any conflict of interest regime ... If a Minister is prepared to make full and continuous disclosure, then he or she ought not to be required to divest himself or herself of a single asset."[4] Noting the mutual financial obligations that contemporary family law placed on married couples, Aird said that the disclosure rules should apply not only to members of the cabinet, but also to their spouses. As well, an independent ethics commissioner could provide consistent interpretations of the conflict rules by having personal meetings with each member of cabinet prior to their taking office. Providing the new ethics commissioner with the powers of a commissioner under the Public Inquiries Act would ensure the impartial investigation of alleged breaches of the legislation. And raising the status of the rules from mere guidelines to legislation would make it possible for the legislature to enforce the rules by applying sanctions against ministers who violated them.

The Peterson government accepted all of this advice when sponsoring the Members' Conflict of Interest Act in the Ontario legislature in 1988. In fact, the government went beyond Aird's recommendations and drafted the legislation so as to apply to *all* members of the assembly, rather than just to cabinet ministers. This expansion of the scope of the conflict-of-interest rules received mixed reviews. Some felt that only cabinet ministers were likely to be in a situation where they could make personal financial gains from public-office duties, and the inclusion of members at large in the rules was a cynical ploy to punish members of the opposition for having exposed the government to the conflict-of-interest scandals with such vehemence. Others felt that MPPs were just as prone as cabinet ministers to conflicts. Although these situations might not be as high-profile as those involving the ministers, collectively members' conflicts of interest, if left unchecked, would continue to erode public confidence in government. As the annual reports of the provincial ethics commissioner will show, the inclusion of MPPs in the legislation has proved to be the right course of action.

With the passage of the conflict-of-interest legislation, John Black Aird became the "interim conflict of interest commissioner" until a permanent commissioner could be appointed, and the Honourable Gregory Evans, former chief justice of the Supreme Court of Ontario, became the first permanent conflict-of-interest commissioner in 1988. His title was changed to "integrity commissioner" in 1994 when the conflict-of-interest act was expanded and renamed the Members' Integrity Act under the stewardship of the Bob Rae government.

According to Gregory Evans, writing in the 1994–95 Annual Report of the Commissioner, the name of the legislation and of the commissioner was switched from "conflict of interest" to "integrity" because the latter represents a broader concept of ethics that goes beyond purely financial matters. "The introduction of conflict of interest legislation is relatively recent, although the issue of integrity in public affairs has existed since the dawn of recorded history ... Public sector ethics are much more than conflicts of interest. They include a sense of loyalty and a respect for public accountability."[5]

The Act prohibits MPPs (including cabinet ministers) from using their public-office position to further their private interests or improperly benefit the private interests of someone else or to use information not available to the general public for this purpose. They must meet with the commissioner on an annual basis to discuss the nature of their own assets and their spouse's assets and to arrange for public disclosure of their non-personal assets. "It is recognized that disclosure ... is an invasion of the member's right to privacy. However, in view of the current public demand for openness in government, it is a necessary invasion."[6]

Only once since 1988 has a member failed to complete the required disclosure statement in a timely fashion. This instance occurred in the fall of 1994, when the commissioner recommended to the Legislature that the Progressive Conservative member for Etobicoke West, Chris Stockwell, be reprimanded after repeated warnings. Stockwell subsequently completed the required disclosure statement.[7]

Members are prohibited from accepting gifts or benefits unless they are simply an incident of protocol, and if these gifts of protocol exceed $200 in value during a year, they must be reported to the commissioner. They are also prohibited from benefiting from government contracts. Those members who find themselves in a potential conflict-of-interest position must immediately withdraw from the situation.

The 1994 amendments to the Act broadened the jurisdiction of the commissioner to include ethical issues beyond financial conflicts of interest. Members are now "expected to perform their duties of office and arrange their private affairs in a manner that promotes public confidence in the integrity of each member," and they are "to act with integrity and impartiality that will bear the closest scrutiny."[8] This wording is broad enough to prohibit special favours to friends and associates that are not of a purely financial nature.

The Act contains more stringent requirements for members of the cabinet, in recognition of their greater responsibilities as impartial administrators of the law and their increased access to situations where abuse of power might occur. Ministers may not engage in an outside business or profession. They may not trade in marketable securities or own a business (unless this is done through a management trust that the commissioner finds acceptable). The acquisition of land while in office is restricted to prevent ministers from taking advantage of insider information. And ministers must follow specific procedures to remove themselves from potential conflicts of interest. After leaving the cabinet, they are not allowed to benefit from government contracts for a one-year period. Many of these requirements, with the exception of the post-employment restrictions, also apply to parliamentary assistants (MPPs who have special duties to assist ministers).

The Act provides for the appointment of an independent integrity commissioner for five-year renewable terms by vote of the legislature. The commissioner is required to produce an annual report, which is an important method of securing the commissioner's accountability. The Commissioner meets with all members as soon as practically possible after each election, explains the purpose and operation of the Act, reviews the financial situation of members and their spouses, and advises them on how to avoid conflicts of interest and other ethical problems.

Has Ontario's ethics legislation gone too far in attempting to regulate political ethics? Ian Scott, Ontario's attorney general in 1988 and the primary author of the legislation, has indicated that the legislation might be unnecessarily strict and that the Liberal and then NDP governments were forced into accepting such a stringent regime by an overly cynical public that had been misled by exaggerated media stories about political corruption.[9] However, most commentators believe that while the danger of over-regulation is real, Ontario's Act is relatively mild. In particular, the commissioner's opinions about the handling of specific ethical problems encountered by elected members and summarized in his annual reports are considered of special value in tackling ethical problems in politics.

At any time, members of the assembly may request the commissioner to provide an opinion as to whether a particular situation presents an ethical problem and if so, how it ought to be resolved. The commissioner also has a mandate to consider "Ontario parliamentary conventions." This latter phrase, which was introduced in the 1994 version of the Act, refers to well-established parliamentary traditions promoting ethical behaviour — for example, MPPs may not attempt to interfere with the decision-making process of an independent agency or a court.

The commissioner is also empowered to investigate, under the Inquiries Act, any complaint received from an MPP about another MPP. The power to investigate complaints received from private individuals is intentionally omitted to avoid opening the floodgates to trivial or poorly researched complaints or to allegations designed merely to grab headlines. (Moreover, Commissioner Evans recommended to the political parties that their whips exercise some discipline over any of their MPPs who might be prone to making groundless complaints.)

When he was in opposition, Ontario NDP Leader Bob Rae was critical of the Liberals's conflict-of-interest legislation for not going far enough. In particular, he was concerned that public disclosure of assets, combined with recusal from potential conflict situations, was not an adequate method to prevent real conflicts of interest. After Rae became premier in the fall of 1990, he issued supplementary conflict-of-interest guidelines for members of the cabinet and parliamentary assistants, which required them to dispose of "any assets, liability or financial interest which causes or could appear to cause a conflict of interest; and all business interests."[10] In contrast, the 1988 Act would have allowed ministers and their parliamentary assistants to keep such assets after public disclosure. In addition, the premier's guidelines prohibited cabinet ministers and parliamentary assistants from violating judicial independence by contacting a judge or interfering with the due process of the law in their contacts with administrative tribunals, prosecutors, or the police.

It is our view that the additional restrictions that Premier Bob Rae placed on his cabinet ministers and parliamentary assistants requiring the divestment of assets were unnecessary. Rae and his party had traditionally thought of divestment as the best way to avoid conflicts of interest and may not have considered seriously enough the advantages of relying on the disclosure-recusal approach found in the Members' Conflict of Interest Act, a method endorsed by both William Parker in the Sinclair Stevens report and by John Black Aird in his 1986 recommendations on the prevention of conflicts of interest. However, the section of Rae's guidelines restricting communication with judges, administrative tribunals, and other officials in the justice system was useful. Although such behaviour is contrary to parliamentary conventions, some members may not be familiar with these traditional rules. The 1994 amendments to the Act incorporated these parts of the Premier's guidelines into the legislation by giving the commissioner the power to provide opinions about the operation of "Ontario parliamentary convention." Because Premier Mike Harris has not issued separate guidelines for his cabinet and parliamentary assistants, the emphasis of the conflict-of-interest rules in Ontario has switched from divestment back to public disclosure and recusal.

Conflict-of-interest commissioner Gregory Evans described his role in the following manner:

> The purpose of any Conflict of Interest legislation should be to provide a greater certainty in the reconciliation of the members' private interests and their public duties in order that they may perform their responsibilities and their duties in a manner which demonstrates complete impartiality and which will establish public confidence in the individual member, and through that promote respect and confidence in the Legislature as a whole.
>
> I believe it is desirable that the Legislature include individuals with broad expertise and experience in diverse facets of public life, and therefore the ethics legislation should not be so restrictive as to preclude such individuals from offering to serve

in the public life of Ontario. Ontario's legislation is not too restrictive.

Now, we do not accept complaints with respect to members from the general public. We occasionally have people calling up wanting us to investigate a certain matter, and we tell them to seek out a member of the opposition to present their complaints to.

Divestiture of assets is an extreme measure which should be resorted to in only the exceptional case. Any management trust should be subject to the approval of the Commissioner, who must ensure that it is an acceptable vehicle for dealing with marketable securities, including shares in public companies. In private companies, the resignation of an elected member as an officer or the director of the company will generally adequately protect the public, because it must be remembered that there is life — or should be — after a political career terminates and a member should not be unduly penalized for his or her contribution to public life.

In Ontario, at the present time, there are additional conflict of interest guidelines imposed by Premier [Rae], which of course can only affect the members of the government caucus. They have caused considerable controversy. I do not deal with conflicts with respect to the Premier's guidelines, other than I sometimes say to a member that he or she had better clear something with the Premier.

While it's true that morality cannot be successfully legislated, an educational program on ethics legislation will better define those gray areas when private interest may impinge on public duty, and can show how the problem could be resolved. I think it would be helpful if all elected members could organize a little educational program for their political and constituency staff, and invite the Commissioner to be present.

The fact is that the legislator basically must be responsible for his or her own behaviour, but when there is a problem or potential problem advice should be sought from the Commissioner. Now in the early days of my office, few people called me. They didn't know I was there or they didn't care. But now we find there are many, many requests asking whether members can do this or that. I think that one of the duties of the Commissioner is to protect the member from getting into trouble. I know we have to represent the public and protect the public, but you're protecting the public if you protect the member from getting into difficulties through prudent advice.

Finally, I think a Commissioner must be independent and responsible only to the Legislature. He or she should have the discretion to determine whether the alleged conflict will influence the member in reaching a decision on any matter in an impartial manner.

I think the Commission serves a useful purpose in Ontario.[11]

In each annual report, Evans has provided a summary of some of the opinions that were requested from him, and of any inquiries that he conducted. Between 1988 and 1996, the commissioner received some 790 inquiries about whether a particular situation might involve a conflict of interest, and if so, how to resolve it. Of these, 740 came from cabinet ministers, parliamentary assistants, and ordinary members of the assembly. Although exact figures are not available, it would appear that roughly a third of the inquiries came from each of these groups. Twenty-four inquiries came from spouses, nine were from former ministers or members, nine were from trustees, six were from a party caucus, and one each came from the cabinet or a legislative committee.

As Evans's remarks indicate, the inquiries from cabinet ministers and other members have been increasing, from 49 in 1988–89 and 40 in 1990–91, to 138 in 1994–95 and 196 in 1995–96. On the other hand, inquiries from spouses have decreased steadily from 11 in 1988–89, to only 1 in 1994–95 and 2 in 1995–96. Clearly, elected members are finding the role of the commissioner increasingly helpful, while spouses are becoming more familiar with the conflict-of-interest rules and have fewer questions about them.

On average, the commissioner found that 25 per cent of the situations inquired about constituted a potential conflict-of-interest. This percentage remained steady at about 17 per cent during the last three years of the Peterson government, and then declined from 16 per cent to 12 per cent during the first two years of Bob Rae's NDP government. But when the NDP was in the second half of its mandate, between April 1992 and April 1995, the proportion of conflict situations increased to an average of 30 per cent of all inquiries, and in 1995–96, during the first year of the Harris government, to 33 per cent. This increase may be an indication that during the years immediately preceding and following the 1995 provincial election, members from all parties were particularly concerned about avoiding potentially embarrassing conflicts of interest, and so inquired about more situations that were potentially troublesome.

The volume of inquiries and of potential conflict-of-interest situations is significant, as it demonstrates the cost effectiveness of expending public funds on a part-time commissioner, a full-time assistant, a secretary, and office overhead, all of which represents an annual expenditure of about $200,000.

The Act also allows MPPs to request the commissioner to investigate alleged violations by other members. During the entire history of the integrity commissioner's office from September 1988 to June 1996, there have been only four instances of an alleged breach of the ethics legislation followed by an investigation. It is remarkable that in eight years there have been fewer allegations of conflict of interest than in 1986, the year prior to the introduction of the original conflict-of-interest legislation. This attests to the usefulness of an independent ethics commissioner who can advise elected members about how to avoid conflicts of interest in their individual situations.

In April 1991, Premier Bob Rae requested Mr. Evans to investigate allegations by the opposition that the minister of community and social services, Zanana Akande, had continued to hold directorships in two corporations, contrary to the Act. Evans reported back within two weeks. He discovered that shortly after her appointment to the cabinet, Akande had sent letters of resignation to the corporations in question and thought that she had therefore fulfilled her obligations under the Act. However, such resignations, to take official effect, must also be filed with the Ministry of Consumer and Commercial Relations, and this Ms. Akande had not done because she was not familiar with the proper procedures. She was therefore in technical violation of the Act, although she had not intended to breach the rules. Akande subsequently filled out the proper forms. The inquiry cleared the air so that Akande was able to continue as minister, until another incident that had nothing to do with a conflict of interest led to her resignation six months later.

Also in April 1991, a member of the opposition alleged that the chair of the cabinet's management board, Frances Lankin, might have violated the act because she had been designated to negotiate on the government's behalf with the Ontario Public Service Employees Union (OPSEU). Lankin had worked for OPSEU as a labour relations negotiator prior to becoming an MPP. Evans found that Lankin had taken appropriate measures to "distance herself from her former position with OPSEU, and withdrew her pension contributions from OPSEU," investing them in a different pension plan.[12] Therefore, she did not have a conflict of interest. The commissioner noted that some might have viewed the situation as an apparent or "perceived" conflict of interest. The Act does not prohibit such perceived conflicts, and rightly so according to Evans, as there is no objective measure of this type of conflict. In our view, however, according to the definition of an apparent conflict developed by B.C. Commissioner Ted Hughes, there was no apparent conflict in the Lankin case, as there was no alleged *quid pro quo* situation.

In the 1992–93 Annual Report, the commissioner noted that he had received an inquiry as to whether Premier Rae's guidelines had been violated by Rae's health minister, Evelyn Gigantes. In June 1994, Gigantes had tried to mediate a dispute among board members of a non-profit housing centre in her Ottawa riding. One of the board members alleged that Gigantes' mediation attempt violated Premier Rae's supplemental ethics guidelines because the dispute between board members was already before the courts. Evans declined to investigate because the premier's guidelines were outside of his mandate. Subsequently, the Standing Committee of the Legislative Assembly investigated the allegations.

The committee, which had a majority of NDP members, concluded that although Gigantes did not attempt to interfere with the judicial process, she had nevertheless violated two of Rae's guidelines: "ministers shall at all times act in a manner that will bear the closest public scrutiny," and they shall perform their duties in "a manner as to maintain public confidence and trust in the integrity of the government." Gigantes had violated the guidelines because the possibility of terminating the legal proceedings was discussed at that meeting, and this conduct "had the potential to lessen public confidence and trust in the integrity of the government ... and in the integrity of the administration of justice."[13] Gigantes resigned from the cabinet but maintained she had done nothing wrong.

Finally, in 1996 it was alleged that Conservative Premier Mike Harris had violated the Act by using funds donated by his constituency association to pay for his golf club membership and a number of other personal expenditures. Evans was asked to investigate by Lyn McLeod, leader of the Liberal party, and by Dave Cooke, house leader of the NDP. Evans found that the matter in question was covered by the Election Finances Act rather than the Members' Integrity Act, and was therefore out of his jurisdiction. In our view, both the Election Finances Act and the Members' Integrity Act are in need of revision to cover loopholes such as the one illustrated by this incident.

Ontario's original experiment with an independent ethics commissioner has been successful by any measure. There have been no major conflict-of-interest scandals since 1988, as compared with several crises during the preceding few years. Members of the legislature are now educated about the nature of conflicts of interest and how to avoid them and receive consistent advice. Ordinary MPPs are using the service as much as cabinet ministers and parliamentary assistants.

Between 1990 and 1996, most of the ethics problems encountered by the Rae and Harris governments did not result from conflicts of interest, but from other breaches of ethical expectations. Eight of Bob Rae's ministers resigned, but none because of a violation of Ontario's conflict-of-interest legislation. Two resignations (that of Shelley Martel and Evelyn Gigantes' first resignation) resulted from a breach of the province's privacy law, and two (Will Ferguson and Peter North) were caused by allegations of sexual misconduct. Zanana Akande resigned because of allegations, later disproved, that the rents she charged as a private landlord contravened Ontario's rent-control law, and Peter Kormos was fired after he posed (dressed) as a "pinup-boy" in *The Toronto Sun*. (The Kormos incident generated a public debate about the propriety of a minister apparently endorsing the exploitation of sex.) One minister, Karen Haslam, quit because she felt she could not support the cabinet's policy on the "social contract," and only one resignation, Evelyn Gigantes' second one, occurred because of a violation of Rae's supplemental conflict-of-interest guidelines. This incident led some media commentators to conclude that Rae's supplemental guidelines were unnecessarily strict, and that Gigantes' attempt to mediate a messy dispute in a housing project was not only appropriate but ethically sound.[14] We agree that as a matter of principle, if an elected member or Minister is called on to mediate a dispute, they are fulfilling an appropriate and important public duty. But if legal proceedings have commenced, a minister should not get involved in mediation unless requested to do so by all parties after legal proceedings have been suspended, which was not the case in the Gigantes affair.

The Gigantes affair is the only instance in which a conflict of interest contributed to the Rae government's credibility problems. Although the legislative committee dealt with the incident in an impartial manner, this is not always the case with legislative committees, as the Senate committee's investigation into the Pearson

Airport deal showed. It would have been better for the allegations against Gigantes to have been investigated by the integrity commissioner, but this would only have been possible if the relevant portions of Rae's guidelines had been incorporated into the Members' Integrity Act. (The Act was eventually amended in this respect, but the changes did not take effect until 1995.) A system that delegates the investigation of some conflict-of-interest allegations to the integrity commissioner and others to a legislative committee might lead to inconsistency and confusion, as well as unnecessary duplication of effort and resulting expenses. According to media reports, the inquiry by the legislative committee cost about $200,000 — more than the entire annual expenditures of the integrity commissioner. The 1994 amendments to the Members' Integrity Act, which broadened its scope to include "Ontario Parliamentary Conventions," in effect incorporated into the legislation the sections of Rae's guidelines that were at issue in the Gigantes affair.

Turning to the Harris government, which took office in 1995, Mike Harris suffered a blow to his credibility when he accepted payments from his constituency association for luxuries that most Ontarians cannot even contemplate — and he accepted these payments while cutting services to the poor. But this is not a conflict-of-interest problem, although it reflects both a weakness in Ontario's election financing law and a question of ethics in public policy.

British Columbia

British Columbia was the second province to create an independent ethics commissioner after Bill Vander Zalm's Social Credit government was rocked by no fewer than seven conflict-of-interest scandals involving cabinet ministers in the late 1980s. The Honourable E.N. (Ted) Hughes became the acting commissioner in October 1990 after the B.C. legislature, in record speed, enacted the Members' Conflict of Interest Act. He was confirmed by a vote of the legislature for a five-year term as the first permanent commissioner beginning in May 1991. Like his counterpart in Ontario, Hughes's position is part-time, and the total expenditure of the office has been less than $200,000 per year.

Hughes's responsibilities under the legislation are very similar to those of Gregory Evans in Ontario, with one exception. A 1992 amendment to the B.C. legislation prohibited *apparent* conflicts of interest as well as real ones: "A member shall not exercise an official power or perform an official duty or function if the member has a conflict of interest or an apparent conflict of interest."[15]

Here is how Mr. Hughes has described his role:

It is my view that independent ethics commissioners are serving an important function. They are not trying to drive good people out of politics because of harsh and unrealistic rules, but on the contrary they are going to be quite a help to good people coming into politics and staying in public life.

I think that the 1990 B.C. ethics act was the only ethics legislation in Canada that was conceived, born, and delivered within 48 hours. I guess a good deal of the thanks for the content of the legislation is the law that was previously passed in Ontario. In the main, the Ontario legislation was copied in our jurisdiction.

We had a provincial election in British Columbia in 1991, and one of the campaign positions of the now Premier was that he was going to see that we had in British Columbia the toughest conflict of interest laws anywhere in the country. That was music to the ears of a good deal of the electorate in British Columbia and so as a result we had fairly substantial amendments passed to our legislation this past session.

Within 48 hours of the announcement of the 1991 election results, Premier-elect Harcourt sent all of the 51 [elected] members of his party copies of the conflict of interest disclosure forms, and they were asked to return those to him within two or three days. After he was sworn in as Premier, he sent me the disclosure forms of the group from which he proposed to pick his new Cabinet, and he asked me to make a report to him of my assessment of potential conflicts on the part of any of those people that he was contemplating taking into his cabinet. When he interviewed the people he decided to take into his cabinet he communicated to them some views that I'd expressed to him, and we immediately had meetings and we got things rectified where that was called for. I think that was really a very useful process.

In an attempt to make this the toughest conflict of interest legislation in the country, we now have in our legislation that an *apparent* conflict of interest is equally as unacceptable as a real conflict of interest....

You'll recall Gregory Evans saying that in Ontario complaints could only be made by members of the Assembly. That's the way it was in British Columbia until the recent amendments came into effect; now anyone can send me a complaint. My office has received dozens and dozens of calls — not all legitimate of course — from members of the public wanting to raise complaints in days gone by so I suspect that this is going to be a real growth industry. But fair enough — if they've got legitimate complaints the public can now come forward with them on their own.

My experience with the 75 current members of the B.C. Legislature — and of course I know them all because I have met with them and will be meeting with them all individually again soon — my own assessment is that today we don't have a rogue amongst them. If that's so, I think that augers well for the future because I'm satisfied that they all want to do the right thing and they've now got, with this legislation, the assistance to make that possible.

The other thing that makes me feel optimistic is that I think we're fast moving into an era where the public isn't going to put up with a lot of kind of shenanigans that might have well gone on in the past. I think the public expects today a higher standard than they once did. I think we've got a far more sophisticated public that are going to call for more changes to bring about ethical standards in the whole operation of government.[16]

In his 1995–96 Annual Report, Hughes admitted that the prohibition of apparent conflicts of interest was controversial among ethics commissioners. Indeed, Gregory Evans, in his annual reports, has criticized the prohibition of apparent conflicts of interest as too vague to administer. However, Hughes maintains that the apparent conflict-of-interest section has not been difficult to enforce. Indeed, he thinks that the higher standard of accountability required by the section should help to reverse the cynicism that many members of the public feel toward politicians.

While serving as acting commissioner, Hughes undertook the Vander Zalm investigation; the incidents investigated occurred prior to the new conflict-of-interest legislation taking effect. However, during his five years as permanent ethics commissioner, Hughes only once found a member in violation of the Act, and even on that occasion did not recommend a penalty. The one violation was the Robin Blencoe affair, an apparent conflict of interest that occurred shortly after the 1992 amendments and resulted from Blencoe's lack of understanding about the nature of an apparent conflict. This nearly perfect bill of health over a five-year period for British Columbia MLAs and cabinet ministers stands in stark contrast to the previous five years, when the government endured what appeared to be an endless series of conflict-of-interest scandals.

In his first annual report (1991–92), Commissioner Hughes described how he dealt with an inquiry from some cabinet ministers as to whether they would create a conflict of interest by participating in the cabinet's decision-making process about changing the regulations under the Compensation Fairness Act. The purpose of the changes was to allow for greater flexibility in negotiating future wage settlements for public-sector employees. Because some cabinet ministers were married to public servants, they were worried about a conflict. Hughes pointed out that the Members' Conflict of Interest Act exempts "an interest in a decision that affects a member as a broad class of electors" from the conflict-of-interest regulations; that is to say if an elected member's personal interests coincide with those of a great many other citizens, then it is not logical to conclude that the member's decision is based on personal interests when it represents the interests of so many others. Hughes decided that public-sector employees represented a "broad class of electors."

In 1993, as a result of the 1992 amendments to the Act, Hughes had the jurisdiction to investigate alleged breaches of the Act brought to his attention by members of the public. All but one proved to be without substance. The exception was the Robin Blencoe affair. In two instances, Hughes was requested to investigate cabinet policy decisions because a policy allegedly provided special benefits to some constituencies and not others or because a policy allegedly provided a special benefit to a company in which the government owned shares. Hughes wrote that his jurisdiction covered only individual ethics issues, not policy issues. (In fact, the ethics of public policy is an important sub-field of ethical politics, but it is certainly outside the jurisdiction of ethics commissioners.) In April 1994, Hughes was, for the first time, requested by an MLA to investigate an alleged breach of the Act. The minister of agriculture, fisheries, and food was cleared of the conflict-of-interest allegations.

During the 1994–95 fiscal year, Hughes received two more requests from members of the legislature to investigate alleged breaches of the Act. The first concerned Mike de Jong, an MLA, who in private life was a lawyer and who represented legal-aid clients. De Jong participated in debates and voting in the legislature about amendments to the act regulating legal aid. Hughes stated that he had to balance the interests of de Jong's constituents in being represented on this issue, as well as the obvious expertise that de Jong could bring to bear, against the possibility that the legislation could affect de Jong's private interests. In this case, Hughes was not satisfied that de Jong's private interests were substantial enough to impair his ability to participate with integrity in the debate, particularly as the amendments that de Jong supported "capped" legal-aid payments.

The second allegation was that Premier Michael Harcourt had been in an apparent conflict of interest by awarding contracts to a public-relations company whose principals were long-term political associates. Hughes found that Harcourt had not involved himself in the awarding of the contracts and moreover that it was under- standable, from the perspective of reasonable observers, that senior staff would "seek out persons with whom the government has a high level of comfort, trust and confidence, which may be based in whole or in part upon sharing similar political views," for public-relations contracts.[17] This particular incident raised the question of whether contracts awarded on the basis of political patronage can ever be considered ethical. Hughes provided a partial answer to that question in his decision about Municipal Affairs Minister Robin Blencoe's apparent conflict of interest: if there is a possible *quid pro quo* involved in a decision about a program established by law, then helping political friends is unacceptable. But in the case of the public- relations firm, a *quid pro quo* was not the issue; rather, it was a question of Premier Harcourt wanting to hire persons of similar political views for public-relations work. Although we reasoned in Chapter 1 that political patronage is ethically unacceptable in a democracy, we made an exception for the political staff of elected members, who are hired to advise on partisan political matters rather than to administer programs established by law. Hughes may have considered that public-relations contracts fall into the same category of political staff. We would agree, with the qualification that public- relations contracts in which partisan considerations are relevant should be narrowly defined to include only contracts that concern the cabinet's desire to express its partisan positions on issues, and not contracts dealing with programs established by law.

The Harcourt case also raised the question of whether the Canadian Charter of Rights and Freedoms applies to ethics commissioners. Hughes had requested a legal opinion on aspects of the Harcourt case from a law firm, and a local magazine requested a copy of the opinion. Hughes denied the request, considering the legal opinion to be confidential advice, and the magazine then went to the B.C. Supreme Court to ask for an order that Hughes release it. The legal action claimed that section 2 of the Charter, which guarantees freedom of expression including freedom of the media, required Hughes to release the documents in question. The resulting judgement of the B.C. Supreme Court was that the conflict of interest commissioner exercised investigative powers on behalf of the B.C. legislature rather than quasi-judicial powers, and therefore the Canadian Charter of Rights did not apply; no decision was made about what effect the Charter would have had it applied. Regardless of whether the B.C. Supreme Court was right about the application of the Charter, the case is indicative of the importance of the public profile of the commissioner.

Hughes completed his term as conflict of interest commissioner in 1996, and in his final annual report he reflected on the past and future of the ethics commissioner's role. He felt that annual meetings between an independent ethics commissioner and MLAs and at least one interview with spouses to discuss the ethics rules could prevent conflicts of interest arising from a lack of understanding of the rules, as the 1991–96 period in B. C. politics demonstrated. However, he stated that conflicts of interest represented just one kind of lapse in ethical conduct. The time had come, he wrote, to expand both the conflict-of-interest act and the role of the ethics commissioner to cover other ethical problems and "fill the void between the distant poles of conflict of interest at one end of the spectrum and criminal conduct at the other end."[18] He recommended that the Act be renamed the "Integrity Act," as in Ontario, and that the new Act should include a clause such as the following:

Public office holders shall act with honesty and uphold the highest ethical standards so that public confidence and trust in the integrity, objectivity and impartiality of government are conserved and enhanced.[19]

Hughes maintains that such a clause would be clearer than Ontario's reference to "parliamentary convention," but would cover the same ground. He pointed to the somewhat lax rules in British Columbia regarding members' expenditures of constituency allowances as an example of behaviour that would be regulated by the Act if such a clause were adopted. Although conflicts of interest now seem to be under control in B.C., other forms of unethical behaviour by politicians could continue to erode public confidence in the integrity of politicians. Hughes believes the continued erosion of public trust will have potentially disastrous consequences. He referred approvingly to a statement by Mr. Justice Isadore Grotsky of the Saskatchewan Court of Queen's Bench, which we quoted earlier and which bears repeating:

> A legislative Assembly comprised of members committed to the principles of honesty and integrity is fundamental to a democratic society as Canadians understand that term.[20]

Hughes also recommended that the ethics legislation be expanded to cover public officials, including independent boards and tribunals, and municipalities.

Like the Ontario example, British Columbia's experiment with an ethics commissioner has been extraordinarily successful in preventing serious conflict-of-interest scandals. Prior to the appointment of the commissioner, a half dozen such scandals rocked the Vander Zalm government, culminating in the resignation of Vander Zalm himself over a conflict of interest. In contrast, since the ethics commissioner began meeting with elected members to discuss compliance with the rules, only one minor violation of the conflict-of-interest code has occurred, and that so minor that no penalty was recommended. But as in Ontario, the focus of public concern about political ethics has shifted to other arenas. The "bingogate" affair — a scandal over a charity that raised money through bingos and other activities and then illegally donated up to $200,000 of the proceeds to the NDP — led to the resignation of Premier Michael Harcourt and to the near-defeat of the NDP government in the 1996 provincial election. This event underscores the inadequacies of party-financing laws, and alleged attempts by party loyalists to cover up the facts of bingogate forced the provincial NDP to ponder the "dirty hands" problem.

Alberta

Alberta enacted its conflict-of-interest legislation in 1991, following allegations of conflict of interest levelled against Premier Don Getty and another cabinet minister, as well as the recommendations of an independent review panel in 1990. However, an ethics commissioner was not appointed until 1992, and the Act did not come into full operation until March 1993. Robert Clark, a cabinet minister in the Social Credit governments of Ernest Manning and Harry Strom in the 1960s, was appointed by the legislature as the first ethics commissioner. He was selected from nearly three hundred applicants for the job by an all-party legislative committee. The role of the commissioner and the legislation is similar to that of British Columbia, except there is no mention of apparent conflicts of interest in the legislation. The annual cost of the office has been less than $200,000.

The position of ethics commissioner was a part-time one until 1995, when the commissioner was also given responsibility for administering the province's new Freedom of Information and Privacy Act. The new combined position became a full-time one.

Clark has described his role as "90% priest and 10% policeman."[21] As with the other ethics commissioners, most of Clark's time is occupied with meeting members, advising them about how to comply with the legislation, and giving opinions about what members fear might constitute potential conflicts of interest. In his 1993–94 Annual Report, Clark reported that he had received twenty-seven requests from MLAs or members of the public to examine alleged violations of the Act, three of which required investigation.

The first concerned a letter of reference that former attorney general Ken Rostad had written for one of his constituents who was about to be sentenced in court. Clark found that Rostad had not breached the Act. The second case was an allegation by the leader of the opposition that Ken Kowalski, minister of public works, had breached the Act by distributing copies of the budget to the Conservative caucus prior to its tabling in the legislature. Clark found that no private interests had been furthered by this situation, although he reported the Speaker's ruling that Kowalski had been in contempt of the legislature by giving his caucus a preview of the budget. Third, Dianne Mirosh, a minister without portfolio, was alleged to have provided her brother, a company president, with insider information that the company used to acquire shares in Syncrude Canada. Clark investigated and found that the minister had taken appropriate measures to ensure that no insider information could be passed on to her brother.

In 1994–95, Clark received forty-three allegations, and again he found that three required investigation. In the first case, the social services minister had provided information to a member of the opposition, Alice Hanson, about a controversial case, and the file contained the name of a social services recipient. Hanson was disturbed that the file contained the recipient's name, in violation of the privacy provisions in the social services legislation. Clark said he had no jurisdiction to review a matter under the Child Welfare Act, and that the new Protection of Privacy Act was not yet in force. However, there was no breach of the Conflict of Interest Act. In the second case, the controversial former minister of public works, Ken Kowalski, was alleged to have breached the post-employment code in the Act by accepting an appointment as chair of the Alberta Energy and Utilities Board. The Act states that ministers may not have business dealings with their former departments until the expiration of a six-month "cooling off" period. Premier Ralph Klein rescinded the appointment prior to Clark's report, but Clark used the occasion to create a broad definition of the kinds of dealings with former colleagues that were prohibited during the cooling-off period. The third case concerned the transportation minister, Peter Trynchy, who was alleged to have arranged a special deal to get his driveway paved at a price not available to the public. Clark found that Trynchy had paid more than the rate paid by the department, but he ruled that in the future, ministers should refrain from entering into private contracts with companies doing business with the government.

In a fourth case, Clark was unable to conduct an investigation himself because of a potential conflict of interest. It was alleged that the president of the Alberta Special Waste Management Corporation (ASWMC) had telephoned a person associated with an individual who had intervenor status before the Natural Resources Conservation Board. The president had allegedly threatened to cut off government contracts to that person's consulting company unless criticism of the ASWMC in a particular report was softened. Clark had at one time been chair of the board of the ASWMC and had recommended the appointment of the president, and so he rightly felt that his investigation would result in a conflict of interest. Premier Klein requested Ted Hughes, the B.C. commissioner, to investigate the situation. Hughes found that the alleged telephone call, as described above, had not occurred. However, he was disturbed that even had it occurred, it would not have breached the conflict-of-interest legislation because no *private* interest of the president would have been advanced. He recommended that Alberta's conflict-of-interest legislation be amended to include a statement to the effect that persons covered by the Act "are expected to act with integrity and impartiality that will bear the closest scrutiny" — an amendment that would apply to the allegation in this case. (He also recommended that a similar amendment be made to the B.C. legislation.)[22]

In the 1995–96 fiscal year, Clark received only sixteen requests for investigations, and he attributed this decrease to a better understanding by MLAs and the public of the nature of conflicts of interest. Again, Clark conducted three investigations, the most notable of which was that of Ralph Klein and the Multi-Corp affair, which is reviewed in Chapter 4. A second investigation concerned an MLA whose company had contracted with the government, contrary to the Act. The MLA had not been aware of the contract until he reviewed his company's accounts, and he then returned the profit to the provincial treasurer and requested Clark to investigate. Clark found that although there had been a violation of the Act, it had been inadvertent and so he did not recommend that the member be penalized. The third case was similar to the second, except that when the MLA discovered that his company had contracted with the government he ensured that the company did not request payment. Nevertheless, Clark found that the Act had been breached, though inadvertently.

Thus, during three full years of operation in Alberta, the commissioner has investigated nine allegations of conflict of interest, and has found only two very minor breaches of the Act. In the Klein case, Clark took personal responsibility for Colleen Klein's failure to report all the circumstances of her acquisition of the Multi-Corp shares, certainly an act of consideration, but in our view overly lenient. In spite of this, the commissioner's office has clearly been successful in helping to educate elected members about conflicts of interest and how to avoid them, has settled a number of issues that might otherwise have continued to fester.

From one perspective, to combine the responsibilities of an ethics commissioner with those of a freedom of information and privacy commissioner makes a lot of sense in the less-populous provinces. After all, conflict of interest, freedom of information, and privacy represent three dimensions of ethical politics. But the concept of a combined office has also generated a good deal of negative commentary in Alberta because the conflict-of-interest role may be eclipsed by the demands of the freedom of information and privacy roles. The combined office should be regarded as an interesting public policy experiment, and the results carefully monitored.

The Multi-Corp affair continued to cast a shadow over the Klein government in spite of the commissioner's exoneration of Klein from any serious wrongdoing, and in November 1995 Klein requested the commissioner to appoint a panel to review the act and recommend improvements. The panel consisted of Allan Tupper, a political science professor at the University of Alberta (and co-author of a book on political corruption), Patricia Newman, Mayor of Innisfail, and Francis Saville, a Calgary lawyer. The review panel's report, which was released in January 1996, recommended major changes to Alberta's ethics legislation.

Echoing developments in Ontario and British Columbia, the panel recommended that the legislation be broadened to cover ethics issues in addition to conflicts of interest. The major recommendations were as follows:

- The Act should be expanded to cover the registration of lobbyists.

- The Act should cover apparent conflicts of interest, as in British Columbia.

- Senior public servants with influence over policy decisions should be covered by the Act.

- Those covered by the Act should be required not only to avoid financial conflicts of interest, but to "act impartially in the performance of their duties."

- The Chairs of standing committees in the legislature and the leader of the opposition should be subjected to the same restrictions that apply to cabinet ministers, such as a "cooling-off" period after leaving public office and before working for related private companies (which period the panel recommended extending from six months to a year).

- Members should be obliged to research relevant information about the financial situations of their spouses, minor children, and associates, in order to discuss how to avoid conflicts of interest with the commissioner.

- In recognition of these changes, the Act should be renamed the "Integrity in Government and Politics Act."[23]

As of November 1996, the Klein government has not indicated which, if any, of these proposals it will adopt.

Newfoundland and Saskatchewan

Newfoundland and Saskatchewan are the most recent provinces to establish independent ethics commissioners, in 1993 and 1994. In both provinces, the legislation and the role of the commissioner are similar to those in the provinces described above, except that in Saskatchewan only members of the assembly can request an inquiry by the commissioner, although the commissioner may also conduct an inquiry on his or her own initiative. In contrast, in Newfoundland investigations can result from requests from members of the house of assembly or members of the public, and the commissioner may also initiate an inquiry. In Saskatchewan, Derrill McLeod, a lawyer in private practice, serves as a part-time commissioner; while in Newfoundland the chief electoral officer, Wayne Mitchell, also serves as the commissioner of members' interests.

By March 31, 1995, the Newfoundland commissioner had conducted two inquiries. The first was the result of a probe from the leader of the opposition, who questioned whether Premier Clyde Wells and another minister were in a conflict of interest when they participated in a cabinet decision to sell Newfoundland and Labrador Hydro Corporation to Fortis Inc., a company in which they had financial interests. Mitchell's investigation revealed that both ministers had at one time owned shares in Fortis, but had placed them in a blind trust acceptable to the commissioner, and neither was aware of whether the trustee had retained the Fortis shares or sold them and purchased different shares. The second inquiry was initiated by the commissioner to determine whether a member had fully reported gifts and benefits received. The Member "co-operated in providing additional information ... I concluded there was no basis to take further action."[24]

The Newfoundland commissioner also faced a dilemma in his first year: the spouse of a member refused to make full disclosure to him, and he had to rely on the member's estimates of the spouse's assets.

Presumably, the spouse considered that the disclosure requirements unnecessarily penalized spouses for being married to members. By the end of the commissioner's second year, however, the spouse had complied fully with the Act, apparently realizing the importance of a procedure that can result in valuable advice for members' spouses in return for the inconvenience of filing disclosure documents.

Neither commissioner has had to recommend punitive measures against a member. The Saskatchewan commissioner has only once had to conduct an investigation of an alleged conflict of interest, and the allegation proved to be groundless. Again, we see examples of how ethics commissioners can prevent conflicts of interest through their meetings with members and their spouses, and how they can settle issues quickly when allegations are made.

Nova Scotia and New Brunswick

The conflict-of-interest legislation in Nova Scotia and New Brunswick empowers the cabinet, in consultation with the chief justice of the province's superior court, to designate a judge to act as the conflict of interest commissioner. In Nova Scotia, members of the house of assembly must complete and file with the commissioner disclosure forms for themselves, their spouses, and their dependent children annually, and within ninety days of any significant changes. This information is available to the public. The commissioner is authorized to respond to members' written queries. As well, the commissioner will investigate alleged violations of the legislation if someone states under oath that they have reasonable and probable grounds to believe that a violation has occurred and can produce sufficient evidence. As a result of an inquiry, the commissioner has the power to levy a fine or to order the return of financial gains accrued as a result of a conflict of interest. The commissioner may also refer the matter to the Supreme Court, and in this circumstance the Supreme Court has the power to declare a member's seat vacant.

An interesting twist to Nova Scotia's legislation is that it also covers the procedures for disclosing contributions to political parties and candidates. The legislation clearly recognizes that conflicts of interest can occur as a result of political donations or donations combined with payments to elected members. Official agents for candidates, riding associations and parties must disclose on an annual basis all political contributions of fifty dollars or more, as well as the names of the contributors. Furthermore, all payments from riding associations and parties to members, their spouses, and dependent children must be disclosed within two months. The disclosures are to be made to the commissioner, or to a chief electoral officer if all parties can agree on appointing such a person.

Nova Scotia's legislation also requires public employees to withdraw from potential conflict-of-interest situations, but they are not required to disclose their assets and liabilities. The law provides for a six-month "cooling off" period before members or public employees can "switch sides" and begin to work for a company that they had dealings with when working in the public sector.[25]

The "designated judge" in Nova Scotia and New Brunswick acts as an independent ethics commissioner. However, because the administration of the conflict-of-interest legislation is only one small part of the judges' duties, they do not initiate the education of members in ethical politics as do the commissioners who are not sitting judges. Indeed, the principle of judicial independence requires the judges to remain more aloof from the members than the independent ethics commissioners in the other provinces. As well, the designated judges do not produce annual reports, which are important educative tools as well as accountability mechanisms. So, although this system is cost effective (the federal government pays the salaries of provincial superior court judges) and the judges provide an assurance of impartiality, this approach does not emphasize education.

Another problem with the designated-judge model is that in the case of a controversy, such as the Richard Hatfield Affair, the judge is inevitably drawn into the political fray, to the detriment of judicial independence.

The Federal Government

The role of the federal ethics counsellor has been evolving for the past twenty years, but this federal official still does not possess the independence from government enjoyed by the provincial commissioners described above. In this context independence means the ability to decide an issue without coercion. Independence is ensured in Ontario, B.C., Alberta, Saskatchewan, and Newfoundland by providing the commissioner with a secure long-term appointment and with accountability to the legislature rather than a member of the cabinet. The federal ethics counsellor is a public servant without special job security, and the incumbent reports to the prime minister.

The first federal ethics counsellor was known as the Assistant Deputy Registrar General (ADRG). This position was created by the Trudeau government in 1974 to process the disclosures of assets of cabinet ministers, which were required by Trudeau's 1973 conflict-of-interest guidelines. The ADRG reported through the minister of consumer and corporate affairs for resources, and for operations through the clerk of the privy council to the prime minister. The ADRG's role in terms of advising ministers about how to avoid conflicts of interest was similar to that of the independent provincial ethics commissioners. However, lacking the high profile of an independent commissioner, the ADRG could not be expected to wield the same authority in advising compliance, as the Sinclair Stevens affair illustrates. It is doubtful that a cabinet minister would succeed in avoiding a meeting with an independent ethics commissioner, as Stevens avoided meeting the ADRG in 1984 and 1986.

Another disadvantage of a commissioner without independence is that ultimately the prime minister settles the difficult issues of interpretation, as Brian Mulroney did regarding his own compliance with the conflict rules in 1988. Such an approach fails to persuade a sceptical public that the federal cabinet is serious about preventing conflicts of interest.

The ethics legislation introduced by the Mulroney government in 1988 and again in 1990 would have created a three-person ethics commission. There were two reasons for such a commission. First, the legislation would have covered not only cabinet ministers and MPs, but also senators and senior public servants. Second, reasonable persons can sometimes have different ideas about what constitutes a conflict of interest, and it was considered that in this regard three heads are superior to one. The Mulroney Conservatives apparently were never very serious about enacting conflict-of-interest legislation, and the legislation died on the order paper.

The Chrétien government promised to establish an independent ethics counsellor with a mandate at least to oversee the legislation regulating the activities of lobbyists. As a first step, in 1993 the ADRG's position was given a higher profile in several ways. The title was changed to "Ethics Counsellor" and the individual was made to report directly to the prime minister. The ethics counsellor was given jurisdiction over ensuring compliance with the Lobbyists Registration Act as well as the prime minister's conflict-of-interest guidelines. The current ethics counsellor is Howard Wilson, a career public servant. At the time of publication, a joint Senate–House of Commons committee was considering what form the independent ethics counsellor's office should take.

In 1992, the ADRG was Georges Tsai, also a career public servant. His comments outline some of the complex issues facing federal policy makers in their attempts to improve the conflict-of-interest rules and enforcement mechanisms:

Modern democracies need for their own sake conflict of interest rules, and they need them principally for two reasons. The first reason is to reassure the public that the public interest will come first, ahead of the private interests of elected officials or public servants. The second is that they can serve as a first line of defence in the protection of the integrity of public office holders, and their reputation.

If elected officials don't have a system of rules then they really don't know what they're allowed to do, because the term, "conflict of interest," is not intuitively crystal clear. Some claim that conflict of interest rules discourage people from entering politics. On the contrary, potential politicians want to know what are the rules of the game and want to have access to sound advice about appropriate behaviour.

Now the conflict of interest rules across Canada come in various shapes, from very general rules which are included just in the Criminal Code to more narrowly focused legislation like that in Ontario and B.C. to guidelines or administrative codes such as the one at the federal level. As well, there are three principles which are involved in any modern conflict of interest regime. You have the principle of avoidance (sell certain assets, resign from outside activities, decline certain kinds of gifts), you have the principle of public disclosure or "sun-shining" (which helps to reassure the public), and you have the principle of honour. Even if the rules were as comprehensive as possible, we would still have to rely on honour — the basic honesty of individuals to report unusual circumstances to the Commissioner, and to avoid conflicts of interest even with regard to permitted activities, gifts under $200, and assets which are considered as exempt to protect privacy. We have to rely on the honesty of the public office holder to discharge his or her official duties in an objective and neutral fashion, putting the public interest first.

All conflict of interest rules cover the obvious elements: assets, outside activities, gifts, preferential treatment, use of government property, and post-employment rules. Then there is the question of how far the scope of the rules should be expanded. Should the rules cover the assets and outside activities of spouses and other dependents? How should we deal with sanctions, monitoring and reporting mechanisms? Are we going to establish a Commission reporting directly to Parliament, or simply appoint a public servant who is credible enough to handle these matters? With respect to the specific tools, it is probably necessary to develop fairly sophisticated techniques such as blind trusts that really work, Chinese walls (mechanisms that prevent conflicts of interest within the same organization), codes of silence, and so on. At times the conflict of interest rules look like a hodgepodge of various elements, so in French I would use a word "ratatouille" — something with all sorts of ingredients and sometimes the end product is quite palatable, and at other times it's a bit difficult to digest.[26]

In Ontario, British Columbia, Alberta, and Newfoundland, the ethics commissioners have recorded in their annual reports some of their opinions on members' inquiries about how to resolve perceived ethical dilemmas. These provide a good deal of insight into the kinds of ethical lapses that might occur if there were no ethics commissioner to provide independent advice to elected officials. A sample of these opinions is reproduced in Appendix III.

The Future of Ethics Commissions

For the most part, Canada's experiments with independent conflict-of-interest commissioners have been a remarkable success. Both Ontario and British Columbia have been free of major conflict-of-interest scandals since the ethics commissioners took office and began meeting individually with elected members to discuss how to comply with the conflict rules. This situation is a stark contrast to the relatively steady diet of conflict-of-interest scandals endured by residents of these provinces during the several years prior to the appointment of the commissioners.

Independent ethics commissioners have been established more recently in Alberta, Saskatchewan, and Newfoundland. Not enough time has elapsed to evaluate their operations, but with the exception of Ralph Klein's difficulties with the Multi-Corp affair, the dearth of conflicts of interest in these provinces since 1993 augurs well for their future. The Multi-Corp affair may be an indication that Alberta's 1991 conflict-of-interest legislation contained loopholes needing remedial action. It may also demonstrate that when the future of a province's first minister is at stake, the local ethics commissioner cannot always be expected to take responsibility for the investigation. Clearly, Ted Hughes's investigation of Bill Vander Zalm was a model of objectivity and thoroughness, but Hughes came to the job with the stature of a retired superior court judge.

The experiences of the independent ethics commissioners have demonstrated the need to ensure that conflict-of-interest legislation covers ordinary members. In Ontario and British Columbia, at least a third of the inquiries about potential conflicts of interest have come from such members. The kinds of problems they raise, as demonstrated by the commissioners' annual reports, tend to be thought-provoking, and so it is crucial for the advice of an expert to be available. And this advice is not expensive, as it costs Ontarians, on average, less than three cents a year on a per capita basis, and British Columbians and Albertans less than ten cents a year each.

Three major areas of controversy surround ethics commissioners and the rules they enforce. First, should "apparent" conflicts of interest be included in ethics legislation and subject to determination by ethics commissioners? On the one hand, British Columbia's Ted Hughes thinks that the prohibition of apparent conflicts raises ethical standards to a level closer to public expectations, and he reports no difficulties in enforcing the rules against apparent conflicts, which have been in place in B.C. since 1992. As well, the B.C. approach toward apparent conflicts has been endorsed by Alberta's Conflict of Interest Review Panel. On the other hand, Ontario's Gregory Evans is sceptical about the usefulness of prohibiting apparent conflicts because, he feels, there can never be a sufficiently precise definition of the concept.

Second, how should complaints about alleged violations of the rules be screened? In Ontario, only members of the provincial assembly may request the commissioner to investigate alleged violations of the Act. Commissioner Evans suspects that his office might be flooded with trivial complaints without such a restriction. But in British Columbia, Alberta, and Newfoundland, where any resident can complain to the commissioner about an alleged violation of the rules, the commissioners report that while they are kept busy with investigating complaints, many of which are indeed ill-founded, they are still able to provide this service while working only part-time. Ted Hughes feels that public access to an ethics commissioner is an important service to democracy.

Third, should members' spouses and families be covered by the ethics rules, and if so to what extent? All five ethics commissioners, in their testimony before the Joint Committee of the Senate and House of Commons on a Code of Conduct in 1995, noted some resistance among spouses when the new ethics rules covering spouses first took effect. However, they also stated that in general, spouses had in time accommodated themselves to the rules and understood their importance. And all are agreed that unless spouses and close family members are covered by the rules, the public would continue to suspect politicians of using public office to provide special favours to their families.

There are two other questions about ethics commissioners that require further thought. The first concerns the implications of the discretionary nature of an ethics commissioner's opinions. Like a judge in a court of law, the commissioner faces areas of discretion in interpreting the ethics legislation. Even the best of ethics commissioners may make errors in judgement. But unlike a court of law, there is no appeal mechanism. (This is not true, however, in the case of the "designated judges" in Nova Scotia and New Brunswick.) It is possible that the formal inquiries of the ethics commissioners might be open to judicial review, but because the main criterion for judicial review of commissioners' decisions is likely to be the standard of "patent unreasonableness," judicial review is not an appropriate mechanism for fine-tuning the decisions of the commissioners.

The five independent provincial ethics commissioners, together with the two territorial commissioners, the two designated judges, the federal ethics counsellor and the director of the ethics and incentives group in the federal Treasury Board have formed a group called the Canadian Conflict of Interest Network (CCOIN). CCOIN provides an annual forum where the commissioners can, if they choose, discuss difficult issues. As well, after getting to know each other through CCOIN, the commissioners are more likely to contact each other between annual meetings for advice on particular ethics problems. This is better than operating in a vacuum. However, it does seem unfair that second opinions are not available to public officials who disagree with the ruling of an ethics commissioner in areas where the ethics rules are open to a variety of reasonable interpretations. Except in the cases of New Brunswick, Nova Scotia, and the federal ethics counsellor, the ethics commissioners technically provide advice to their legislatures through their investigations, and so the ultimate appeal is to the legislature. However, from a practical perspective, it is unlikely that a legislature would overrule the advice of a commissioner. It would make sense that the members of CCOIN could be empowered, by appropriate provincial legislation, to act as an appeal body for opinions of individual ethics commissioners. For example, CCOIN could set up on an ad hoc basis a three-person appeal tribunal, not including the commissioner whose decision was being appealed.

A second problem may sometimes occur when an ethics commissioner finds himself or herself in a conflict-of-interest position while investigating an alleged violation of the ethics legislation. Such a conflict may arise if the commissioner has been personally involved in some way in the situation being investigated, as was the case with Robert Clark when faced with an investigation of the Alberta Special Waste Management Corporation. Or a commissioner may find that one of the issues in an inquiry is the advice that he or she had tendered to a member during a private meeting about avoiding a conflict of interest. Further, a particular commissioner might feel that it is inappropriate for him or her to conduct an investigation into an allegation involving the provincial premier. When these kinds of situations arise, it would make sense for a commissioner from another jurisdiction to conduct the inquiry. There is no reason why the designation of alternate commissioners could not become a regular part of the system of investigating ethics in politics.

In spite of the success of the ethics commissioners, there is still a great deal of public cynicism about the ethical standards of politicians. In his 1995–96 Annual Report, Ted Hughes lamented that "... the level of cynicism, suspicion and lack of trust in politicians ... seems to continue without significant diminution."[27] And Gregory Evans, in his 1994–95 Annual Report, wrote that the central ethical issue in Canadian politics "... is not corruption of public servants, but the increasing public cynicism of our political system and those who serve in it ... The Canadian media ... has become increasingly negative. Whether it only expresses public opinion or is instrumental in forming it, the result is that we are left with the view that a number of our politicians are lazy, incompetent and dishonest."[28]

From our perspective, there are three main reasons why public cynicism persists in spite of ethics commissioners's success in reducing the incidence of conflict of interest. The first is that the prevention of conflicts resolves only part of the political ethics problem. If the rules regulating lobbyists or election financing or other integrity issues are lax, then ethics scandals will simply shift from conflicts of interest to another arena. Moreover, unless politicians develop their own personal codes of conduct, they will remain prone to lapses of integrity in spite of the most comprehensive ethics rules imaginable. Second, in the public view all politicians tend to get tarred with the same brush. If ethics rules are tightened up in one jurisdiction and not in another, the reputation of politicians in the first jurisdiction is still likely to be tarnished. Third, occasionally, egregious blunders in political judgement that deserve reproach are not covered by the legislation enforced by ethics commissioners. Two such cases surfaced in the summer of 1996. In Alberta, Premier Ralph Klein organized a premiers' conference in Jasper. Klein arranged for the premiers' travel, lodging, entertainment, and food costs to be picked up by a number of large corporations. Figuring that he was saving the taxpayers' money, Klein had Canada's leading politicians accept gifts from companies that frequently seek government business. Premier Frank McKenna got involved in much the same thing when he accepted a fully paid trip to the Atlanta Olympics from IBM. Recognizing the impropriety once the press made it an issue, McKenna reimbursed IBM for the expenses.

Accordingly, there is a need to broaden the roles and jurisdictions of the ethics commissioners. The Ontario commissioner's jurisdiction has already been expanded to cover Ontario parliamentary conventions. Hughes' final annual report recommended expanding the ethics rules not only to cover more general integrity issues in British Columbia, but to cover municipalities as well. And the Alberta Conflict of Interest Review Panel recommended expanding the scope of the Alberta rules and the Alberta commissioner's responsibilities along the lines of Hughes's recommendations.

Emphasizing the role and strengthening the mandate of independent ethics officers to curtail abuses of power are steps in the right direction. Nevertheless, the institutionalization of ethics commissioners is not sufficient to deal with such problems as broken promises and dirty hands. We discuss these ethical lapses when we turn to an especially thorny issue of political integrity in the next chapter.

Dirty Hands

In March 1993, a Somali youth who had infiltrated a Canadian compound in Somalia was killed by Canadian peacekeepers. Sixteen-year-old Shidane Arone was tortured and beaten to death. In 1994, Private Kyle Brown was convicted of manslaughter and torture in connection with Arone's death and sentenced to five years of imprisonment. In 1996 Major Tony Seward was sentenced to three years for telling his men on the night of Arone's death that it was all right to abuse prisoners. But five soldiers who stood by and watched while Arone was being tortured were later promoted. In 1994, the Canadian Airborne Regiment was disbanded, and Mr. Justice Gilles Létourneau of the Federal Court of Appeal was appointed to head a commission of inquiry into the Somalia mission. The inquiry was delayed on several occasions by the legal manoeuvres of some of those under investigation. Testimony before the inquiry alleged that senior military officers tried to prevent the inquiry from obtaining certain documents, ordered other documents destroyed, and approved the release of misleading letters. And when Corporal Michel Purnelle tried to leave his post with the Royal 22nd Regiment in May 1996 to provide information to the inquiry, he was arrested and detained by the military.

Canada's chief of defence staff, General Jean Boyle, admitted before the Somalia inquiry that defence department staff accountable to him "did not comply with the spirit of the law" when they misled a CBC journalist who was investigating military documents.[1] Mr. Justice Gilles Létourneau, the chair of the inquiry, suggested that there was a "mentality to alter documents" to conceal evidence in the defence department's public affairs branch.[2] We believe the evidence accumulated by the Létourneau commission indicates that senior members of the Canadian military were determined to cover up the facts out of a conviction that it was crucial to safeguard the reputation of Canada's peacekeeping forces and its military command structure at any cost, including that of honesty. Testimony at the inquiry also revealed that some senior members of the military believed that keeping the lid on the killing of Arone was important to Defence Minister Kim Campbell's campaign for the Conservative leadership. There is a similar disposition in many political leaders to "circle the wagons" and protect "their" institution, system, or party against revelations of wrongdoing, and that inclination is facilitated through a reliance on "dirty hands."

Doing Wrong in Order to Do Right

Perhaps the most serious challenge to integrity in politics comes from leaders who believe that they are justified in using duplicitous measures and other immoral tactics to accomplish goals that they believe will advance the public good. Such leaders flout laws and moral conventions for the sake of goals they consider to be so important (for example, safeguarding national unity, protecting the security of the state from foreign invasion or subversion, countering terrorist or racist organizations, bolstering confidence in the dollar) that failing to achieve them will result in disaster. The use of deceit, trickery, and force has a long tradition in politics and has been justified by a number of thinkers — the best known of whom is the Italian political theorist Niccolo Machiavelli — as necessary for the greater good. In other words, these political thinkers have argued that it is sometimes necessary to do wrong in order to do right because the ends justify the means.

When lying, breaking promises, and concealing the facts are carried out in the name of the public good, the political leaders who commit or authorize and justify such acts are known as politicians with "dirty hands." The image of dirt, which can also be understood to mean blood (that is, someone with blood on his or her hands), conveys the notion that the actor is tainted or guilty of doing something terribly wrong in his or her dealings with others, in contrast to someone whose conduct is above-board and whose hands are clean. In this chapter, we will review and criticize the justifications for dirty-handed behaviour. We will consider several famous examples of dirty-handed politics, including Watergate and the Iran-Contra scandal in the U.S. and the RCMP "dirty tricks" campaign in Canada, and we will argue that dirty-handed behaviour has no justification in a peace-time democracy.

Machiavelli observed that in the exercise of power

> Everybody recognizes how praiseworthy it is for a ruler to keep his word and to live a life of integrity, without relying on craftiness. Nevertheless ... in practice ... those rulers who have not thought it important to keep their word have achieved great things, and have known how to employ cunning to confuse and disorientate other men. In the end they have been able to overcome those who have placed store in integrity.[3]

Machiavelli was describing sixteenth-century Italian politics as he saw it. And he made it clear that this context was one of widespread corruption marked by intense factionalism, violence, intrigue, and duplicity. But as the preceding quotation makes clear, it is not only when dealing with dishonest opponents that dishonesty is usefully employed. What Machiavelli tells us is that in the real, tough world of politics, honest politicians, like nice guys, often finish last.

In *The Prince*, Machiavelli wasn't satisfied to present only a joltingly realistic picture of the struggle for power in his times. He also offered counsel — recommendations and advice — to would-be rulers. And rather than criticize duplicity and ruthless behaviour, or direct leaders to reorient their conduct, Machiavelli counselled more of the same: if people want power they have "to learn how not to be good"[4] because "a wise ruler cannot and should not keep his word when doing so is to his disadvantage." Such a ruler "is often obliged in order to hold on to power, to break his word, to be uncharitable, inhumane, and irreligious ... he should do right if he can; but he must be prepared to do wrong if necessary."[5]

There are various ways of summarizing this extreme version of what is treated philosophically as consequentialist ethics but which also has much to do with an actor's purposes, intentions, and commitments to a cause. Proponents of this philosophy believe it is not what you do to reach a goal, but reaching it that matters. It is not how you play the game but the result that is everything. And in politics as with many other competitive games the most sought-after result is winning. "So if a ruler wins wars and holds on to power," says Machiavelli, "the means he employs will always be judged honorable and everyone will praise him." It is very important to remember that the political scene of Machiavelli's reflections and recommendations was one where conduct was unconstrained by constitutional rules or democratic values and procedures. In sixteenth-century Italy people didn't gain office through democratic elections. They were either handed power or seized it. Power seekers got away with doing nasty things because, according to Machiavelli, there was no rule of law. Furthermore, Machiavelli assumes that the determination of the preferred outcome or goal as well as the choice of the means necessary to achieve it are the prerogatives of leaders. And when the public comes into the picture, their overwhelming concern, like that of their leaders, is with a politician's success in either gaining or consolidating power. In the end, the only thing that counts is a successful outcome. "In the behaviour of all men, and particularly of rulers, against whom there is no recourse at law, people judge by the outcome."[6]

This is not to say that Machiavelli was uninterested in the nature or the value of the outcomes sought by rulers. There is ample evidence in his writings to indicate that he hoped strong leaders would reduce rampant corruption, establish a system of law and order, and rid Italian states of foreign armies and influence. However, his position is that one needs to be in power first to be able to accomplish these worthy goals. So before everything else, the primary goal and the first priority is attaining and/or maintaining power. This seems at first glance to be a general truth about all politics and all politicians everywhere and at any time. But, as we shall argue below, the logic involved in both the prescriptive and descriptive elements of Machiavelli's analysis — a logic of the morality of dirty hands — is incompatible with the principles of democracy that inform our politics. When dirty hands come into play, it is because democratic norms are being either ignored or flouted.

Two characteristics of the "dirty hands" approach to political action need to be emphasized if we are to appreciate its appeal to practitioners and commentators. Both characteristics underlie the belief of many people that committing dirty deeds is justified in various conditions. First, "dirty hands" is different from an amoral or cynical — an "anything goes" — approach to politics.[7] The willingness of decision makers to act immorally or illegally stems from the notion that at a certain point, in extreme situations, a different and higher morality takes precedence, one that is especially applicable to the struggle for power and one that trumps all other moral considerations.

Second, the assumption of a higher morality or overriding principle or set of principles is believed to distinguish public life, with its special calling and professional responsibilities, from normal, everyday life activities. This distinction is sometimes referred to as the difference between public duties (and public morality) on the one hand and private duties (and private morality) on the other. Both of these concepts — the notion that some moral principles trump or override others and the idea that there are two moralities, one that is particularly suited to politics and one that applies outside of politics — are closely related and overlap. The alleged higher morality — which ironically legitimizes committing base acts — is associated with the special duties and more complex ethics that come into play once one enters the realm of politics.

Modern Machiavellians: Politics as War

A long list of political thinkers and actors over the past five hundred years have subscribed to Machiavelli's views on how politics is and should be conducted. Modern Machiavellians believe that the obligation to "do wrong in order to do what is right" is an ethical paradox or dilemma that lies at the heart of politics and which has to be confronted by all conscientious, responsible leaders. The dirty hands position seems to have no single ideological home. It has been advocated by left-wingers, right-wingers, and those in the centre of the political spectrum. "All means are good when they're effective," says Hoederer, a central character in Jean-Paul Sartre's aptly named play, *Dirty Hands*.[8] Hoederer is the leader of a communist party in an East European state emerging from the carnage of the Second World War. He is a modern-day Machiavelli who boldly articulates a justification for dirty hands. He contends that in the struggle to achieve worthy, desired ends, any leaders worth their salt will have to get their hands not only dirty but bloody. Only infantile idealists and the indecisive think they can govern innocently.

Early in this century the German political sociologist Max Weber (who is generally considered a liberal for his times) argued that, because "the decisive means for politics is violence," a special kind of morality applied to and needed to be applied by politicians: they must "be willing to pay the price of using morally dubious means, [even] dangerous ones" that could have "evil ramifications."[9]

Communist revolutionary leader and theorist Leon Trotsky took the position that all measures that united the revolutionary working class and contributed to advancing the revolutionary goal of liberation were not only "permissible," they were also "obligatory."[10] An almost identical rationale was set out by Barry Goldwater, the U.S. Republican party's 1964 presidential candidate. In his nomination

acceptance speech at the Republican convention, Goldwater proclaimed that "extremism in the defense of liberty is no vice." Here
is the view that there is a world of difference between "their" morality and "ours." And because "theirs" is criminally deficient and
dangerous (really a bogus morality) "we" can do anything to make
"ours" triumphant.[11]

Goldwater's maxim, though ridiculed by his Democratic party
opponents at the time, accurately summed up the mentality that
informed American foreign policy throughout the Cold War with the
Soviet Union. This dirty-hands mentality also figured significantly
in the United States' prosecution of its hot war with Vietnam. As
David Halberstram pointed out in his book on the principal decision
makers in the Kennedy and Johnson presidencies of the 1960s, a
central component of their Cold War thinking, which influenced U.S.
tactics and strategy throughout their dealings with Cuba and Vietnam, was

> the idea that force justified force. The other side did it and so
> we would do it; reality called for meeting dirty tricks with dirty
> tricks. Since covert operations were part of the game, over a
> period of time there was in the high levels of the bureaucracy,
> particularly as the CIA became more powerful, a gradual ac-
> ceptance of covert operations and dirty tricks as part of normal
> diplomatic-political maneuvering.[12]

Policies that make use of dirty hands seem to be especially appropriate to warfare and relations between antagonistic sovereign states:
deception, dirty tricks, the ruthless use of force, and even at times
the sacrifice of your own soldiers might be required to vanquish a
powerful enemy. However, one of several dangers encountered in a
defence of unscrupulous acts to combat another country's aggres-
sions is the tendency to slide from the arena of foreign policy ma-
noeuvrings to domestic politics. In fact, Machiavelli drew no
distinction between the politics of one realm and the politics of the
other. To him, all politics was about war, and leaders needed to know
how to fight. Trotsky, Weber, Hoederer, Kennedy, Johnson, and
Goldwater all share Machiavelli's perspective on the essential demands of statecraft. So too do ostensibly democratic theorists like
American political scientist Michael Walzer, who declares that "the
men who act for us and in our name are often killers," and who claims

that the defining characteristic of a moral politician is that he has dirty hands and knows it.[13]

Now if we accept this perspective we must concede that politics is more often than not another name for war and the politician a warrior; and such a view has clear implications, for, as Thomas Hobbes stated 350 years ago, "force and fraud, are in war the two cardinal virtues."[14] So, according to the tough-minded adherents of dirty-hands strategy, only those willing and able to use these "virtues" as tools have what it takes to attain their goals. A skilful politician will be prepared and know how and when to fight dirty against an unscrupulous opponent. If politics is often a dirty game, then even good politicians will have to get their hands dirty if they want to bring about desired, good ends. And getting dirty involves a wide ambit of action: misleading all or some of the public, lying, concealing information, breaking promises, flouting the law, using and abusing individuals or entire groups of people, and killing. Some or all of these acts are not only acceptable to those who advocate the use of dirty hands, they need to be done, given particular situations, and therefore, they ought to be done. They are the morally right things to do because they bring about a great good or prevent disasters. And the great good outweighs and compensates for the deviousness and the harm some people are subjected to along the way.

The trouble with this perspective is that force and deception are not tools of democratic politics; they are tactics and strategy in warfare. When politicians start dirtying their hands, they have abandoned their democratic sensibilities and succumbed to the protective/aggressive instincts and ruthless determination of embattled warriors. Their behaviour is a consequence of the breakdown of politics or the absence of conditions and processes of democratic practice.[15]

Let's look at some of the forms that a dirty-hands approach to effective conduct takes. While this is a book about Canadian politics, some of the examples that follow are from the United States. There are several reasons for including American cases. First, Watergate and Iran-Contra are classic contemporary cases of dirty-handed thinking and practices. Second, it is no secret that Canada's intelligence gathering networks and security services have long had a close working relationship with American agencies and, like our country's foreign and defence policy leaders, have been greatly influenced by U.S. foreign policies and priorities. Third, like so many things American, trends in campaign styles and tactics are often imitated by Canadian party strategists. Finally, a focus on Watergate, Iran-Contra, and dirty campaigning provides us with useful reminders of what we should avoid importing into our political culture.

Exigencies of War

Dirty-hands tactics are most often used in war:

- An advance squad is ordered into an area to draw enemy fire and almost certain death — they aren't told this is highly probable — but the foray permits a large battalion to take up an advantageous position elsewhere and also permits headquarters to pinpoint the whereabouts of enemy positions for air strikes. Consequently, some soldiers are sacrificed for a "good cause." The World War II tragedy of the Canadian army's Dieppe Raid comes to mind in this context: on August 19, 1942, five thousand men of the 2nd Canadian Infantry were sent across the English Channel to land on the shores near Dieppe, a small city on the northwest coast of France. The point of the raid was to test the German defence installations. Within nine hours over nine hundred Canadian soldiers were killed and almost two thousand were forced to surrender. From the perspective of the architects of allied strategy, the sacrifice and suffering of so many could be risked because of what could be learned. Generals dirtied their hands with their soldiers blood. War historians have argued about the reasons for the débâcle, but many have held the view that the lessons learned from the failed assault did prove helpful in later amphibious attacks, especially the June 1944 D-Day landing at Normandy.

- U.S. planes drop atomic bombs on Hiroshima and Nagasaki in order to end the Second World War and avoid losing thousands of American troops; so the sacrifice of hundreds of thousands of Japanese civilians was regrettable but "worth it" (though clearly not to the Japanese populations of those cities).

These examples apply cost-benefit calculations to dirty-hands situations and deliberations. It is a cost-benefit analysis that rationalizes ruthlessness and deception; it sacrifices principles and people to higher causes. The classic examples come from war.

In these cases, of course, the people who pay the costs — with their lives — are not involved in the decisions affecting them. This

is war, after all, not democracy. The enemy is not invited to participate in decision making, nor are one's own soldiers. Nevertheless,
so long as they are mindful of the criteria for a just war on one hand
and what constitutes just conduct *in* war on the other (though there
is room for disagreement, and of course pacifists would reject both
categories), there will be times in extreme situations like Dieppe and
Hiroshima when leaders may be justified in authorizing covert operations, deception, concealment, and the use of force that may
unavoidably harm innocents, non-combatants, and even their own
civilian and military population.

Dirty Campaigning

Election campaigns that resort to false promises, tricks, and negative
advertising provide further examples of dirty hands. The metaphor
of war is unfortunately easy to apply to election campaigns: "the
battle for the ballot" involves "mobilizing" workers and supporters,
pits one side's "troops" against the other's, and provides "ammuni-
tion" (that is, excuses and arguments) for denigrating and duping the
enemy, while concealing a party's real intentions.

Making False Promises

An all too common dirty-handed manoeuvre is to promise to do one
thing during an election campaign and then do the opposite once
elected:

- Lyndon Johnson campaigned for the U.S. presidency in 1964 by
  claiming that he was the candidate committed to peace in contrast to his opponent who would immerse America in war. All
  the while his administration was planning to escalate the war in
  Vietnam, which it did shortly after Johnson's victory.

- Pierre Trudeau campaigned against wage and price controls in
  the 1974 federal election, only to introduce them within months
  of being re-elected.

- Brian Mulroney treated free trade with the United States as a
  non-issue in his campaign of 1984. He explicitly dismissed it,
  only to embrace it once in office.

- The Liberal Party, when in opposition during the early 1990s,
  continually berated the Conservatives for introducing the GST

and indicated they would replace it; Liberal members promised that the tax would go if they were elected. After becoming the governing party they contended that there was no viable alternative to the GST, though it might be improved through harmonization with provincial sales taxes.

- The first NDP government in Ontario history decided a public automobile insurance system was off their agenda within a year of making it a central plank in their election campaign.

Having convinced themselves of the importance of their goals politicians may often sincerely believe that their election and/or re-election is in the public interest; and so they lie, "justifiably" and with good intentions, assuming that the truth is too complex for the voter or that a different position (the one they really hold) is not yet acceptable but will be eventually.

In opposition to this line of reasoning, American philosopher and ethicist Sissela Bok's critical comment on Lyndon Johnson's deception about Vietnam applies as well to Trudeau's phony campaign against wage and price controls, Mulroney's misleading comments on free trade prospects, Chrétien's attack on the Tory GST policy, and Bob Rae's skittish commitment to a government-run auto insurance system. Whether or not their policy reversals were meant to be in the public interest

> Deception of this kind strikes at the very essence of democratic government. It allows those in power to override or nullify the right vested in the people to cast an informed vote in critical elections. Deceiving the people for the sake of the people is a self-contradictory notion in a democracy, unless it can be shown that there has been genuine consent to deceit.[16]

In time of war it is arguable that citizens in a democracy will expect their government and military command to conceal many things, engage in covert activities, and deceive their own citizens when such actions are necessary to deceive an enemy. And in peace-time citizens accept (that is, consent to) police use of unmarked cars and radar traps to catch speeders and stake-outs to monitor and prevent criminal activities. But the false promises referred to above are all examples of a party's posture during a democratic election when people expect to make decisions on the basis of what a party is committing itself to do if elected. The idea that in each of these cases the electorate was somehow complicit in an elaborate con game orchestrated by the political parties is difficult to fathom. The proposition that it is democratic for citizens to disenfranchise themselves by suspending their critical decision-making rights and capacities is logically and practically incoherent. It is tantamount to saying that as an expression of their freedom, free persons will voluntarily submit themselves to slavery. "Democratic dirty hands," like "free slaves," *is* an oxymoron, but ethical politics is not.

The law of contracts does not apply to political promises, so a failure to honour political commitments is not illegal, just immoral. Under our political rules the only recourse "betrayed" voters have is to wait until the next election to punish a government that breaks its election promises. In the meantime, however, issues may change, the party has an opportunity to fudge its policies again, and it may offer retroactive excuses for why it changed its position. The comment of a Liberal cabinet minister on Sheila Copps's victory in a Hamilton by-election provides an example. The by-election was held because Copps was embarrassed into resigning by an earlier pledge to do so if her party kept the G.S.T. Without a shred of evidence to back her up, Revenue Minister Jane Stewart said Copps's victory was another indication that "Canadians are beginning to realize the G.S.T. is a necessary evil."[17]

The examples of politicians making false promises show how elected officials can thumb their noses at their electorate. Parties tend to espouse issues that have considerable resonance with voters who want clear alternatives, but party leaders may not really be committed to implementing the alternatives in the first place. Even if we assume they are motivated by public spiritedness — that they break their promises because they genuinely believe that keeping them won't benefit the public or that they believe *their* governing, rather than that of another party, is best for the country — it still amounts to double-dealing and scorn for the democratic process. Indulging in bogus promises purportedly in the interests of the people is almost always a deception that serves only the interests of the party or party leaders.

Deceptive and Negative Advertising

Political advertising in the mass media and especially on television has become a central feature of election campaigns. While alerting voters to the disastrous consequences they will face if they elect the wrong party has long been a staple of electoral tactics, a new emphasis has recently developed on deceptive and negative advertising that exaggerates the other party's or party leader's failings. It is in keeping with a dirty-hands approach to electoral competition.

- In the 1988 American presidential election, George Bush's campaign team created posters and TV ads stating that his opponent Michael Dukakis "opposed virtually every weapons system developed." The Bush organization also ran a series of television ads that carefully juxtaposed words and pictures to imply that Dukakis as governor of Massachusetts granted furloughs to 268 first-degree murderers who went out to rape and kidnap. As Kathleen Jamieson points out in her study of deceptive campaigning in America, these were patently false claims and Bush's team knew it. Dukakis's campaign ran ads indicating that Bush had voted to "cut" Social Security, which was also untrue.[18]

- In the Canadian general election of 1993, the Tories ran a television ad that focused attention on Jean Chrétien's face. As a result of a childhood disease one side of his mouth droops. The Tory ad implied that electors couldn't trust a man who looked like that.

Normal regulations and laws against false advertising and defamatory statements don't apply to political campaigning, so these ads are not illegal, but they are certainly sleazy. These examples show that at least some key members of election campaign teams are so bent on winning that they will authorize and/or devise any ad — however inaccurate or unfair — that they think will garner votes for their side.

One positive result of the Conservative's negative advertising attack on Chrétien was that it proved counter-productive. Hundreds of thousands of Canadian voters and many Tory politicians were so disgusted by the perceived cruel and shameful attempt at character assassination that the ad was pulled within days of its appearance.

Dirty Tricks and Watergate

The Watergate scandal is a dramatic example of how a dirty-hands, state-of-siege mentality combined with a "win at all costs" orientation infected U.S. domestic politics and the Republican party's campaign strategy. Watergate led to a demand for the impeachment of President Richard Nixon that ultimately resulted in his resignation.

Soon after he took office in 1968, Nixon and his top advisors became concerned about leaks to the press of government documents and strategies relating to the war in Vietnam. To counter these leaks, they set up their own intelligence gathering unit called "the plumbers." A former National Security Council advisor named Daniel Ellsberg had released hundreds of pages of documents, which later came to be known as the Pentagon Papers, that added up to a history of American government decision making and obfuscation regarding the war. In an effort to smear Ellsberg's reputation, the plumbers broke into the office of his psychiatrist. What they were after and what they didn't find were medical records that might tarnish Ellsberg's credibility. The enemy was no longer the Soviet Union and their "proxies" but other Americans.

In fact, the Nixon White House had drawn up an "enemies" list of prominent Americans who were actively involved in mobilizing opposition to the war and to the Nixon administration. It wasn't long before the targeted enemy became the opposition Democratic party. It was full of "bad" guys, and their victory in a presidential election would be "bad" for America. So the plumbers were authorized to break in to the national headquarters of the Democratic party (located in an office tower known as The Watergate) and plant listening devices so they could find out what the enemy was up to. But the break-in was botched, and the plumbers were caught in the Democratic party offices and arrested by local Washington police on June 17, 1972.

Just four days after the plumbers were caught, President Nixon told his chief of staff that he didn't think there would be an uproar across the country. "Breaking and entering" said Nixon (on the audio tapes confiscated from his office), "is not a helluva lot of crime." Furthermore, he said that "[m]ost of the people" would not be outraged by "the Republican committee trying to bug the Democratic Headquarters," because they would "think that ... this is routine — that everybody's trying to bug everyone else: it's politics."[19] In other words, Nixon felt Americans believed that it was normal and acceptable for all parties to use dirty tricks to get elected. He was wrong. He was forced to resign and almost all his lieutenants who were involved in the plumbers' activities and the attempted cover-up of those activities were disgraced and sent to jail.

Despite the notoriety of the Nixon years and heightened concern about ethical conduct on the part of senior decision makers in the

U.S., the dirty-hands defence resurfaced with the Reagan administration's involvement in the Iran-Contra affair in the 1980s.

For Reasons of State and National Security

The term "reason of state." (in French, *raison d'état*) refers to the idea that the interests of the state, especially its national security, are the first priority for political leaders and therefore come before all other moral considerations. The reason of state argument is often adopted by prime ministers, presidents, and defence ministers to defend state secrecy and covert operations; it also serves those associated with spy agencies as a ready justification for their activities, no matter how morally questionable they may be.

RCMP Dirty Tricks

Around the same time as Watergate and two decades before the Iran-Contra affair, Canada's security intelligence division of the RCMP was operating very much along the lines first followed by Nixon's plumbers and later by Oliver North and his associates. Over a period of approximately five years beginning in the early 1970s — but in a few instances stretching back to the 1950s — our national police force committed a long list of underhanded and dirty-handed illegal acts.

This was a time of considerable anxiety on the part of government security agencies and conservative forces in society in general. The 1960s in North America had been marked by the Black civil rights movement, mounting protests against the war in Vietnam, an anti-nuclear weapons consciousness, campus radicalism, and the development of articulate and militant socialist and anarchist student groups demanding major social change. Many of these movements had offshoots in Canada, but in addition, many Canadians became critical of what they saw as American imperialism and the Americanization of Canada's culture, economy and foreign policy. A left-wing segment of the NDP known as the Waffle called for an independent and socialist Canada and received considerable coverage in the media and on campuses across the country; some left-wing magazines and radical activists spoke about the need for an extra-parliamentary opposition, given what they regarded as the conservative nature of parliamentary parties and the truncated nature of participation offered by traditional electoral politics. On top of all this, Quebec nationalism was becoming a powerful force, and a small but articulate and, in a few instances, violent portion of the nationalist movement was agitating for a socialist revolution. In October 1970, two small cells of the Front de Libération du Québec (FLQ) — which didn't number much more than the membership of the two cells — kidnapped first James Cross, the British trade commissioner in Montreal, and then Pierre Laporte, a cabinet minister in the Quebec government. Laporte was subsequently murdered by his kidnappers.

As a response to these events and movements our security forces decided to "protect" Canada in much the same way the conspirators involved in Watergate and Iran-Contra sought to defend America. Here are some examples of their protection:

- In a joint operation, officers from the Quebec Provincial Police, the Montreal Police force and the RCMP broke into the offices of a left-wing news agency in Montreal and stole various documents and files.

- The RCMP broke into offices containing Parti Québécois membership lists and financial information, where they copied and removed some material.

- The RCMP criminal investigations branch conducted about four hundred break-ins without warrants, mainly in B.C.

- The RCMP spied on the NDP Waffle and other left-wing movements and placed operatives on campuses.

- The force electronically bugged MPs. The most famous incident was the bugging of the solicitor-general who was responsible for the RCMP.

- In contravention of the Post Office Act of the time, hundreds of pieces of mail were opened by security investigators.

- Several agents burned down a barn that they believed was a meeting place for radicals.

- Some officers stole dynamite.

- Security personnel engaged in a campaign of disinformation by sending out phony communiqués with false signatures of Que-

bec radicals that were calculated to incite other radicals to violence.

- When trying to recruit informers, officers used threats and force
to get co-operation.

- They obtained confidential medical files on various left-wing
leaders to spread rumours about their mental stability.

- They organized surveillance of almost all candidates running for
election.

- The force was found to be in possession of papers that had been
stolen from a left-wing Toronto research organization called
Praxis, which had its offices broken into and torched in December 1970. Seven years later, a Tory back-bencher revealed that
the Canadian government in the early 1970s — much like the
Nixon government in the U.S. — had compiled an enemies list
of twenty-four people who were associated with a so-called
extra-parliamentary opposition. The list had apparently been
based on names found in Praxis files. To this day the break-in
and arson remain unsolved.

- The force had a paid informant in a neo-nazi Toronto organization called the Western Guard. The informant did more than
inform; he took an active role in a swastika-painting and window-
smashing series of raids on offices and homes of Jews and
communists.[20]

The McDonald commission of inquiry into the illegal activities found
that our security force shared the same kind of cold war, siege
mentality that was exhibited by American administrations and intelligence agencies. The inquiry also made apparent the presence and
danger of a principled absoluteness or zealousness in regard to what
was believed to be the justness of the cause. When the former chief
of security services in Quebec testified before the commission he
said his officers were accustomed to breaking the law in order to
protect the country. "We were used to living with certain illegalities.
They were so commonplace they were no longer thought of as illegal." When he was asked by one of the commissioners how he felt

about breaking the law, the officer replied that one either "betray[s] one's duty to protect the public or break[s] the law."[21]

What was clearly lacking in the training and standards of the force and what also seemed neglected by the force's political masters was a serious appreciation of the rule of law. Mr. Justice Bora Laskin in a unanimous judgement of the Ontario Court of Appeal in 1969 declared:

> The recognition of 'public duty' to excuse breach of the criminal law by policemen would involve a drastic departure from constitutional precepts ... Legal immunity from prosecution for breaches of the law by the very persons charged with the public duty of enforcement would subvert that public duty.[22]

It is true that politicans have public duties that the rest of us don't have. They make laws, we don't; they can instruct police to carry machine guns rather than pistols, we can't; they can authorize a government intelligence agency to eavesdrop on our e-mail, telephone conversations, even our talk around the dinner table and in the bedroom; they can pass or revoke laws that reward companies that specialize in strike-breaking; they can exclude or permit the hiring of replacement workers when unions are on strike; they decide whether highway patrols will use photo radar to catch speeders or not, whether there will or won't be inspections of the safety of the vehicles we drive and the food and water we consume, if bridges and roads are constructed and maintained, whether the taxation rules are progressive or regressive, and if our health care system is functioning properly. What this should tell us is that public officials have a greater — not lesser — responsibility to be scrupulously honest with citizens than most of us have in our day-to-day dealings because their actions affect far more people and are authoritative, and because they have a fiduciary trust to uphold.

One very practical and central problem that surfaced in the investigation of RCMP dirty tricks was the dilemma a police officer faces when asked to carry out orders that require laws to be broken: the officer is subject to internal discipline if an order is disobeyed and liable to prosecution for a criminal offence if it is obeyed. This appears to be a classic case of a professional being caught between a rock and a hard place in trying to discharge public duties.

The Canadian Bar Association in 1980 tried to address the issue of an officer's duty when confronted with orders to commit dirty deeds: "The solution to the dilemma is not to give an immunity to prosecution for obedience to orders. The solution is to give immunity from disciplinary action for obedience to the law."[23] The Association's recommendation is as pertinent for whistleblowers, moral politicians, and honest cops today as it was then.

Yet an examination of the incidents of RCMP wrongdoing indicates that practically none of the Mounties found it difficult to extricate themselves from the dilemma addressed by the Bar Association. And this was apparently the case because they didn't think there really was much of a dilemma. There was no evidence that any Mounties either questioned or refused orders that involved lawbreaking. A Mountie who was involved in the 1972 barn-burning proudly told the McDonald commission of inquiry that he and his fellow undercover officers did what they did because "The ends justified the means at that time." The conviction that their actions were right (even though illegal) was reinforced by the general understanding that involvement in such activities would not hurt one's career progress. To the contrary, there were numerous examples of officers being promoted for carrying out their duties.

So one of the prime inducements as well as one of the seductive traps of dirty-handed activity by intelligence officers and security personnel is the opportunity to combine career security with national security, personal interest with the national interest. The same Mountie who offered the Machiavellian dirty-hands rationale told the McDonald commission that most of his comrades who were involved in surreptitious activities continued to have very good careers.

It is in the interest of both the officer giving the orders and subordinates carrying them out to conceal their activities not only from the targets of their skulduggery but from the purview of any impartial third party. They believed that what they were doing was in the public interest, so the deception and concealment were also justified.

The parallel with politicians and especially those with cabinet-level powers is close. A politician who refuses to go along with her party when it lies or makes false promises has to choose between fidelity to principles of integrity and democratic accountability or loyalty to her party. If she chooses the former she risks party discipline, exclusion from the caucus, and losing the opportunity to run for the party again. If she is a cabinet minister she risks betraying cabinet solidarity and being stripped of her portfolio. Again, if she can be convinced by colleagues that the motives for lying or other breaches of integrity are "good" ones, because the public good will be advanced, then she may still feel troubled but also righteous about the regrettably necessary, unpleasant thing(s) done.

Despite all the revelations brought to light by two commissions of inquiry into RCMP dirty tricks (one set up by the Province of Quebec, one a federal government royal commission), none of the solicitors general who were responsible for the RCMP and not a single member of the federal cabinet felt obliged to resign, nor was one asked to do so by the prime minister. Instead, the politicians in charge either claimed ignorance of RCMP wrongdoing or implied that in trying to deal with potential threats to national security members of the security forces might have erred slightly on the side of over-zealousness — which was excusable given the circumstances — but otherwise were doing the job they were meant to do.

A number of senior RCMP officers testified that they believed they were doing what the government of the day wanted and expected them to do, although there may have been no explicit instructions to that effect. When faced with the stubborn refusal of the Trudeau government to take responsibility for the huge number and succession of dirty tricks, the McDonald Royal Commission blamed the security force for getting out of control.

Nevertheless, in a clear admission that something was terribly wrong with the direction of Canada's security service, on July 14, 1984, the Trudeau government replaced the RCMP's Security Service with a civilian agency, the Canadian Security Intelligence Service (CSIS). In an attempt to avoid a repetition of RCMP errors and to keep the security service under control, the CSIS Act mandated a review agency, the Security Intelligence Review Committee (SIRC), and another monitoring office, the inspector-general, to conduct investigations and review CSIS activities. As was the case with the RCMP security services, CSIS and its "watchdog" agencies were accountable to the solicitor-general. In addition, Parliament set up a sub-committee on national security, which in Reg Whitaker's words, is "a kind of watchdog on the watchdog ... but leaving the detailed investigative task to SIRC with its privileged access to CSIS information."[24]

The Iran-Contra Scandal

Between 1984 and 1986 key figures in the Reagan administration were secretly involved in activities that contravened congressional stipulations and Reagan's own stated policies. The president's national security advisor, Admiral John Poindexter, and Poindexter's assistant, Lieutenant Colonel Oliver North, with the co-operation of the director of the Central Intelligence Agency (CIA) and various agents organized a scheme to sell arms to Iran in exchange for the release of Americans who had been kidnapped in Lebanon by Iranian-backed terrorists. They also organized the channelling of funds from the arms sales and other sources to support rebels in Nicaragua who were called "Contras" (because they were against the socialist Sandinista Government, which the U.S. opposed).

The first part of the scheme was clearly at odds with President Reagan's public condemnation of Iran as a terrorist nation and his efforts in getting congress to pass a law forbidding the sale of arms to Iran. And the second part, the financial and military support of the Contras, violated an explicit congressional ban against such activities.

Once the conspiracy was exposed and the principals in the covert operations were subjected to congressional investigations and criminal indictments, many commentators were surprised at how brazen North and Poindexter were in maintaining the justness of their deceit. On a number of occasions, North indicated that lying was second nature to anyone involved in covert actions. In testimony before one of the congressional hearings into Iran-Contra, North declared that

> it is very important ... to understand that this is a dangerous world; that we live at risk and that this nation is at risk in a dangerous world ... By their very nature covert operations are a lie. There is great deceit, deception practiced ... [and] the effort to conduct these covert operations was made in such a way that our adversaries would not have knowledge of them or that we could deny American association with it, or the association of this government with those activities. And that is not wrong.[25]

Asked if the operations weren't also designed to be kept from Americans, North replied that this was the only way they could be kept from the enemy. And when he was asked how he could defend his actions in terms of democratic principles, his response echoed the rationale of the Nixon White House in establishing the plumbers: he did it, he said, "because we have had incredible leaks, from discussions with closed committees of the Congress." In other words, anyone outside a tight circle of committed loyalists and specialists in deception was suspect. Summing up the cost-benefit rationale for the operation, North stated that "we had to weigh in the balance the difference between lies and lives." And in response to congressional committees, and later when he defended himself against twelve criminal charges in a jury trial resulting from the affair, North offered the defence of a dutiful soldier: he was properly following orders from his superiors and everything he did was authorized from above.[26]

When professional liars like North are put on the defensive, they claim that if people only understood their motives better and the situations with which they have to deal, they would be viewed as great patriots having to spread noble lies. They ask that we defer to their judgement and trust them. The trouble with their claims, unfortunately, is that the very nature of their arguments and practices prevents the public from evaluating the seriousness of the situation or worthiness of the motives, means, or goals. And we are being asked to trust those who are masters of deception. An appeal for trust is difficult to uphold when it comes from such a source.

There is an additional factor that came to light in the Iran-Contra machinations: the individuals and companies that fronted the trading made profits of $16 million, but curiously, only about $4 million was funnelled to the Contras. It is not unfair to infer that in this case dirty hands found their way into pockets filled with money, thus casting additional doubt on the supposed nobility of the cause.

On sound democratic grounds, citizens should be wary of deferring to bureaucratic, political or policy elites, because such people find it easy to treat their own particular interests as equivalent to the general interest. Their cause — getting re-elected, securing immunity from public scrutiny and immunity from criminal investigations — is seen to be at one with the nation's cause. "The freer they are from public scrutiny and public judgment," notes Robert Dahl, "the more likely they are to be corrupted" by the exercise of power.[27] Dahl adds that the corruption is not necessarily venal. But as was the case in the Iran-Contra scandal, using the necessity of protecting state secrets as a cover certainly facilitates concealing private aggrandizement.

The Heritage Front Affair

Ten years and one month after its creation, CSIS became the subject of allegations of misconduct on a par with the RCMP's earlier dirty tricks campaign. An August 25, 1994, Brian McInnis, a former journalist who had been press secretary to Conservative solicitor-general Doug Lewis, told a television audience that he had given *The Toronto*

Star a classified cabinet briefing memo from CSIS. The memo indicated that a paid CSIS informer was helping organize activities of the white-supremacist, neo-Nazi Heritage Front organization. According to McInnis, he blew the whistle on the CSIS operation because he was disgusted that a government agency was contributing to strengthening a racist group. In an interview with one of the authors, McInnis said surveillance of a subversive group is one thing, organizing it quite another.[28]

Four months after McInnis went public, SIRC submitted a report to Parliament stating that CSIS had acted properly in targeting the Heritage Front for infiltration and that its informant generally did a good job. According to SIRC, the informant, Grant Bristow, and his handler "deserve[d] our thanks" despite the fact that Bristow was part of a telephone-harassment campaign that "tested the limits of what we believe Canadian society considers to be acceptable behaviour for someone acting on behalf of the government."[29]

The difficulty in establishing accountability and control of CSIS activities was evidenced by the very different reports prepared by the three organs investigating the affair. As indicated above, SIRC, in its approximately 200-page report, *The Heritage Front Affair*, essentially condoned CSIS's methods of surveillance. In a special report to the solicitor-general, the inspector-general indicated that there had been serious security breaches in the office of the former solicitor-general, suggesting that McInnis was a "potential security problem." Both the SIRC and inspector-general reports raised questions not about CSIS but about the whistleblower and the media. The Parliamentary sub-committee on security, however, criticized CSIS for failing to notify the Reform party leader that his party had been targetted for infiltration by the Heritage Front, or to inform members of Toronto's Jewish community that they were on a hit list drafted by members of the neo-Nazi group. The committee also noted that CSIS waited six days before alerting Metro police to the threats.[30] Equally troubling was the release of a video by Heritage Front leader Wolfgang Droege that seemed to indicate Grant Bristow was a major organizer of the group and an instigator of various racist activities. The evidence of the video would appear to vindicate McInnis's decision to blow the whistle on the CSIS file. Whitaker has suggested the Heritage Front affair indicates a crisis of accountability in the new security service. We think it also shows that dirty-hands are once again manipulating events behind the scenes.

The Shelley Martel affair

Shelley Martel was the twenty-eight-year-old minister of northern development in the Ontario NDP government in December 1991. Around that time the government had reached an agreement with the Ontario Medical Association that included a cap on medical billings of over $400,000 a year. This greatly upset some doctors in the province and particularly a number of high-billing specialists in Martel's home riding of Sudbury. The Sudbury doctors were continually criticizing the NDP government. In turn, members of the government saw such doctors as threatening the viability of the health care system.

At a party in Thunder Bay, Martel got into an argument with a Tory organizer who felt the government was treating the physicians unfairly. Martel apparently responded that she knew of a Sudbury doctor who was probably guilty of over-billing and that the government was thinking of charging him.

This seemed to indicate that Martel had confidential health ministry information, as well as confidential information from the attorney general's office. Within days, Martel's comments at the party were in the news and the legislature. As Thomas Walkom reported, it became a "full-fledged political scandal" within a week.[26] Martel's reputation and career took a nosedive, and the situation was exacerbated when she voluntarily asked to take a lie detector test to show that she was telling the truth when she said she lied about having information about the doctor. A legislative committee eventually concluded that she had told the truth about having lied, and so she stayed in the cabinet. But in 1994, Ontario's privacy commissioner reported that Martel had violated that Privacy Act in another incident, and she resigned.

According to Walkom, the Martel affair, combined with the government's flip-flop on auto insurance and its surprising support for casinos, shattered the NDP's reputation for integrity, and the party never recovered the public's trust thereafter. Comparing Richard Nixon, Oliver North, and the RCMP dirty tricks to the foolishness of a rookie Ontario cabinet minister seems like equating the outrageous with the ludicrous, and not a little unfair. Indeed, Martel's conduct pales beside that of the individuals we've discussed previously. The point of including Martel's behaviour as a case of dirty hands is to emphasize what can happen even to a talented, generally conscientious young politician when the perceived rightness of the cause and the treatment of a dissenter as an enemy overshadow all other considerations.

The kind of militaristic thinking that justifies attacking some for the benefit of others or for a great cause can too easily be applied by politicians bent on restructuring society. And when this happens, important democratic principles are forfeited. What Shelley Martel did on a small scale is now being implemented on a large scale in the public policy of debt-fighting neo-conservative governments. Only this time it is not a doctor being attacked but hundreds of thousands of people on welfare and unemployment insurance. A resolutely militant approach to achieving one's objectives can be applied to economic programs as well as to national security matters. A cost-benefit analysis that pits "short-term pain" against "long-run gain" has affinities with the logic of dirty hands. If adopting a particular measure or set of measures will result in the provision of more goods and services, which can then be counted as units of satisfaction for the majority, whether some people may be harmed in the process and whether the end product is shared fairly are secondary considerations.

For example, the current wars being waged by most governments across Canada against deficits and public debts are hurting the most vulnerable members of society and offering the least to the least advantaged. This is because increased unemployment and reduced support of the indigent are regarded as costs that are necessary to reduce both government debt and taxes. This calculative rationality either displaces moral considerations, or goes hand in hand with a narrow moral view that advocates disciplining those who are regarded as too lazy or too slow to adapt to a changing economy. A militaristic toughness is combined with paternalism to orchestrate an ideologically driven program. The poor are told that this program is good for them and if they don't comply with the war aims they will be no better than the enemy — and in the minds of those who want to cut welfare spending the enemy are all those who resist such "reforms" and stand in the way of relying on the work ethic and market forces to resuscitate the economy.

Public policies that overlook the respect owed to the least advantaged in society are morally blind. Those that do take the least advantaged into account but consider that an increase in their suffering is for the greater good are, from our perspective, immoral. Only those policies that apply equal concern and respect to all social strata, with a particular concern for the least advantaged, meet the test for ethical politics. Such policies may well result, during budget-conscious times, in reducing some benefits to the poor, but presumably benefits for the advantaged would be cut even more.

Dirty Hands versus Democratic Trust

When we say that public office is a public trust with fiduciary obligations we mean that elected representatives assume the role of trustees, with the duty of acting for the sole benefit of the citizens who elected them. And that, in turn, means they must not allow their decisions to be influenced by anything other than the welfare of the citizenry they have undertaken to serve. As John Locke asserted in his *Second Treatise*, a representative government founded on consent has "only a Fiduciary Power to act for certain ends," and the people have every right to remove or alter it "when they find [that it acts] contrary to the trust reposed" in it.[32]

Furthermore, the trust relationship associated with democracy should not be confused with the blind faith expected of religious fundamentalists or the blind trust established for corporate investments on behalf of public servants who want to avoid conflicts of interest. With respect to information and considerations that bear on decisions made in citizens' interests, the fiduciary duty of a government is to provide full and frank disclosure at all material times. In the examples of fraud or real conflicts of interest covered in Chapter 4, there was a clear breach of fiduciary duties. But the betrayal of trust that accompanies the use of public office for private purposes does not seem to fit the case, generally, of dirty-handed politicians who genuinely believe that they are acting for the common good and do not seek or receive a special favour in return.

The two types of corrupt practices overlap, however, because the nature of the trust relationship has been undermined in similar ways — though for different reasons. In both cases the truth is concealed from us or we are deliberately misled. Elected officials have failed in their fiduciary duty to keep us properly informed. Even when they think they are doing what is in our best interests, they are still abrogating the terms of the relationship between trustee and beneficiary. We elect politicians not to do as they please but to do what pleases us. We don't authorize our trustees to lie to us about where our money and our investments are. We don't elect them to treat us like children or compliant lambs ready to be shepherded this way or that way. We elect them assuming that we deserve to be treated with mutual respect, that they will look after our best interests, and that they must be accountable to us in so doing.[33]

Democracy provides a public space for differences of opinion over policy options, debate over strategic goals, and argument about the range of alternatives and their practical and moral appropriateness. Democratic sensibilities acknowledge and encourage a public discourse replete with appeals and arguments meant to persuade, to mobilize opinion and support, to direct collective preferences this way rather than that. What energizes representative democracy is persuasion not manipulation, force of argument not force of arms, honest politics and not lies and deception.

Except for the most extreme exigencies of war or insurrection, what democracy rules out is the right of any elite, whether self-appointed or elected, to decide what and how much information the public can be trusted to have — when it can handle the truth and when it needs to be lied to. This means that governments cannot arrogate to themselves the role of moral guardian or parent. Paternalism and democracy are like fire and water: they don't mix. A defence of dirty hands turns on paternalism and turns off democracy. Dirty-hands advocates claim that morally dubious acts are committed because not doing them would be disastrous. But what could be more disastrous than the breakdown of democracy and the absence of trustworthiness?

Compromise

It is sometimes thought that a compromise is tantamount to dirty hands in the sense that compromising means selling out or abandoning one's principles and therefore betraying the trust of supporters/electors who expected such principles to be promoted. As one advocate of compromise has stated, "Arrangement of compromise belongs today to specialists ... the politicians. Let these moral middleman do this dirty work for you."[34] According to this double-edged meaning of compromise, democratic politics and dirty-handed negotiations go together. But there is another understanding of compromise, which holds that "dirty work," in the sense of sacrificing one's moral integrity, is not required by the give and take of democratic politics.

The idea of compromise as reaching a reasonable middle way or balance between extreme demands has some affinities with the notions of moderation and the "golden mean" that Plato and Aristotle recommended as great practical virtues. Neither were democrats, however, so close parallels should be avoided. But the kernel of an important idea is there: moderate political policies usually result in better political outcomes than extremist politics.

In her 1993 Massey Lecture, Jean Bethke Elshtain notes a discussion she had with a former Czechoslovakian dissident who was elected to the Prague Parliament after the 1989 "velvet revolution." The new MP said that compromise is something of fundamental importance to a democracy — something that many Czechs weren't used to but would have to learn. "In a democracy, compromise is not a terrible thing. It is necessary. It lies at the heart of things because you have to accept that people are going to have different views, especially on the most volatile matters and the most important issues."[35]

Ambivalence about the meaning and value of compromise is nicely underlined by Arthur Kuflik, who notes that "compromise" has both "a pejorative and honorific sense." He outlines four criteria that indicate when it is morally right to try to accommodate views and positions different from our own. He says we should be prepared to scale down our own demands and be prepared to accept those of others whenever our priorities

- are reflections of "non-moral interest rather than considered moral conviction,"

- are "based on moral convictions that we now perceive to be mistaken,"

- are clearly ones that need balancing "against other legitimate claims" to achieve a "more comprehensive view of the matter that is in dispute," or

- are clearly biased because of our emotional closeness to a situation. We need to ask what our views would be if we could look at the situation objectively, imagining that there is no dispute, realizing "that reasonable differences of opinion are possible, and that a peaceful settlement achieved through a fair process that fosters mutual understanding and respect is of great moral significance in its own right."[36]

Kuflik emphasizes that what need *not* be compromised according to these criteria is moral integrity. Extrapolating from Kuflik, we would say that willingness to compromise, within limits, is a fundamental democratic disposition that complements the democratic sensibilities of accepting majoritarian decisions, respecting minority rights, and treating others as equals. Compromise facilitates decision making and is an estimable procedure for resolving conflicts respectfully and peaceably. The process of compromise actualizes the proposition that ethical decision making in politics often requires not only tolerance of differing interests and claims, but mutual accommodation. Sometimes parties may choose to work out their differences through direct negotiated settlement, and sometimes they may elect to bring in an impartial third party to mediate or arbitrate. Regardless of the approach to settlement, everyone will not necessarily see eye to eye on tough questions; rather, the disputants will probably have to accept some things they don't like or want.

Kuflik adds that in some instances compromise is not only inappropriate, "it is reprehensible."[37] His example is the Munich accord that Neville Chamberlain arranged with Adolph Hitler just prior to the start of World War II. Insofar as compromise implies searching for a middle way and splitting differences, there are clearly some midpoint solutions that are unacceptable. It won't do to accommodate an abusing parent or husband intent on continuing the abuse. Authorizing police or crown attorneys to reach an agreement with a wife batterer not to press charges as long as the abuser reduces the incidence of abuse by, for example, 50 per cent, is not an acceptable compromise. A compromise that countenances prejudicial or ill-treatment of someone is not a moral one. These distinctions illustrate the notion that compromising one's morality is the opposite of a moral compromise.

There is both a procedural and substantive aspect to any compromise, and both have to meet certain conditions if a particular compromise is to count as morally acceptable. An honourable democratic compromise, as we intimated earlier, is one that recognizes limits. And the limits that apply are our commitment to moral integrity and the principles of democracy. Clearly, what must be avoided are compromises that countenance deception or bribery. As well, a compromise is unacceptable if it sanctions the threat or use of force to frustrate the will of the majority, to violate fundamental human rights, or to distribute primary social goods unequally without advancing the life chances of the least advantaged. Such compromises do not meet the criteria of honourable, democratic principles. In this regard, forging a successful moral compromise consistent with democratic principles is one thing and achieving success with dirty hands quite another.

The notion of compromise that we have in mind encompasses both process and outcome and exemplifies mutual respect and co-operation among participants who treat each other as equals interested in reciprocal benefits. As Kuflik notes, this is closely related to key ingredients of John Rawls's theory of justice.

Rawls's takes what we would call a welfare liberal approach to developing principles that everyone can agree on as fair. Rawls's formulation is not very far from ideas that are often associated with democratic socialism, but is considerably at odds with a competing classical liberal notion that has been resuscitated lately by both neo-liberals and neo-conservatives.

The classical liberal perspective associated with Thomas Hobbes, David Hume, and Adam Smith has become enormously influential among contemporary economists and governing elites. It makes much of the importance of compromise in a different sense. This approach begins with an assumption about human nature: that the majority of people are naturally self-centred and self-interested, with very little empathy for others; they are "egoists." The compromise here (referred to as a "social contract" by some and as "conventions" of civil association by others) is one in which these purely self-interested individuals agree among themselves to give up various pre-political, individual freedoms and hand over the rights of making rules and enforcing them to a third party — a government — in return for security. This view treats social rules as the result of a compromise fashioned by individuals who feel vulnerable to each other's predatory inclinations. They therefore want to establish a secure level playing field where those with the requisite will and abilities can, if they choose, pursue a life of self-aggrandizement, the unintended consequences of which would be to everyone's benefit.

Rawls decries this kind of self-centredness and articulates principles that place heavy stress on consideration of others' interests and well-being. The worth of social duties like mutual respect and mutual aid he says "is not measured by the help we actually receive but rather by the sense of confidence and trust in [others'] good intentions and the knowledge that they are there if we need them. Indeed, it is only necessary to imagine what a society would be like if it were publicly known that [these duties were] rejected."[38] These duties and sensibilities are in stark contrast to a classical liberal's inclination to leave most important matters to the market, to an egoist's reflex to treat the self at the expense of others, and a fanatic's readiness to put a cause before people. For such individuals the principle of mutual respect and the democratic values and procedural safeguards associated with it are of secondary importance. Given this perspective, it comes as no surprise that so many of those involved in ethics scandals in Canadian politics over the past decade — Sinclair Stevens, Bill Vander Zalm, Grant Devine — are associated with neo-liberalism or neo-conservatism.

Conclusion

The examples we have considered demonstrate the dangers involved in accepting dirty-hands justifications for deceiving citizens. The dirty-hands defence is extremely elastic. It includes cases in which individuals knowingly do something wrong and plan it in advance, and cases in which something goes wrong as a result of incompetence or human error and the officials involved decide a cover-up is in order; it applies to election campaign trickery and false promises which, ironically, have parallels with the dirty tricks and disinformation campaigns waged by covert security/intelligence agencies.

If we accept the argument that those in charge, or — in the case of political parties in an election — those who believe they should be in charge, can lie to us because they have our best interests at heart, *even* when they cover up actions that have jeopardized our interests, then we can never require them to account honestly for what they do or to correct their mistakes. Nor can we be informed participants in the decisions that affect us.

Dirty-hands practices destroy integrity. When lying, deception, and breaking promises become regular practices, the bonds of trust among citizens, as well as between citizens and their representatives, become unraveled. John Stuart Mill was right when he spoke of "the trustworthiness of human assertion," as the foundation of "social well-being" and its "insufficiency" as the greatest factor threatening "civilization, virtue and everything on which human happiness on the largest scale depends."[39]

Breaking promises and deceiving the electorate undermines the trust relationship between citizens and their representatives. These actions betray the fiduciary responsibility that governments are obligated to fulfil. The result may be success for a party or faction but it signals a failure of democratic processes. The downside of this failure is considerable: the deterioration of the trust relationship contributes to cynicism, and the provision of opportunities increases for charismatic charlatans to preach salvation through simplistic solutions about the cleansing of politics. This failure leads to a loss of faith in the role of governments, an erosion that seems to be happening in Canada and the United States. If no politicians do the positive things they promise, the electorate understandably will be receptive to calls for the downsizing of government initiatives and institutions and to the temptation to leave everything up to the market, because at least businesses have a clear agenda to produce useful, saleable goods and services and to make a profit for their shareholders.

However, there is also an upside to citizen reaction to government perfidy. While many politicians have debased the democratic currency, they haven't managed to alter the electorate's demand for honest politics. Recent evidence of voters handing overwhelming defeats to governments with reputations for dishonesty — British Columbia's Social Credit government in 1991, Saskatchewan's Conservative government in 1991, and the federal Conservative government in 1993 — demonstrates the electorate's indignation and irritation with phony governments and their inclination to punish them by choosing alternatives.

Religious fundamentalists answer to their God, military officers to their commanders, revolutionaries to history, and egoists to themselves, but politicians in a democracy are accountable to the people. Dirty-handed conduct subverts both the process that ensures accountability and the maintenance of trust. Dirty-handed politicians undermine the principles and values that are integral to democracy and that is why their conduct is unacceptable and incompatible with honest politics.

In Pursuit of Honest Politics

Relatively few Canadians today would consider a career in politics to be potentially one of the noblest achievements of a lifetime. In a 1996 survey of Canadians conducted by Professor Maureen Mancuso and others, 51 per cent of respondents said that judges are more ethical than the average person, while only 17 per cent thought that MPs were.[1] Undoubtedly, if Canadians were asked what they want their children to be when they grow up, "politician" or "statesperson" would score near the bottom of the list, if it appeared at all. Yet politicians need to earn precisely the opposite reputation — one for honesty and trustworthiness — if our democracy is to regain its health.

If politics is regarded as sleazy and dirty, then dishonest people will be drawn to it. On the other hand, if politics is considered a respectable and worthy profession, it will attract the best and the brightest that society has to offer. But politics cannot be regarded as admirable unless its practice is considered by and large ethical.

Our view is that honest politics is not only attainable in a democratic country, it is essential if the fundamental democratic value of mutual respect is to be taken seriously. It is often said that ethical politics is an oxymoron. Yet this is usually said in frustration. Serious ethical deficiencies exist in Canadian politics because the infrastructure needed to support honest politics is, depending on the issue, either partly built, neglected, or non-existent.

There are some who will conclude that any attempt to improve ethical standards in Canadian politics is as futile as teaching good manners to swine. However, it should be remembered that at one time, judges did not enjoy a high reputation. During various periods prior to the advent of judicial independence in the Anglo-Canadian legal tradition, judges had a reputation for being corrupt, prone to accepting bribes, and amenable to undue influence. Today, thanks to a general acceptance of the importance of the principles of fairness and impartiality in the courts, and the attention that judges themselves attach to ethical issues, judging is one of the most respected professions in our society. Many good lawyers aspire to become judges, in spite of a possible drop in pay, because a judicial appointment is symbolic of a successful career. The same transformation needs to occur — and we believe can and must occur — with respect to elected officials.

In this chapter we suggest what remains to be done to promote high ethical standards in the political practices of elected officials in Canada. These changes pertain to six areas: ethics commissioners, ethics legislation, codes of ethics, ethics audits, ethics education, and greater political accountability.

Ethics Commissioners

Canada's experiments with ethics commissioners have been reassuring with regard to conflict-of-interest issues, which up to now have been the commissioners' primary concern. With few exceptions, the creation of the office of an independent ethics commissioner has marked the dividing line between frequent conflict-of-interest scandals and an almost complete absence of significant conflicts.

There are several reasons for the success of the commissioners. Most important is their role in counselling elected members. Because the commissioners meet with individual members in confidence to advise them about avoiding the potential conflicts of interest that might arise from their personal financial situations, the members receive a dose of preventive medicine that was previously unavailable. The commissioners also provide a quick and impartial means of resolving allegations of conflict of interest. Finally, the commissioners appointed have all been competent and experienced individuals. In particular, the first two appointments — Gregory Evans in Ontario (1988) and Ted Hughes in British Columbia (1990) — have become role models for the more recently appointed commissioners in Alberta, Saskatchewan, and Newfoundland. As former judges, Evans and Hughes were keenly aware of the importance of the impartiality principle in a democracy and its incompatibility with real conflicts of interest.

The exceptions to the general success of the ethics commissioner system are the Multi-Corp scandal in Alberta and the organization of the premiers' conference in Jasper, both of which involved Premier Klein, and Premier McKenna's IBM-paid trip to Atlanta's

Olympics. In the Alberta cases, it appears that the advice Klein received from his recently appointed ethics commissioner was either inadequate or based on insufficient information. In the Multi-Corp case, Klein did not consult with Commissioner Robert Clark prior to Colleen Klein's acquisition of the Multi-Corp shares, and when they eventually reported the acquisition, they failed to mention that the shares had not been paid for or that the agreed cost of acquisition was significantly below market value. The Kleins' apparent lack of concern about their situation underlines why an ethics commissioner is not only potentially useful, but necessary.

In the case of the Jasper conference we agree wholeheartedly with *The Globe and Mail* editorial writer(s) who noted that, although the Alberta ethics commissioner apparently found nothing wrong with the practice of private companies sponsoring the activities of government leaders, private sponsorship of public discourse means that when a sponsoring firm wants something from government that one of its ministries is in a position to supply, "which is the reason the firm makes donations, that ministry may be more favourably disposed." Furthermore, the message to Canadians is, "here is your government, brought to you by the private sector."[2]

Two provinces — Nova Scotia and New Brunswick — have appointed judges as ethics commissioners. In our view, this approach is better than having no ethics commissioner at all, but not as effective as appointing a retired judge or someone else outside the judiciary to the position. Sitting judges cannot become as involved in the educational role as the other ethics commissioners due to their need to maintain judicial independence and to avoid being drawn into political controversy, as in the case of Richard Hatfield. The cause of judicial independence is not furthered by a situation that exposes judges to potential political controversy. And this clearly bears on Premier McKenna's initial acceptance of IBM's sponsorship of his trip to Atlanta.

To raise ethical standards in Canadian politics, independent ethics commissioners must be appointed in the jurisdictions that do not yet have them: Manitoba, Quebec, and the federal Parliament. As well, it would be helpful for Nova Scotia and New Brunswick to replace their designated judges with independent ethics commissioners who do not also have judicial appointments. To make an ethics commissioner a cost-effective venture in the smaller provinces, the commissioner's role might be combined with that of the chief electoral officer as is the case in Newfoundland, or with an information and privacy commissioner, as in Alberta. But careful thought should be given to the potential disadvantages of a combined role, such as a possible loss of focus. A part-time commissioner might be preferable in the smaller jurisdictions.

We agree with Commissioners Evans and Hughes that the ethics commissioners' responsibilities should be expanded beyond conflicts of interest to include integrity issues in the broad sense. In particular, the provinces should consider legislation to ensure that the relation between lobbyists and public officials conforms to the ethical standards of a democracy. The ethics commissioners are the logical candidates to take on educational and investigatory roles pursuant to such legislation.

Finally, it is critical that there be effective conflict-of-interest legislation and ethics commissioners at the municipal level right across the country. The slower the provincial governments are to bring their municipal governments within the scope of effective ethics legislation, the more likely it is that serious allegations of conflict of interest — most notably involving the development industry — will continue to fester and to erode confidence in municipal governments.

While expanded roles for independent ethics commissioners offer great potential, there are also limits to what they can reasonably be expected to accomplish. They can provide preventive advice with regard to conflicts of interest, lobbying, and possible undue influence resulting from political donations, but they are not necessarily in the best position to tackle broader issues of integrity, such as those related to election promises or dirty-handed politics. Some ethics issues can best be addressed by political parties themselves developing codes of ethics, by the voters at election time, and by citizens playing a more participative role in politics *between* elections.

Ethics Legislation

In addition to our recommendation that the jurisdictions currently lacking conflict-of-interest legislation should remedy this deficiency, more effective legislation is required at the provincial and municipal levels to shed light on the activities of lobbyists, and at all levels to eliminate patronage and undue influence related to party financing. As well, careful thought should be given to appropriate whistleblowing legislation.

The new federal rules for regulating lobbyists, combined with the development of effective codes of ethics for lobbyists, ought to go a long way toward preventing undue influence in policy development and in the awarding of federal contracts. If the rules prove effective, then scandals involving federal lobbyists on the scale of the Airbus controversy or the Pearson Airport deal are less likely to occur again.

The federal legislation regulating lobbyists represents one of the few areas in which federal ethics rules are superior to provincial rules. The provinces would be well-advised to copy the federal example in their own jurisdictions and to include the municipalities in such legislation. Requiring lobbyists to disclose who they are, what issues they are working on and for whom, and how much they are being paid promotes open, honest government with very little public expenditure.

The potential for a relation between contributions to political parties and public office favours is still a problem in most parts of Canada. Even though all significant contributions are now made public on an annual basis, this publicity has not been enough to prevent undue influence or the appearance of it. Contributors expecting public office favours in return for their financial largesse need only take the heat once a year, along with dozens of other large donors, and it is rarely possible to prove an explicit connection between a contribution and a favour.

We think that Ontario and Quebec are on the right track in placing limits on contributions from individual sources. Moreover, there are good arguments for legislation that permits only individual donations and does not allow businesses or unions to make political contributions. If contribution limits are low enough (somewhere between $500 and $5,000 annually would be acceptable, although a limit of $1,000 is preferable), then the possibility of undue influence is negligible unless the rules are broken. And with Patti Starr's jail term setting an example, we think that such rules are likely to be taken seriously. Furthermore, placing limits on single-source contributions would certainly encourage all political parties to establish a broader base of support, and such a move could only be good for democracy.

One of the greatest potentials for undue influence related to political contributions concerns contributions to candidates at leadership conventions. All political parties should limit single-source contributions to $1,000 and should ensure that contributions are made and publicized prior to the final counting of the ballots at their leadership conventions. And if the parties themselves don't act in this regard, then their leadership financing rules should be set by legislation.

We can see no legitimate role for patronage appointments or the awarding of contracts based on patronage, with the very minor exception of positions directly related to partisan politics. If cabinet ministers and members of provincial assemblies wish to hire their political friends to work in constituency offices or as ministerial assistants, or to fulfil small public-relations contracts, this practice might be acceptable as long as the numbers of political staff are limited.

However, all hiring related to the implementation of a program established by law and the awarding of all contracts related to such programs should be conducted in an impartial manner. Otherwise, the rule of law becomes a hollow slogan that contributes to disillusionment and cynicism about politics. The legislative provisions that stipulate hiring based on merit should be extended to include what are now patronage jobs controlled by the federal and provincial cabinets.

It will take a colossal effort to wean Canadian political parties from the patronage habit, and many readers may consider this goal an impossible dream. But three decades ago, conflicts of interests were generally accepted as part of politics, and today they are not. Three decades ago, nearly all judicial appointments at the federal and provincial levels were based on patronage, and today far fewer are. It takes time to turn around the ship of state, and we hope that thirty years from now, patronage will not only be a thing of the past in Canadian politics, but our grandchildren will wonder why we put up with this obvious abuse of democracy for so long.

Whistle-blowing

Legislation should also be considered with regard to "whistle-blowing." A whistle-blower is someone who openly or secretly releases confidential information about an illegal or harmful act — potential or actual — outside the regular channels in his or her organization. A public servant may be in a position to expose the illegal or unethical acts of an unelected public official or an elected politician. More rarely, elected public officials are in a position to blow the whistle. Whistle-blowing can offer an opportunity to act with integrity in public life — not only to stop a dirty-handed act, but also to prevent fraud, a real conflict of interest, or undue influence.

Most people who work in a large organization will find themselves at some point wondering whether they should blow the whistle. In one sense, whistle-blowers appeal to the same logic as dirty-handed politicians — they are devoted to serving a cause that they believe requires them to go outside normal channels of accountability and responsibility. The difference is that the actions of whistle-blowers are meant to publicize and reveal wrongs, while dirty-handed politicians attempt to conceal them. The decision to blow the whistle is rarely an easy one because it pits loyalty to the organization and to one's superiors against what is perceived to be the good of the larger community. From the perspective of the basic democratic value of mutual respect, the respect that an employee owes to peers and superiors is challenged by the respect owed to society at large, and so competing moral claims are at stake. Added to this dilemma is the possibility that whistle-blowers may have to leave their jobs, either because they are fired or because they will find it too uncomfortable to carry on after taking action. The decision as to whether to blow the whistle may effect the whistle-blower's family as well. And as Kernaghan and Langford have pointed out, there is a very fine line between legitimate whistle-blowing and deliberate obstruction of the organization.[3]

H.L. Laframboise, a former federal assistant deputy minister, has argued that whistle-blowing is only justified "if the act [reported outside the organization] is abhorrent to peer group values. Without that distinction a community would disintegrate into a collection of mutually suspicious informers."[4] He considers that whistle-blowers are usually "compulsive moralists" who "grieve everything grievable, appeal every competition they lose, incite other employees to complain, and generally make nuisances of themselves."[5] We think Laframbroise has overstated the dangers of whistle-blowing and that his standard — peer group values — is certainly inadequate. Given this standard, it might not have been acceptable for a member of the Canadian Airborne Regiment to blow the whistle on those torturing Shidane Arone in order to save his life: the testimony before the Létourneau inquiry indicated that many of the members of the regiment saw nothing wrong with this behaviour.

From our perspective, potential whistle-blowers have an ethical responsibility first to discuss the activity raising concern with the person or persons carrying it out or with their superiors, unless such a discussion is likely to lead to even greater harm. For example, those in the Canadian Airborne Regiment who were aware that captured Somalis were being tortured had a moral responsibility to object to these acts to the soldiers involved or to their superiors, or both, unless they had good reason to believe that such action might have led to an intensification of the torture. In that case, not only would they have been justified in contacting the media or an MP, they had an ethical responsibility to do so. Fortunately, many situations where whistle-blowing is contemplated do not involve nearly so much potential harm, and often raising the issue with the appropriate people inside the organization will rectify the harmful act or behaviour.

The problem is that many of us do not think we have the necessary interpersonal skills to carry off a discussion about a possible ethical breach, and so we blow the whistle because it is easier than facing the perpetrator of the harmful act or our boss. Even more commonly we do nothing. Some federal and provincial government agencies have officials designated as "ethics counsellors." In addition to their regular employment, they are available to provide confidential advice about ethical dilemmas faced by workers in their organization. We feel that this innovation has great potential value, as long as the ethics counsellors have the opportunity to gain a solid understanding of ethics issues and legislation, have the appropriate interpersonal skills, and have the support of their organization.

The U.S. federal government and several states have legislation to protect legitimate whistle-blowers from retaliation. Ontario became the first province with such a law when the Rae government enacted "Whistleblowers' Protection" legislation in 1993. The legislation authorizes the legislature to appoint a lawyer as an independent "counsel" for a five-year term. The purpose of the counsel is to consider confidential information from Ontario public employees about "serious government wrongdoing" that violates a law, "represents gross mismanagement; ... causes a gross waste of money; ... represents an abuse of authority; or ... poses a grave health or safety hazard ..."[6] Upon examining such information, the counsel may require the head of a provincial agency to prepare a report on the matter and can request further reports until counsel is satisfied. Alternatively, counsel may advise the employee that the allegations appear to be groundless, or that it would be more appropriate to bring the allegations to an official in the employee's agency, the police, the ombudsman, or the freedom of information and privacy commissioner. If an agency head prepares a report, however, the counsel can make it public. If employees have blown the whistle in good faith, they are protected from "adverse employment action," and if they feel that they have been punished for whistle-blowing, they can have the matter arbitrated through their collective agreement, or take the issue to the Labour Relations Board.

The Ontario whistle-blowing legislation has never been implemented because neither the Rae government nor the Harris government has taken the steps to appoint a counsel. The federal government in the U.S. has had similar legislation for years, but it may not have been very effective in preventing reprisals. For example, between 1979 and 1984, only about 1 per cent of complaints received from federal employees about unjustified reprisals for whistle-blowing resulted in corrective action.[7]

While an independent counsel along the lines of the the Ontario model might prove to be an effective avenue for promoting integrity among appointed public officials, elected officials in jurisdictions with ethics commissioners already have someone they can turn to for advice. The ethics commissioners are authorized to investigate matters involving a conflict of interest, and with regard to other issues they might agree to act as an informal sounding board. Cabinet ministers who decide to blow the whistle on cabinet colleagues must first resign, however. And the ultimate defender of elected officials who blow the whistle is the public, who must decide at election time whether an elected whistle-blower deserves re-election, as well as whether members who did not blow the whistle when they had the opportunity deserve their jobs back. The verdict of the people of Saskatchewan is clear — Conservative cabinet ministers and MLAs should have blown the whistle on the expense fund fraud, and their failure to do so has cost most of them their jobs and has done untold damage to their party.

Codes of Ethics

Among the recommendations of the Royal Commission on Electoral Reform and Party Financing in 1991 was the proposal that Canadian political parties develop their own internal codes of ethics. To date, no party has adopted what we could properly call a code of ethics. This is regrettable, because the less the parties are able to ensure high ethical standards themselves, the more likely it is that ethical standards will have to be imposed from the outside. As well, many aspects of ethical politics can be more effectively handled by the parties than by an outside body.

Codes of ethics are important for three reasons. First, even with the most carefully drafted legislation regarding conflicts of interest, lobbying, and party financing, unscrupulous people will find loopholes. It is far better to have brief, easy-to-understand legislation that politicians can be trusted to comply with most of the time, than complex legislation designed to plug every loophole. Like the Income Tax Act, complex laws do not make for inspiring reading, they open the door to those who specialize in getting around the legislation rather than complying with it, and they cause resentment.

Second, integrity issues such as lying, negative advertising, and dirty-handed politics are difficult if not impossible to control through legislation. The best way to promote integrity in public life is for elected officials to take primary responsibility for setting standards.

Third, the process of developing a code of ethics is an education in itself. Those involved in developing such codes need to think carefully about the basic principles of democracy and how they relate to the party's objectives and activities. If carefully planned, this process can lead to the internalization of ethical values, and this is a powerful weapon on behalf of integrity.

Janet Hiebert suggests that political parties would benefit in a number of ways from having such codes. For example, Canadian parties are decentralized organizations, and codes of ethics could help to foster a greater sense of national purpose. Moreover, Canadian parties have often been embarrassed by over-zealous partisans who unwittingly tarnish the party's reputation, and codes of ethics would help to prevent such incidents.[8]

The only major party in Canada with a code of ethics is the Reform Party, but as Hiebert points out the Reform Party's code does not fulfil the functions expected of a good code of ethics. It is basically a pre-screening device to ensure that candidates do not have embarrassing reputations, and it does not apply to rank-and-file members.

It is worthwhile to consider why the parties have resisted developing these codes. Hiebert suggests that party activists tend to see their parties as private organizations with little public accountability. This perception of political parties may seem odd to those who consider that parties play such a pivotal role in setting the public policy agenda that they must be accountable not only to their members, but also to the general public. The view that parties are essentially private organizations could be explained in part by the rather dismal reputation of contemporary politicians which draws a disproportionate number of self-interested persons into politics. Being self-interested, they would tend to emphasize the private rather than the public nature of their party. For example, Allan Kornberg's study of the twenty-fifth Canadian Parliament found that between a third and a half of the members of the Conservative and Liberal parties were motivated to enter politics primarily by personal reasons, such as a desire to advance their own careers. Only the New Democrats were motivated primarily by a desire to serve the public and to advance the party's ideology.[9] And Maureen Mancuso's study of British MPs in the late 1980s shows that a third of them had fairly low ethical standards; she refers to them as "entrepreneurs." These MPs viewed their office almost as a business, rather than a calling ... In the grey areas of conflict of interest, and in determining the scope of activities that can be conducted in the name of constituency service, these particular MPs were guided by the principle of "anything goes."[10] It would not be surprising to find that a significant number of elected officials in Canada are similarly motivated. It would be hard to persuade the "entrepreneurs" in political parties that codes of ethics are desirable.

This opposition to codes of ethics may change if one political party develops a credible code and attracts significant new public support because of it. Eventually, the other parties might feel pressured to develop their own codes in order to maintain public support and could end up competing to establish the most effective code.

Some party activists may fear that a code of ethics would prevent their party from responding flexibly to the unethical practices of other parties and some journalists. The constraints of a code of ethics could place so many shackles on a party that it might be annihilated by the dirty tricks of its enemies. But as we argued in Chapter 7, this type of justification of dirty-handed politics equates politics with war, where winning tends to be more important than the means employed to win. And in spite of the bravado of some party militants, politics is *not* war — it is a competitive process to determine which citizens are best fitted to be entrusted with the onerous duties of running a government. The principle of mutual respect holds that even those who appear not to respect others nevertheless deserve to be treated with respect. This is why, for example, it is important for the justice system in a democracy to treat accused and convicted persons fairly and according to law. In this way the values of democracy are promoted through example. In our view, a political party that intelligently pursues honest politics is more likely to lead by example — and thereby encourage the other parties and the less ethical elements in the media to raise their standards — than to be defeated by ethical constraints.

Another fear of some party members is that a code of ethics could be a recipe for disaster since the media and members of opposing parties will be quick to point out the ways in which the party fails to live up to its code. From this perspective, a code of ethics could do more harm than good to the party's electoral fortunes. This is a valid concern, and our reply to it is that everything depends on how a party develops and implements its code of ethics. A code should be the result of a bottom-up, not top-down, exercise. The parties would be wise to involve their local organizations in drafting these codes over a period of time long enough to foster a healthy internal debate; a process lasting one or two years would not be unreasonable. A thorough internal airing of ethical issues can foster an acceptance and internalization of ethical standards so that party members will be less likely to embarrass the party by violating the code. Effective and fair enforcement procedures are also needed. For example, the parties should ensure that each of their constituency associations has an ethics counsellor who can both advise on ethics issues and consider complaints from party members and the public, and that a national co-ordinating mechanism for these local ethics counsellors is put in place. Penalties for violating the code could vary from a reprimand to suspension of membership.

What form should a party code of ethics take? It should be brief and clear. There should be a statement outlining the basic principles of democratic government together with the basic values of the party from which the more specific elements of the code are derived. A definition of conflict-of-interest would be useful, along with a statement affirming the duty of party members to remove themselves from conflict-of-interest situations. Similarly, there should be a definition of undue influence and a condemnation of activities that promote undue influence, especially in relation to the financing of election and leadership campaigns. The importance of providing equal opportunities for all party members to participate in party activities, regardless of their gender, race, ethnicity, age, physical disability, or sexual orientation should be stressed. There should be a commitment to respect the activities of other parties and their members, especially during election campaigns, along with constraints on negative advertising. A statement affirming the value of integrity and condemning dirty-handed politics would be useful. And the enforcement mechanisms of the code need to be explained. This list does not exhaust the topics that a party's code of ethics might cover, but we think that the issues discussed above should all be considered.

Ethics Audits

One way to promote accountability in politics is the use of periodic ethics audits. In 1995, the auditor general of Canada published its first ethics audit of the federal public service. The audit included a survey of public servants to assess their awareness of ethics-related rules and issues in the public sector pertaining to conflicts of interest and fraud. The audit also reviewed the extent and effectiveness of ethics training programs in the federal public service. The report indicated that ethical standards among federal public servants were relatively high, but areas of weakness were detected. For example, a tenth of those surveyed saw nothing wrong with accepting a free weekend of skiing from an agency receiving benefits from their department, and nearly a third saw nothing wrong with hiring a relative on a $20,000 untendered contract. Recommendations were made for dealing with these ethical deficiencies through better ethics training. The auditor general would not be the appropriate agency for conducting an ethics audit of elected members or a political party, but the auditor general's report demonstrates both the practicality and the utility of the ethics audit concept.[11]

Elected officials at every level, as well as political parties, could benefit from periodic ethics audits. An objective set of procedures could be developed to evaluate the extent to which a particular government or a particular party was adhering to the generally accepted ethical standards of a democracy. Such ethics audits could be conducted by an independent research organization, such as a public policy research institute or a centre for practical ethics affiliated with a university.[12] Our view is that such measures would go a long way toward ensuring public accountability for ethical standards in politics.

Ethics Education

As the American philosopher and democratic theorist John Dewey emphasized, education should be about "the formation of character, intellectual, moral and esthetic, and not just training in skills and the importation of information."[13] For Dewey, building a democratic character is the purpose of a democratic education. Our aim in this book has been to make a contribution to that kind of education by focusing on the democratic value of mutual respect and the principles and obligations that flow from it, along with the necessary ethical supports that will help sustain and strengthen the workings of our democracy.

It is desirable that as many public officials as possible have a solid grounding in the principles of ethical democratic politics and the process of ethical reasoning prior to becoming politically involved. To assume that elected officials can learn what they need to about ethical politics in a crash course after they are elected is wishful thinking. Elected officials are often too busy for courses, and bad habits may already have set in. From this perspective, the basics of ethical politics need to be covered in courses that deal with Canadian government and politics in high schools, colleges, and universities.

Unfortunately, in reality the word "ethics" is rarely mentioned in such courses today. This situation needs to change, and we think that the change is inevitable. In the 1970s, human rights issues were rarely mentioned in Canadian government courses; today, they are considered central. We expect a similar growth of interest in ethical politics as the agencies for promoting honest politics, such as ethics commissioners, become better known and as more teaching materials become available.

Political Accountability and Responsibility

Just prior to the 1993 federal election, the Campbell government appointed Justice Horace Krever of the Ontario Court of Appeal to "review and report" on all aspects of the blood system in Canada, including the contamination of blood supplies with the AIDS virus and the hepatitis C virus in the early 1980s. In December 1995, after over 200 days of public hearings, the inquiry's legal counsel sent notices to twenty institutions (such as the Red Cross, governments, and pharmaceutical companies) and seventy-five individuals (including many former health ministers) outlining more than three hundred allegations of misconduct that might be included in the final report. They were told that they would have until February 1996 to rebut the allegations. Most of those who received the notices filed lawsuits against Krever, claiming that he did not have the power to assess blame. In June, a Federal Court judge decided that Krever did have the power to assess blame, but if that decision is appealed then Krever's final report could be delayed for months or even years. By mid-1996, the inquiry's budget had grown from an initial $2.5 million to $14 million, and it had heard from 350 witnesses. Half of the witnesses were victims, and many of them were frustrated by the legal manoeuvres that prevent Krever from commenting on who might have been responsible for their plight.

On May 9, 1992, twenty-six miners were killed in an underground explosion in Nova Scotia's Westray Mine. The provincial government appointed a commission of inquiry, but a challenge to the inquiry's powers that went all the way to the Supreme Court of Canada prevented public hearings from starting until November 1995. Even then, some officials from the company's office refused to testify on the grounds that a Nova Scotia inquiry could not force them to appear. Most officials who testified blamed others for the explosion, claiming that there was nothing they could have done. Former Nova Scotia premier Donald Cameron blamed the workers and the union. However, the inquiry uncovered a close relationship among certain members of the Cameron government and Westray officers; it also uncovered considerable support for the company from the Conservative federal government. Eventually, the Nova Scotia government apologized to the families of the victims for the way the Westray matter was handled.

As in the Somalia case, two themes are common to both these inquiries. First, a concerted effort was made by some individuals to prevent the full details from becoming public. Second, few of those involved have been willing to take responsibility for the dreadful things that occurred. They claim they were either following orders, the wrongdoing was someone else's responsibility, or it couldn't have been helped. This type of ethical breach has been called the problem of "many hands":[14] so many people are involved at various stages of decision making and policy implementation that those supposedly in authority claim not to have authorized or known about particular transgressions. In the Canadian system of parliamentary democracy, however, the involvement of many people should not count as an excuse, a point emphasized by former health minister Monique Bégin, who wrote to the Krever commission to say that responsibility for governmental policy and mistakes must lie with ministers, not just their subordinates.

Accountability and responsibility are closely related and generally complementary. To be accountable is to be answerable. In a democracy, elected politicians are answerable first and foremost to the public and secondly to their party organization. The question of how politicians are accountable is almost as important as to whom they are answerable. They are accountable through and at elections and by being required publicly to disclose their records and their reasons for seeking support. Responsibility, while sometimes taken to mean the same thing as accountability, refers to fulfilling the job requirements of a politician, which may include overseeing the jobs other public servants are commissioned to fulfil.

One of the key constitutional conventions in Canada is ministerial responsibility. It holds cabinet ministers responsible for the quality of administration in their departments. And if serious administrative problems occur in the department, including ethical problems, the minister must take the blame rather than blame others.

One of the traditional methods of holding ministers accountable is question period. While we believe in the value of question period, we are dismayed by the political gamesmanship that has devalued its potential effectiveness in the House of Commons and several provincial legislatures. It is clear that official inquiries are far superior to question period when the objective is fact finding, scrutinizing political mismanagement, and exposing cover-ups.

While we are not supporters of the traditional view that a minister must always resign as punishment for departmental administrative errors, we are disturbed by the current tendency of federal and provincial ministers to shirk responsibility and to refuse to admit that ethical breaches or administrative foul-ups have occurred. The refusal of any federal solicitor-general to take responsibility for the RCMP dirty tricks campaign of the 1970s, or of most federal and provincial health ministers to take any blame for Canada's tainted blood scandal, is unacceptable. To err is human; to admit error and devise a plan to ameliorate the situation is the ethical route because it is honest and respectful of those who have suffered from the error. On the other hand, for opposition politicians to insist on the resignation of ministers who take the ethically high road in such situations is itself morally reprehensible.

While laws and courts are useful in protecting constitutional rights, nullifying jurisdictional trespass, checking criminality, and enforcing contractual obligations, there is no law to penalize and no court that will punish politicians who break their promises. The electorate is responsible for holding politicians to account. We need a vigorously attentive and participatory citizenry, but there are scant resources and opportunities for citizen participation outside of well-recognized and well-financed interest groups and lobbyists. As a result, except for those who have the means to organize or join pressure groups, most citizens are rendered voiceless between elections and are unable to halt what they regard as betrayals and repugnant acts until well after they have been committed. We think a system that invites citizens to take the initiative in demanding referendums and recalls — in a similar sense to the way citizens are invited and expected to take part in elections — will encourage citizens to participate more in the decisions that affect them.

The case for referendums as supplements to official elections is based on two general points. First, referendums are a means of exerting popular democratic control over a government that has chosen either to reverse the position it took when seeking election, or to introduce a major program or constitutional change that cannot be properly addressed in an election campaign. Second, referendums are democratically educative and effective in promoting the value of legitimate governance as a result of participation in collective decision making, deliberation, mutual respect, and self-worth.[15] Much to the dismay of Canada's political elites, the referendum on the Charlottetown Accord proved to be an enormous success with respect to both these points. Canadians in all walks of life got involved in the democratic process. The pros and cons of the accord were debated around dinner tables, in offices, classrooms, and factories. And the result was that an initiative to change the nature of the country was halted when a majority of voters across the nation indicated their disapproval.

A recall procedure would enable voters to recall MPs, including cabinet ministers, who have failed to live up to the expectations of their constituents. Most recall procedures involve three steps to remove a sitting member of a legislature. First, a certain proportion of the electorate is required to sign a petition calling for a recall vote. Second, once a valid petition is collected, constituents then vote on whether their representative is to be recalled (that is, required to resign his or her seat). Third, if a majority of voters support the recall, a by-election is called. Careful thought must be given to the proportion of voters needed to trigger a recall vote. In 1994, legislation was passed in B.C. that gave voters the right to trigger a recall election if 40 per cent of eligible voters sign a recall petition in a three-month period.[16] However, the 40 per cent threshold may be too high. A more reasonable figure, as Peter McCormick has recently argued, is probably 25 per cent. This would mean that in an average federal riding 15,000 people would have to sign a recall petition, which as McCormick points out is neither inconsequential nor prohibitive.[17] Recall provisions would serve as a constant reminder to elected officials that they have an ethical responsibility to take their election promises seriously.

Another method of promoting ethical accountability is the appointment of commissions of inquiry in cases of serious allegations of ethical breaches, if such allegations are outside the mandate of an ethics commissioner. The commissions of inquiry into the RCMP dirty tricks campaign, Sinclair Stevens's conflict-of-interest problems, the activities of the Canadian peace-keeping force in Somalia, the tainted blood scandal, and the Westray Mine explosion all illustrate how such inquiries can expose violations of integrity and promote ethical accountability.

Toronto Star columnist Richard Gwyn has suggested that reliance on commissions of inquiry is leading to protracted, expensive, and highly legalistic ventures in fact-finding concerning political responsibility. Gwyn warns that such inquiries contribute to the erosion of an older, traditional sense of *civitas*, or civic duty.[18]

In a somewhat related sense, John Langford and Allan Tupper have indicated their concern that increased reliance on codes of conduct, ethics commissioners, ethical education, and principles like the ones we've been emphasizing throughout this book might result in future Canadian governments being "ethically bombarded to death" by utopian "democratic sanitizers."[19]

Our position is that the more obstacles in the way of corrupt practices and the more incentives to ethical politics there are the better. Our examination of the way politics is conducted across the country does not indicate that our elected office-holders are overburdened with rules and regulations, but rather that they require better and more useful checks and guidelines to help them carry out the jobs they were elected to do.

Conclusion

Although this book has focused on the ethical deficiencies in Canadian politics and their remedies, we should not forget that in spite of the defects, the ethical standards of many Canadian politicians are actually quite high compared with other countries. Monique Bégin is an excellent example of a highly responsible and honest politician. Bégin was minister of health and welfare in successive Trudeau governments. In August 1996, she sent a letter to Justice Krever, head of the inquiry into the tainted blood fiasco. Bégin waived any immunity that Justice Krever might grant and noted that she should be asked to testify if her former civil servants were called on to do so.

> If you have to lay the blame, I consider it my duty to take my share of the responsibility. The notion of "ministerial responsibility" is the cornerstone of our executive government. Justice is offended if people at the top are not held responsible for their actions, but employees at less serious levels of the hierarchy are. Public ethics requires that those at the top be accountable.[20]

This is a clear illustration of how responsibility and accountability need to be brought together.

Another outstanding example is Warren Allmand, who has been a moral gadfly within government circles for more than three decades. Allmand, who has served as solicitor general, minister for Indian affairs, and consumer affairs minister, was dismissed as chair of the House of Commons justice committee on September 1995 by the Liberal party whip because he voted against the government's budget. According to Allmand, the Liberal budget was a disavowal of the party's Red Book promises, and he felt an obligation to hold firm to his principles. "You have to, and I'll continue to do so, if I think we are violating the principles of our party or we are going against what we promised in the election. I'll continue to support the platform I ran on."[21] Ethical politics is important to most Canadians, and voters are rarely willing to provide ongoing support to governments with a record of corruption. Failing to provide an adequate infrastructure for ethical politics is an invitation to those with baser motives to take advantage of the system.

By making more extensive use of ethics commissioners, improving ethics legislation, encouraging political parties to develop codes of ethics, promoting ethics audits and greater ethical accountability, and enhancing the quality and quantity of ethics education, we can set the stage for an era in the not-too-distant future when ethical politics is considered as much a hallmark of our political system as free elections and judicially monitored human rights.

All of the ethics safeguards in the world will not help a country where too few of its citizens possess a democratic character. A democratic character is one that is supportive of mutual respect and the democratic principles that derive from it. It is also community-minded, tolerant, and moderate, a personality that is as concerned about others as about self, and therefore values social equality. It defends minority rights, finds exploitation of the disadvantaged unacceptable, and values freedom and integrity. Fighting political battles fairly and being a good loser are essential to the democratic character. To the extent that citizens feel that they are treated fairly, they have trust in democratic institutions, even when they are on the losing side of a decision. Yet all of us are susceptible to letting our own personal agendas interfere with our public responsibilities. To the extent that we are able to control the "me first" urge in our public duties, we exemplify a sense of democratic character. According to Robert Putnam, party activists need to place loyalty to fellow citizens ahead of loyalty to the party. George Kateb describes this democratic character trait as one of "engaged detachment," and this outlook militates against the temptation to get involved in dirty-handed politics.[22]

Some may consider the quest for democratic character to be a hopeless ideal. The debate about whether human beings are, ought to be, or possibly can be mutually interested rather than singly self-interested is older than recorded history. But until recently, it has been a debate mainly among males. Most mothers we know, as well as fathers who take parenting seriously, have no doubts about the reality and the value of a concern for others.[23]

There are many factors that, combined, promote a democratic character: A loving and nurturing family environment that engenders a sense of moral consciousness,[24] an education that helps us to understand groups we might otherwise be suspicious about out of ignorance,[25] and enough involvement in community activities to help us appreciate the problems and outlooks of our fellow citizens.[26] But even if these character traits are present in society in significant quantities, their potential energy cannot be harnessed to promote and protect democracy without ethical leadership. The ethical tone of a regime is enormously influenced by those at the top — the premier or prime minister, the cabinet, and the top public servants. Leaders who are considered self-interested and untrustworthy create a malaise in governing circles that tempts public servants to behave unethically to protect themselves.[27] And these factors combine to erode the public's trust in government as a whole. Conversely, if those at the top are perceived as fair and honest, then these values tend to permeate the entire society.

But it is worth remembering that in a democracy, leadership comes from and is representative of the citizenry. As our leaders have a duty to function as moral actors, so all citizens also have a duty to see to it that they live up to their obligations and practise the ethics and principles of democracy.

Appendix I
Workshops on Ethical Politics

The authors organized three workshops on ethical issues in politics between 1992 and 1994 at York University with assistance from the Social Sciences and Humanities Research Council of Canada. The purpose of these workshops was to provide a forum for academics, public officials, politicians, and journalists to analyse current expectations about ethical politics and to identify areas needing reform. These workshops provided the impetus for this book, and a number of references in the book are to workshop sessions. The workshop topics and participants are shown below.

Workshop I: Conflicts of Interest
November 21, 1992

Session I: The Concept of Conflict of Interest

Chair: Ian Greene, York University
Participants:
Ian Scott, M.P.P. and former Attorney General of Ontario
Stevie Cameron, journalist, *The Globe and Mail*
Patrick Boyer, M.P.
Andrew Stark, University of Toronto

Session II: Conflict of Interest Commissions, Codes, and Statutes

Chair: Skip Bassford, Dean, Atkinson College, York University
Participants:
Hon. Gregory Evans, Ontario Conflict of Interest Commissioner
Eldon J. Bennett, lawyer
Charles Campbell, lawyer
Georges Tsai, Assistant Deputy Registrar General, Government of
  Canada

Session III: Conflict of Interest Dilemmas

Chair: Harry Arthurs, former president of York University
Participants:
Marc Rodwin, University of Indiana
Stephen Bindman, journalist
Michael Vaughan, Treasury Board of Canada
Valeria Alia, University of Western Ontario

Session IV: Conflicts of Interest, Patronage, and Party Financing

Chairs: Reg Whitaker and Donald MacNiven, York University
Participants:
Donald C. MacDonald, Chairman, Ontario Commission on
  Election Finances
Geoffrey Stephens, journalist, *Toronto Star*
Allan Tupper, University of Alberta
Janet Hiebert, Queen's University
Kenneth Gibbons, University of Winnipeg
James Lightbody, University of Alberta

Session V: Where Do We Go from Here?

Chair: David Shugarman, York University
Participants:
James Gillies, York University (former federal cabinet minister)
Hon. Ted Hughes, Ethics Counsellor, British Columbia
Wes Cragg, York University
John Langford, University of Victoria

Workshop II: Dirty Hands
December 12, 1993

Session I: Do We All Have Dirty Hands?

Kai Neilsen, University of Calgary
Ronald Biener, University of Toronto
David Shugarman, York University

Session II: Dirty Money

Les Green, York University
Wes Cragg, York University

Session III: Thinking Right, Practising Welfare

Evan Simpson, McMaster University

Michael McDonald, University of British Columbia
Michael Yeo, Westminster Institute

Session IV: Does Politics Require Dirty Hands?

Leah Bradshaw, Brock University
Sharon Sutherland, Carleton University
Kai Neilsen, University of Calgary

Workshop III: Gender and Ethics
April 30, 1994

Session I: Employment Equity and Gender Expectations

Chair: David Shugarman, York University
Participants:
Les Jacobs, York University (equal opportunity and gender
  disadvantage)
Don MacNiven, York University (an affirmative action dilemma)
Jamie Cameron, York University (ethics, law, and the judiciary)

Session II: Gender Ethics, Elected Officials, and the Media

Chair: Ann Denholm Crosby, York University
Participants:
Michael Atkinson, McMaster University (gender differences in
  ethical standards)
Valerie Alia, University of Western Ontario (gender ethics issues
  in journalism)

*Session III: Feminist Ethics: Extending the Boundaries of the
Gender Ethics Debate*

Chair: Margaret Moore, Waterloo University
Participants:
Mary Powell, Laurentian University (voices of women and men in
  the classroom)
Sandra Whitworth, York University (gender, ethics and
  international relations)
Isa Bakker, York University (gender ethics and economic policy)

Session IV: Dealing with Violence and Harassment

Chair: Ann Denholm Crosby, York University
Participants:
Pat Marshall, Chair, Canadian Panel on Violence against Women
Melanie Joyner, York University (wife abuse and public policy)

Session V: Ethics and New Reproductive Technologies

Chair: Ian Greene, York University

Participants:

Bernard Dickens, University of Toronto (ethics, law, and new reproductive technologies)

Martin Thomas, York University (empirical evidence of sex selection: informing the ethical debate)

Micki Thomas, Toronto Hospital (ethical issues in prenatal diagnosis)

Thelma McCormack, York University (the Baird Report: D.O.A.)

Appendix II
Excerpts from Codes of Conduct

A. Federal Conflict of Interest and Post-Employment Code

The following code applies to federal cabinet ministers, parliamentary secretaries, ministerial staff (except public servants), and some governor-in-council appointees.

Government of Canada
Conflict of Interest and Post-Employment Code for Public Office Holders
1994

1. This Code may be cited as the Conflict of Interest Code.

2. The object of this Code is to enhance public confidence in the integrity of public office holders and the decision-making process in government
   (a) while encouraging experienced and competent persons to seek and accept public office;
   (b) while facilitating interchange between the private and the public sector;
   (c) by establishing clear rules of conduct respecting conflict of interest for, and post-employment practices applicable to, all public office holders; and
   (d) by minimizing the possibility of conflicts arising between the private interests and public duties of public office holders and providing for the resolution of such conflicts in the public interest should they arise.

3. Every public office holder shall conform to the following principles.

Ethical Standards

(1) Public office holders shall act with honesty and uphold the highest ethical standards so that public confidence and trust in the integrity, objectivity and impartiality of government are conserved and enhanced.

Public Scrutiny

(2) Public office holders have an obligation to perform their official duties and arrange their private affairs in a manner that will bear the closest public scrutiny, and obligation that is not fully discharged by simply acting within the law.

Private Interests

(4) Public office holders shall not have private interests, other than those permitted pursuant to this Code, that would be affected particularly or significantly by government actions in which they participate.

Public Interest

(5) On appointment to office, and thereafter, public office holders shall arrange their private affairs in a manner that will prevent real, potential or apparent conflicts of interest from arising but if such a conflict does arise between the private interests of a public office holder and the official duties and responsibilities of that public office holder, the conflict shall be resolved in favour of the public interest.

Gifts and Benefits

(6) Public office holders shall not solicit or accept transfers of economic benefit, other than incidental gifts, customary hospitality, or other benefits of nominal value, unless the transfer is pursuant to an enforceable contract or property right of the public office holder.

Preferential Treatment

(7) Public office holders shall not step out of their official roles to assist private entities or persons in their dealings

Insider Information

(8) Public office holders shall not knowingly take advantage of, or benefit from, information that is obtained in the course of their

official duties and responsibilities and that is not generally available to the public.

Government Property

(9) Public office holders shall not directly or indirectly use, or allow the use of, government property of any kind, including property leased to the government, for anything other than officially approved activities.

Post-Employment

(10) Public office holders shall not act, after they leave public office, in such a manner as to take improper advantage of their previous office.

(The code continues with 20 pages of compliance measures.)

B. British Columbia Members' Conflict of Interest Act

The following legislation applies to all members of the Legislative Assembly in British Columbia, including cabinet ministers.

Members' Conflict of Interest Act
Chapter 54, Statutes of British Columbia, 1990
(as amended in 1992)

2.

(1) For the purposes of this Act, a member has a conflict of interest when the member exercises an official power or performs an official duty or function in the execution of his or her office and at the same time knows that in the performance of the duty or function or in the exercise of the power there is the opportunity to further his or her private interest.

(2) For the purposes of this Act, a member has an apparent conflict of interest where there is a reasonable perception, which a reasonably well informed person could properly have, that the member's ability to exercise an official power or perform an official duty or function must have been affected by his or her private interest.

2.1 A member shall not exercise an official power or perform an official duty or function if the member has a conflict of interest or an apparent conflict of interest.

3. A member shall not use information that is gained in the execution of his or her office and is not available to the general public to further or seek to further the member's private interest.

4. A member shall not use his or her office to seek to influence a decision, to be made by another person, to further the member's private interest.

5. This Act does not prohibit the activities in which members normally engage on behalf of constituents.

6.
   (1) A member shall not accept a fee, gift or personal benefit, except compensation authorized by law, that is connected directly or indirectly with the performance of his or her duties of office.
   (2) Subsection (1) does not apply to a gift or personal benefit that is received as an incident of the protocol or social obligations that normally accompany the responsibilities of office.
   (3) Where a gift ... exceeds $250 in value ... the member shall immediately file with the commissioner a disclosure statement ... indicating (a) the nature of the gift or benefit, (b) its source, and (c) the circumstances under which it was given and accepted.

7. (1) The Executive Council ... shall not knowingly (a) award or approve a contract with, or grant a benefit to, a former member of the Executive Council ... until 24 months have expired after the date when the former member of the Executive Council ... ceased to hold office...

8. (1) A member of the Executive Council shall not,
   (a) engage in employment or in the practice of a profession,
   (b) carry on a business, or
   (c) hold an office or directorship other than in a social club, religious organization or political party, where any of these activities are likely to conflict with the member's public duties ...

9. (1) A member who has reasonable grounds to believe that he or she has a conflict of interest in a matter that is before the Assembly or the Executive Council, or a committee of either of them, shall, if present at a meeting considering the matter,
  (a) disclose the general nature of the conflict of interest, and
  (b) withdraw from the meeting without voting or participating in the consideration of the matter ...

(Sections 10 through 16 deal with the appointment of a Commissioner of Conflict of Interest and authorize the Commissioner to review members' disclosure statements, issue opinions, and conduct inquiries.)

17. (1) If the commissioner finds
  (a) after an inquiry ... or (b) that a member has refused to file a disclosure statement within the time provided ... the commissioner may recommend, in a report that is laid before the Legislative Assembly
  (c) that the member be reprimanded,
  (d) that the member be suspended for a period specified in the report,
  (e) that the member be fined an amount not exceeding $5 000, or
  (f) that the member's seat be declared vacant until an election is held in the member's electoral district.
(2) The Assembly shall consider the commissioner's report ...
(3) The Assembly may order the imposition of the recommendation of the commissioner under subsection (1) or may reject the recommendation ...

C. Lobbyists' Code of Conduct

Following are excerpts from a draft code of conduct issued by the federal Ethics Counsellor on August 6, 1996. It will be revised after recommendations from a parliamentary committee. After the revised code is published in the *Canada Gazette*, lobbyists will be required to comply with it.

Transparency

1. Identity and purpose
   Lobbyists must, when making a representation to a public office holder, disclose the identity of the individual or organization on

whose behalf the representation is being made, as well as the reasons for the approach.

2. Accurate information
   Lobbyists must provide information that is as accurate, current and factual as possible, to public office holders, clients, employers and the public. Moreover, lobbyists must not knowingly mislead anyone, and must use proper care to avoid doing so inadvertently.

3. Disclosure of obligations
   Lobbyists must indicate to their clients, employers or organizations, their obligations under the Lobbyists Registration Act, and their requirement to adhere to the Lobbyists' Code of Conduct.

4. Fees and expenses
   Consultant lobbyists shall disclose fully to their clients the nature and approximate amount of all anticipated fees and charges, prior to entering into any undertaking.

Confidentiality

5. Confidential Information
   Lobbyists must not divulge confidential information unless they have obtained the informed consent of the parties concerned, or disclosure is required by law or is requested by the Ethics Counsellor's Office for the purpose of applying this Code.

6. Insider information
   Lobbyists shall not use any confidential or other insider information obtained in the course of their lobbying activities either to the disadvantage of their client, employer or organization, or to their own financial or other advantage.

Conflict of Interest

7. Competing Interests
   Lobbyists shall not represent conflicting or competing interests without the informed consent of those whose interests are involved.

8. Disclosure

More specifically, consultant lobbyists must advise their clients in writing of any actual, potential or apparent conflict of interest, and obtain the informed consent of each client concerned before proceeding or continuing with the undertaking.

9. Improper influence

Lobbyists must not place public office holders in a conflict of interest, by proposing or undertaking any action which would constitute, or could be reasonably perceived as, an improper influence on a public office holder.

D. Examples of support for whistle blowers in codes of ethics:

"Organizations should protect from retaliation responsible and conscientious public employees who, after much forethought, disclose information about situations potentially harmful to the public interest. Agencies should focus on the message not the messenger ..."

> Policy statement of the National Council of the
> American Society for Public Administration.

The United States Code of Ethics for Government Service calls on all government employees and office holders to "expose corruption wherever uncovered" and to "put loyalty to the highest moral principles and to country above loyalty to persons, party or Government department."

Appendix III
Opinions of Ethics
Commissioners

The following is a sample of the opinions provided by the ethics commissioners in Ontario, British Columbia, Alberta, and New-foundland in response to inquiries received from members of the legislature, cabinet ministers, parliamentary assistants, or spouses of one of these groups. Selected opinions have been published in the annual reports of the commissioners to provide general guidance to those who find themselves in similar situations. Because Ontario has had an ethics commissioner for the longest period of time, most examples are from that province.

Ordinary members:

1. *Situation:* An Ontario MPP is asked to attend the opening of a mine in his constituency and is offered a charter airline ticket valued at $600. Is it a conflict of interest to accept the ticket?
   Decision of Commissioner: The event is in the MPP's constituency, so accepting the ticket does not contravene the Act. However, the airline ticket is a gift, and the donor and value of this gift must be publicly disclosed. (The public disclosure should help to ensure, through public and media vigilance, that the MPP acts impartially toward the mine with regard to his or her public duties.) (Ontario, Annual Report 1990–91, 9)

2. *Situation:* An Ontario MPP is a teacher on a leave of absence. The legislature is about to consider changes to the legislation governing the teachers' pension plan. Is it a conflict for the MPP to participate in these deliberations?
   Decision of Commissioner: Because the MPP is a member of a "broad class of electors" — teachers — no conflict would arise through participation in the proposed legislative changes. (In other words, the MPP would not be in a position to do special

favours to himself or herself, as the legislation would affect all teachers.) (Ontario, 1990–91, 8-9)

3. *Situation:* An Ontario MPP is offered a complimentary membership in a local yacht club.
   Decision of Commissioner: There are no official duties involved. Acceptance of this gift would contravene the Act, even if publicly disclosed. (Ontario, 1990, 6)

4. *Situation:* A constituent was unhappy that the Court of Appeal for Ontario had dismissed his appeal from the Divisional Court with no reasons. He wanted his MPP to raise the issue in the legislature to try to force the Court to give reasons.
   Decision of Commissioner: The Divisional Court did give reasons, and the Court of Appeal is not required to give reasons. "As the constituent intended to pursue further appeal procedures, it would be inappropriate for the member to make any comments or intervene in any manner ... To do so would be considered as interference with the judicial process and place the member in a conflict of interest." (Ontario, 1991–92, 6)

5. *Situation:* A constituent believes he has been harassed by a government agency in Ontario, and complains to his union. The constituent is not entirely happy with how the union is handling his case, and wants the MPP to call the government agency on his behalf. The MPP feels that calling the agency would be inappropriate, and suggests that the constituent work through the Human Rights Commission.
   Decision of Commissioner: The MPP's advice was correct. "The Commission and the union have processes in place to deal with these issues. It would be inappropriate for the member to contact the government agency employer, as it may be interpreted as an attempt to influence or interfere with these processes." (Ontario, 1994–95, 7)

6. *Situation:* Several Saskatchewan MLAs are leasing crown land for farming or recreational purposes. Do these leases represent a conflict of interest?
   Decision of Commissioner: There is no conflict of interest because the leases were entered into prior to these persons being elected to the legislature. (Saskatchewan, 1994, 2)

7. *Situation:* The homes or businesses or several MLAs from
Southern Alberta were damaged during severe floods in 1995.
Would it be a conflict of interest for these MLAs to apply for
assistance under an emergency provincial flood assistance
program?
Decision of Commissioner: As long as Members do not use their
offices to acquire benefits beyond those received by others in
the same situation, there is no conflict of interest. (Alberta,
1995–96, 8)

8. *Situation:* Alberta MLAs receive an invitation to attend a
conference in a foreign country. All expenses will be paid by an
independent organization in the host country. The Members are
invited because of their positions as elected members.
Decision of Commissioner: Because the subject of the conference
is not a topic likely to be debated in the Alberta legislature, and
because there would be considerable benefit to the province, the
Member, and the Members' constituents because of the
Members' attendance, there is no conflict of interest. (Alberta,
1995–96, 9)

9. *Situation:* Should payments from political parties to the party
leaders be disclosed under the Act, even if the payments are to
reimburse expenses incurred by the member?
Decision of Commissioner: It would be prudent to disclose these
payments. (Alberta, 1992–93, 8)

10. *Situation:* Four B.C. MLAs were invited by a forest company
and its union to visit the company's operations. Transportation
and lunch would be provided.
Decision of Commissioner: Clearly, the knowledge gained by such
a visit would help the members to carry out their
responsibilities more effectively and efficiently. Thus, there is
no conflict of interest. (British Columbia, 1992–93, 16)

11. *Situation:* A professional association wishes to honour a B.C.
MLA by providing the MLA with an honorary membership;
this included waiver of annual membership fees. Is this
permissible?
Decision of Commissioner: Waiver of the annual fee would be a
benefit that could result in a conflict of interest. The association

should consider another way of honouring the MLA (which it did). (British Columbia, 1992–93, 19)

12. *Situation:* A British Columbia MLA owns a home close to a proposed housing development over which there are environmental concerns requiring the attention of the provincial government. The MLA wishes to advance personal concerns as well as concerns of constituents to appropriate provincial agencies. Is this permissible?
Decision of Commissioner: The MLA can act as a conduit for letters received from constituents. However, the MLA should refrain from making personal representation to provincial agencies, as this could be interpreted as undue influence. (British Columbia, 1992–93, 20)

13. *Situation:* A member's constituent has a son who has been charged with a criminal offence. The constituent requests the member to send a letter of reference regarding the son to the judge.
Decision of Commissioner: It would be inappropriate for the member to provide a letter of reference unless the member knows the accused personally and is "familiar with the charges … and the circumstances surrounding them." If the member has evidence that would assist the court, then the member should be subpoenaed to give oral evidence in court. (Ontario, 1992–93, 11)

Cabinet Ministers:

1. *Situation:* A Ontario cabinet minister's son does consulting work for a company which intends to apply for a provincial government contract. Does this cause a conflict?
Decision of Commissioner: There is no conflict of interest as long as the bidding process is fair and competitive. However, if the son's company wins the contract, the Commissioner should be notified so that the matter could be reviewed if necessary. (Presumably, the Commissioner would consider whether potential conflict of interest situations might arise so that he could advise about how to resolve these in an appropriate fashion.) (Ontario, 1990–91, 9-10)

2. *Situation:* An Ontario Minister has been sent free passes from the Metro Toronto Conservation Authority, and the Canadian National Exhibition. Should he accept them?
   Decision of the Commissioner: To accept the pass from the CNE would violate the Act, as "it is not a benefit related to the responsibilities of his office either as a Minister or an MPP." The Conservation Authority pass may fall into a different category, however. The Authority is not related to the Minister's departmental duties, but if there is a conservation area in his constituency, then it is related to his duties as an MPP. If the pass is accepted and is worth over $200, then the Act requires the Minister to publicly disclose its receipt. (Ontario, 1994–95, 7)

3. *Situation:* An Ontario Minister planned to distribute a publication to her constituents concerning constituency matters, and wanted to use the title of "Minister" at the top of the publication. Is this appropriate?
   Decision of Commissioner: Because this is a constituency publication, the use of the title, "Minister," is not acceptable. "The business a member conducts in a constituency office should not in any way be mixed with the business conducted" as a Minister, Parliamentary Assistant or a member of a committee. (Ontario, 1994–95, 7)

4. *Situation:* A former Newfoundland Minister of Municipal and Provincial Affairs wished to accept a consulting contract with the Minister of Employment and Labour Relations regarding occupational health and safety. Newfoundland legislation requires former ministers to obtain a waiver from the Commissioner if they wish to do business with the government prior to the expiration of a one-year "cooling off" period.
   Decision of Commissioner: The waiver was granted because the former Minister had worked in the occupational health and safety field prior to becoming a Minister, and because his duties as Minister of Municipal and Provincial Affairs had nothing to do with occupational health and safety. (Newfoundland, 1993–94, 3)

5. *Situation:* Can B.C. cabinet ministers purchase 1992 British Columbia Savings Bonds?

Decision of Commissioner: Yes, except for the Minister of Finance and Corporate Relations, because the Minister has the power to set interest rates. (B.C., 1992-93, 19)

Parliamentary Assistants:

1. *Situation:* An Ontario Parliamentary Assistant (PA) and spouse are invited to a social function sponsored by an interest group affected by Ministry policy. The cost of the event, including transportation from Toronto, will be covered by the group.
Decision of Commissioner: It would violate the act to accept payment for the cost of the event and transportation, as attending the event is not simply an incident of protocol. The gift of transportation and the charges for the event might compromise the Assistant's impartiality. (Ontario, 1994–95, 6)

2. *Situation:* A constituent requests an Ontario PA to write a letter supporting an application for funding from the Ministry which the PA is responsible for.
Decision of Commissioner: Writing such a letter would not be appropriate, as it may be interpreted as an attempt to influence the outcome of the funding decision by Ministry personnel. (Ontario, 1994–95, 7)

3. *Situation:* An Ontario PA wonders whether she can become a member at large, or a Board member, of a foundation. The foundation in question sometimes challenges the validity of certain Ontario laws in court.
Decision of Commissioner: A cabinet minister is prohibited by the Act from becoming a Board member of a foundation. But a PA, in general, is free either to become a Board member or a member at large of a foundation. However, because this particular foundation sometimes sponsors court challenges of Ontario laws, it would not be appropriate for the PA to become a Board Member of this particular foundation. (Ontario, 1994–95, 8)

Spouses:

1. *Situation:* An Ontario Parliamentary Assistant's spouse wants to apply for a provincial order-in-council position. Would this application put the Assistant in a conflict position?

Decision of Commissioner: There is no conflict of interest.
(Ontario, 1991–92, 9)

2. *Situation:* An Ontario Minister's spouse was requested by a
   government agency to run a workshop for a fee of $3,500. Is
   this acceptable?
   Decision of Commissioner: The government agency had offered
   the workshop contract to two other consultants, but neither was
   available, and it was difficult to find another consultant with the
   specialty possessed by the Minister's spouse. Under the
   circumstances, no favouritism was shown to the Minister's
   spouse because of his connection to the Minister, and so it
   would be acceptable for the spouse to sign the contract.
   (Ontario, 1990–91, 8)

3. *Situation:* An Ontario MPP's spouse wished to serve as a
   volunteer member on two local boards which received
   provincial government funding. Is this acceptable?
   Decision of Commissioner: Serving on the boards would be
   acceptable as long as the spouse does not "participate in any
   discussions or lobbying with respect to the funds from the
   Provincial Government." (Ontario, 1991–92, 12)

4. *Situation:* The spouse of a B.C. MLA wonders whether it
   would be acceptable to apply for a public service position for
   that he/she is qualified for.
   Decision of Commissioner: Yes, as long as the position is not in a
   ministry in which his/her spouse was the Minister or had
   Parliamentary Secretarial responsibilities. (British Columbia,
   1992–93, 17)

Notes

Chapter 1

1. *Globe and Mail,* 9 November 1995, A1; and 29 May 1996, A4; and Toronto Star, 27 October 1996, A8.
2. *Toronto Star,* 12 January 1978.
3. Dworkin 1978, 180-2.
4. Rawls 1971.
5. Held 1987.
6. Ibid., 268.
7. McQuaig 1993 and 1996.
8. Preston Manning, "The Reform Party Faces Its Future," statement by Preston Manning. Ottawa, 6 May, 1996. Mimeo.
9. Macpherson 1965.
10. Supreme Court of Canada, *A. G. Canada v. Lavell* [1973] 38 *Dominion Law Reports* (3d) 481.
11. Polyviou 1980.
12. Greene 1989, 165ff.
13. Peter Russell, Joseph Fletcher, Philip Tetlock and Paul Sniderman, provided this information based on their studies of attitudes towards civil liberties in Canada. The surveys were done with the Institute for Social Research at York University and published work based on the studies includes Sniderman et al 1993, and Sniderman et al 1996.
14. Marchak 1981.
15. Bayefsky 1985.
16. Malszechi 1995, and see Bashevkin 1985.
17. Long 1985.
18. Greene 1989, 55.
19. Ibid. ch.8.
20. Dworkin 1978.
21. Pateman 1970.
22. *Globe and Mail,* 4 April 1996, A1.
23. Ibid., 14 October 1995, A9.
24. Hughes 1996.
25. Evans 1995, 15.

26. Canada, Senate of Canada, *Proceedings of the Special Joint Committee on a Code of Conduct.* Issue 9. Ottawa: Queens Printer for Canada, 1 November 1995, 9.
27. Chief Justice Lyman Duff in the Alberta Press Bill case, Re Alberta Statutes [1938] Supreme Court Reports 100.
28. Fallows 1996.
29. Salutin 1996.
30. *Globe and Mail,* 20 July 1996, A1.
31. Carter 1996, 74.
32. Ibid.
33. John Nunziata, newsletter to York South constituents (untitled). Ottawa, September 1996.

Chapter 2

1. The Hon. Madam Justice J. MacFarland, Commissioner, Report of a Judicial Inquiry Re: His Honour Judge W. P. Hryciuk, A Judge of the Ontario Court, Provincial Division, 1993. Mimeo.
2. Canadian Judicial Council, Press Release, Halifax, 20 September 1996, 2.
3. Canadian Bar Association, Committee on the Appointment of Judges in Canada, *The Appointment of Judges in Canada.* Ottawa: Canadian Bar Foundation, August 1985; Russell and Zeigel, 1989.
4. Hughes 1996, 1.
5. Re Manitoba Language Rights (Order), [1985] 2 Supreme Court Reports 347.
6. Rawls 1971, 235-242.
7. Shugarman 1989.
8. Locke 1980, 71,75 (sec.136, 142).
9. David Smith 1987.
10. Jones and de Villars 1994.
11. Supreme Court of Canada, *Martineau v. Matsqui Institution Disciplinary Bd.* (No. 2) [1980] 106 *Dominion Law Reports* (3d) 385 at 412. Recently, the Supreme Court has expanded the scope of natural justice rather than develop a separate doctrine of fairness.
12. Jones and de Villars 1994, 215.
13. Wilson 1980.
14. Thompson 1993, 370.
15. Presentation by Ted Hughes, see Appendix I.
16. Rawls 1971.
17. *Globe and Mail,* 17 July 1996, A10.
18. *Toronto Star,* 15 June 1996.
19. Kernaghan and Langford 1990.
20. Public servants, however, already had the benefit of appropriate statutes and regulations. See Kernagan 1974.

21. Mill 1972, 6.

Chapter 3

1. Whitaker 1987.
2. Weber 1958.
3. Whitaker 1987, 66.
4. Howard 1994.
5. Cameron 1994, 183.
6. Ibid., 404.
7. Ibid. and Simpson 1988.
8. Greenspon 1995 and Howard 1994.
9. Law Reform Commission of Canada 1991, 39.
10. Ibid. 39n9.
11. Tu 1996.
12. Canada, Assistant Deputy Registrar General, *Conflict of Interest and Post-Employment Code for Public Office Holders.* Ottawa: Ethics Counsellor, 1994. See also Appendix II.
13. Parker 1987, 29.
14. Starr and Sharp 1984.
15. Kernaghan 1974, 531.
16. Kernaghan 1973, 6.
17. MacEachen 1973.
18. Starr and Sharp 1984.
19. Cameron 1994.
20. John Black Aird, *The Aird Report.* Toronto: Premiers Office, 1986. Mimeo.
21. Hughes 1994.
22. Stanbury 1991.
23. Ibid., 39ff.
24. Ian Greene 1991, 110.
25. *Vancouver Sun,* 31 March 1990, B3.
26. *Toronto Star,* 22 June 1989, A14.
27. *Calgary Herald,* 6 April 1989, A10.
28. *Winnipeg Free Press,* 28 August 1988, 9; and *Vancouver Sun,* 26 August 1988, A1.
29. *Globe and Mail,* 8 August 1987, A8.
30. *Vancouver Sun,* 8 August 1984, B3.
31. Greene 1991, 124.
32. Cheney and Brazao 1995.
33. Stark 1992, 517-8.
34. From the annual reports of the Lobbyists Registration Act, 1993–95. See Canada, Industry Canada, Lobbyists Registration Branch, 1996.

Chapter 4

1. Cameron 1994, 93.
2. Ibid., 98.
3. Montreal *Gazette,* 10 February 1987, A2.
4. *Globe and Mail,* 12 May 1993, A9; and 13 May, A1.
5. Parker 1987, 39.
6. Ibid., 69-70.
7. Ibid., 42-5.
8. Ibid., 258, and see 232-7.
9. Ibid., 259.
10. Ibid., 271, 341.
11. Ibid., 341.
12. Ibid., 312.
13. Ibid., 313.
14. Ibid., 315.
15. Ibid., 316.
16. Ibid., 326.
17. Ibid., 349.
18. Ibid., 29.
19. Ibid., 360.
20. Ibid., 348.
21. Ibid., 353.
22. Black 1988.
23. Parker 1987, 350.
24. Ibid., 355.
25. Ibid., 357.
26. The Hon. E. N. Hughes, QC, *Report on the Sale of Fantasy Garden World Inc.* Victoria: Office of the Conflict of Interest Commissioner, April 1991. Mimeo, 40, and 26.
27. Ibid., Appendix 1.3.
28. Ibid.
29. Ibid., 56.
30. Ibid., 57.
31. Ibid.
32. Ibid., 58, 59.
33. Ibid., 59.
34. Ibid., 60.
35. Greene 1988.
36. Parker 1987, 23.
37. *The Daily Gleaner* (Fredericton), 15 September 1980, 1.
38. Ibid., and see also 16 September 1980, 1; 17 September, 1; and 6 November, 1.
39. Parker 1987, 35.
40. Ibid., 37, emphasis in original.

41. Statutes of British Columbia, 1992, Chapter 54, Member's Conflict of Interest Act, Section 2(1) (see Appendix II). Also, presentations by Ted Hughes and Gregory Evans, see Appendix III.

42. Ibid., Section 2(2).

43. The Hon. E. N. (Ted) Hughes, QC., *Opinion of the Commissioner of Conflict of Interest on a Citizen's Complaint of Alleged Contravention of the Member's Conflict of Interest Act By the Honourable Robin Blencoe, Minister of Municipal Affairs, Recreation and Housing.* British Columbia, Office of the Commission of Conflict of Interest, August 1993. Mimeo, 35.

44. Ibid., 22.

45. Ibid., 23.

46. Ibid., 29, 30.

47. Ibid., 32-6.

48. Ibid., 37-8.

49. Ibid., 39.

50. Hughes 1994, 12.

51. Rusnell 1995.

52. Robert Clark, *Report of Investigation into Allegations Relating to The Honourable Ralph Klein, Premier.* November 1995. Mimeo.

53. Allan Tupper (chair), Patricia Newman and Francis M. Saville, *Integrity in Government in Alberta: Towards the Twenty-First Century.* Report of the Conflicts of Interest Review Panel. Edmonton, 11 January 1996. Mimeo. See also *Globe and Mail,* 5 November 1996, A7, 6 November 1996, A2, and 12 November 1996, A3.

54. *Maclean's,* 25 December 1995-1 January 1996, 38.

55. Montreal *Gazette,* 14 March 1996, A11.

56. *Globe and Mail,* 13 March 1996, A4.

57. *Toronto Star,* 1 May 1996, A12.

Chapter 5

1. *Globe and Mail,* 2 February 1989, A2; 11 February, A3; 13 February, A1; 15 February, A1; 16 February, A1; and 20 February, A1.

2. Ibid., 22 March 1991, A4; 19 April, A6; 28 June, A8.

3. Ibid., 13 February 1989, A1; 15 February; 16 February, A1; and 20 February, A1; *Toronto Star,* 16 June 1989, A1, A12; 17 June A9, D1; 21 June, A25.

4. *Toronto Star,* 16 June 1989, A12; Globe and Mail, 7 July 1989, A1; and 22 March 1991, A4.

5. *Globe and Mail,* 11 February 1989, A3.

6. *Toronto Star,* 11 June 1989, A10.

7. Cameron 1994, 72-85.

8. The Hon. Gregory T. Evans, Integrity Commissioner, Report Re: Mr. Michael Harris, M.P.P., Nipissing. Toronto: Office of the Integrity Commissioner, May, 1996. Mimeo, 5.

9. Flanagan 1996.

10. *Globe and Mail,* 7 Sept. 1988, A5.

11. Cameron 1994, 36, 37.

12. Ibid., 41, and see 31-41.

13. Montreal *Gazette,* 10 Oct. 1985.

14. *Globe and Mail,* 3 June 1986 and 29 July, A10, A13.

15. Lightbody 1993, 199.

16. Ibid., 207.

17. Ibid., 207-211.

18. Presentation by Kenneth Gibbons, see Appendix I.

19. *Globe and Mail,* 8 August 1989, A1; and 9 August, A10.

20. Ibid., 11 December 1987, A1; and 18 December, A19.

21. Ibid., 20 September 1994, A8; and 21 September, A1.

22. Ibid., 18 May 1994.

23. Ibid., 20 September 1994, A8.

24. Ibid., 11 August 1994, A10.

25. Presentation by Gregory Evans, see Appendix I.

26. Nixon's report appears as Appendix E in Canada, Senate of Canada, 1995. Both the majority and minority reports also appear in Canada, Senate of Canada, 1995. The passages quoted are at E-9.

27. Cameron 1994, 371.

28. Minority Report, II-29 (in Canada, Senate of Canada, 1995).

29. Majority Report, 39 (in Canada, Senate of Canada, 1995).

30. Ibid., 68.

31. Minority Report, II-35.

32. Ibid., II-35-7.

33. Ibid., II-42.

34. Ibid., II-44.

35. Ibid., II-42-3.

36. Ibid., II-49.

37. Cameron 1994, 376, 381.

38. Minority Report, II-52.

39. Ibid., II-60, 63, 116.

40. Ibid., II-98.

41. Appendix E in Canada, Senate of Canada, 1995, E-6-9.

42. Ibid., E-10.

43. Canada, Senate of Canada, 1995, v.

44. Majority Report, 120-3 and Minority Report, II-102-104.

45. Cheney and Brazao 1995; *Calgary Herald,* 20 November 1995, A3.

46. Ibid.; Cameron, 24.

47. Carolyn Abraham, "Bribes rampant in aerospace industry," Southam News World Wide Web service (http://www.southam.com/) 22 December 1995.
48. Evans 1994, 3.

Chapter 6

1. Ontario, Standing Committee on Public Accounts, Report on the Allegation of Conflict of Interest Concerning Elinor Caplan, MPP. September 1986, 62.
2. Ibid., 66.
3. Ontario, Standing Committee on the Legislative Assembly, Report on Allegation of Conflict of Interest Concerning René Fontaine, MPP. September 1986, 28-9.
4. John Black Aird, *The Aird Report.* Toronto: Premier's Officer, 1986. Mimeo, 38, 51.
5. Evans 1995, 1-2.
6. See the Member's Integrity Act, *Statutes of Ontario* 1994, Chapter 38.
7. Evans 1995, 5, 14.
8. Member's Integrity Act, *Statutes of Ontario* 1994, Chapter 38, parts III, IV (preamble).
9. Presentation by Ian Scott, see Appendix I.
10. Ontario, Office of the Premier, Premier's Conflict of Interest Guidelines. 12 December 1990. Mimeo.
11. Presentation by Gregory Evans, see Appendix I.
12. Evans 1992, 13.
13. Ontario, Standing Committee on the Legislative Assembly, Report Regarding Allegations of Breach of the Premier's Conflict of Interest Guidelines Made Against Evelyn Gigantes, MPP and Minister of Housing. Legislative Assembly, Queen's Park, August 1994.
14. Sheppard 1994 and Mittelstaedt 1994.
15. *Statutes of British Columbia,* 1992, Chapter 54, Member's Conflict of Interest Act, Section 2(2).
16. Presentation by Ted Hughes, see Appendix I.
17. British Columbia, Office of the Commissioner of Conflict of Interest, Opinion of the Commissioner of Conflict of Interest Pursuant to Section 15(1) and 1(1) of the Members Conflict of Interest Act. Victoria: Office of the Commissioner of Conflict of Interest, 17 April, 1995. Mimeo, 28.
18. Hughes 1996, 8.
19. Ibid., 9.
20. Ibid., 1.
21. From *Canadian Parliament Review* (Winter 1995), reproduced in Hughes 1996, 25-32, 29.
22. Clark 1995.

23. Allan Tupper (chair), Patricia Newman and Francis M. Saville, *Integrity in Government in Alberta: Towards the Twenty-First Century*. Report of the Conflicts of Interest Review Panel. Edmonton, 11 January 1996. Mimeo.

24. Newfoundland and Labrador, House of Assembly, 1994; and for the Saskatchewan reports see McLeod 1995.

25. Province of Nova Scotia, Members and Public Employees Disclosure Act, Disclosure Guidelines for Members of the House of Assembly, Members of the Executive Council and Leaders of Political Parties. Halifax: Queens Printer, 1993; and see New Brunswick, Conflict of Interest Act, *Statutes of New Brunswick,* 1978, C-16.1 (as amended in 1980) and Regulation 83-134.

26. Presentation by Georges Tsai, see Appendix I.

27. Hughes 1996, 6.

28. Evans 1995, 2.

Chapter 7

1. *Toronto Star,* 30 August 1996, A10.

2. Ibid.

3. Machiavelli 1995, ch.18, 53.

4. Ibid., ch. 15, 48.

5. Ibid., ch. 18, 55.

6. Ibid.

7. The term Machiavellian is often used to refer to personalities, attitudes, styles, and actions that are dismissive of the place of morality or codes of conduct in politics. Indeed, at times in his writings Machiavelli himself seemed to exemplify this cynical, *realpolitik* view of the nature of public life, whereby everything is about the struggle for power and morality has no function except as a ruse. But as we have tried to stress, there is another side to a Machiavellian approach to leadership, one that argues the need to do unsavoury things for the sake of the public good.

8. Sartre 1955, 223.

9. Weber 1958, 121.

10. Trotsky 1969, 37.

11. White 1965, 261.

12. Halberstram 1972, 496.

13. Walzer 1973, 164.

14. Hobbes 1968, book 1 ch. 13.

15. For further elaboration of our argument here see Shugarman 1990.

16. Bok 1978, 182.

17. *Toronto Star,* 20 June 1996.

18. Jamieson 1992.

19. *Toronto Star,* 18 May 1993.

20. McDonald 1981.

21. *Toronto Star,* 12 Jan. 1978.
22. *R. v. Ormerod* [1969] 2 *Ontario Reports* (C.A.), 230.
23. *Toronto Star,* 24 July 1980.
24. Whitaker 1996, 288.
25. These quotes are taken from the transcript of congressional committees of inquiry into Iran-Contra. They are cited by David Nacht in an excellent analysis of the conspiracy and its unravelling. We have relied heavily on Nacht for our own account, see Nacht 1990, 56.
26. Nacht 1990.
27. Dahl 1989, 338.
28. Interview with David Shugarman, York University, 31 July 1996.
29. *Globe and Mail,* 16 December 1994.
30. *Toronto Star,* 20 June 1996.
31. Walkom 1994, 236.
32. Locke 1980, 77-78 (sec. 149).
33. For an important comment on the nature of trust in government see Cox 1991-2.
34. Smith 1942, quoted in Benjamin 1990, 172.
35. Elshtain 1993, 60.
36. Kuflik 1979, 51-52.
37. Ibid.
38. Rawls 1971, 339.
39. Mill 1972, 21.

Chapter 8

1. The survey of 1419 Canadians was conducted in February 1996 by Maureen Mancuso, Michael Atkinson, André Blais, Neil Nevitte and Ian Greene as part of the Canadian Political Ethics Project, with support from the Social Sciences and Humanities Research Council.
2. *Globe and Mail,* 21 August 1996.
3. Kernaghan and Langford 1990, 95.
4. Laframboise 1991, 74.
5. Ibid., 76.
6. *Statutes of Ontario* 1993, Chapter 38, Part IV, 28, 13.
7. Caiden and Truelson 1988.
8. Hiebert 1991.
9. Kornberg 1967.
10. Mancuso 1995, 51.
11. Auditor General of Canada 1995.
12. We announce here a potential conflict of interest: we are both members of York University's Centre for Practical Ethics.
13. Dewey 1988, 297.
14. Thompson 1987, 40ff.

15. For a recent study of the pros and cons of referendums see MacDonald 1991.
16. British Columbia, *Statutes of British Columbia,* Recall and Initiative Act (Bill-36), 1994.
17. McCormick 1991.
18. Gwyn 1996.
19. Langford and Tupper 1993, 16, 17. The case for adding institutionalized checks on our governors does not depend on choosing between a larger or a smaller state. It calls for re-orienting the structures and processes of government to make them more democratic. In this regard more generally, see Albo 1993.
20. *Globe and Mail,* 21 August 1996, A1.
21. *Toronto Star,* 19 September 1995, A19.
22. On democratic character see Putnam 1993 and 1995, Kateb 1981 and Rainer Knopff, "Courts and Character," presented at the annual meeting of the Canadian Political Science Association, Brock University, 2-4 June 1996.
23. Held 1990.
24. From the perspective of Jean Piaget's study of child psychology, an acceptance of mutual respect tends to occur between the ages of eight and twelve. David Richards describes this age as a time when "there evolves mutual respect between equals: respect based on the feelings that others are equally competent in the exercise of their moral capacities of judging and acting in terms of 'the norm of reciprocity and objective discussion'" (Richards 1971, quoting Piaget 1932).
25. Sniderman 1975.
26. Pateman 1970.
27. Zussman and Jabes 1989.

Selected References

Adorno, Theodore, et al. 1969. *The Authoritarian Personality.* New York: Norton.

Albo, Greg, David Langille and Leo Panitch, eds. 1993. *A Different Kind of State? Popular Power and Democratic Administration.* Toronto: Oxford University Press.

Appleby, Timothy. 1995. "World's Awash with Scandals," *The Globe and Mail.* 16 December, A1.

Auditor General of Canada. 1995. "Ethics and Fraud Awareness in Government," chapter 1 in *Report of the Auditor General of Canada to the House of Commons.* Ottawa: Minister of Supply and Services, May.

Bashevkin, Sylvia B. 1985. *Toeing the Lines: Women and Party Politics in English Canada.* Toronto: University of Toronto Press.

Bayefsky, Anne. 1985. "Defining Equality Rights," in Anne F. Bayefsky and Mary Eberts eds., *Equality Rights and the Canadian Charter of Rights and Freedoms.* Toronto: Carswell.

Benjamin, Martin. 1990. *Splitting the Difference: Compromise and Integrity in Ethics and Politics.* Lawrence, Kansas: University Press of Kansas.

Black, Conrad. 1988. "Over-reaction to Problems Discriminatory," *The Financial Post.* 24 March, 16.

Bok, Sisella. 1978. *Lying: Moral Choice In Public and Private Life.* New York: Pantheon.

Buckler, Steven. 1993. *Dirty Hands: The Problem of Political Morality.* Brookfield, Vermont: Avebury, Ashgate.

Caiden, Gerald E. and Judith A. Tuelson. 1988. "Whistle Blower Protection in the USA: Lessons Learned and to be Learned," *Australian Journal of Public Administration* (June) 121.

Callahan, Joan C. ed. 1988. *Ethical Issues In Professional Life.* New York: Oxford University Press.

Cameron, Stevie. 1994. *On the Take: Crime, Corruption and Greed in the Mulroney Years.* Toronto: MacFarlane Walter & Ross.

Campbell, Kim. 1996. *Time and Chance.* Toronto: Doubleday.

Canada. Ethics Counsellor. 1994. *Conflict of Interest and Post-Employment Code for Public Office Holders.* Ottawa: Office of the Ethics Counsellor, June.

Canada. Industry Canada, Lobbyists Registration Branch. 1996. Annual Report (Annual Report of the Lobbyist Registration Act). Ottawa: Minister of Supply and Services.

Canada. Senate of Canada. 1995. *Report of the Special Senate Committee on the Pearson Airport Agreements.* The Senate of Canada: December.

Carter, Stephen L. 1996. "The Insufficiency of Honesty," *Atlantic Monthly* 227:2 (February) 74-76.

Cassidy, Michael, ed. 1991. *Democratic Rights and Electoral Reform in Canada.* Volume 10 of the Research Studies of the Royal Commission on Electoral Reform and Party Financing. Toronto: Dundurn.

Cheney, Peter and Dale Brazao. 1995. "Moores King of Movers, Shakers," *Toronto Star.* 3 December, A18.

Clark, Robert C. 1993. *Annual Report 1992–3.* Office of the Ethics Commissioner, April.

———. 1994. *Annual Report 1993–4.* Province of Alberta, Office of the Ethics Commissioner, April.

———. 1995. *Annual Report 1994–5.* Province of Alberta, Office of the Ethics Commissioner, May.

Cox, Archibald. 1991-2. "Ethics In Government: The Cornerstone of Public Trust," *West Virginia Law Review* 94:2 (Winter) 281-300.

Dahl, Robert, A. 1989. *Democracy and Its Critics.* New Haven, Conn.: Yale University Press.

Dewey, John. 1988. "Philosophy and Education," in Jo Ann Boydston ed., *The Later Works, 1925–1953.* Volume 5, 1929–1930, 289-298. Carbondale Ill.: Southern Illinois University Press.

Dicey, A.V. 1902. *Introduction to the Study of the Law of the Constitution.* London: Macmillan.

Dworkin, Ronald. 1978. *Taking Rights Seriously.* Cambridge: Harvard University Press.

Elshtain, Jean Bethke. 1993. *Democracy on Trial.* Toronto: Anansi, Massey Lecture Series.

Evans, The Hon. Gregory T. 1992. *Annual Report 1991–2.* Legislative Assembly of Ontario, Commission on Conflict of Interest, June.

———. 1994. *Annual Report 1993–4.* Legislative Assembly of Ontario, Commission on Conflict of Interest, June.

———. 1995. *Annual Report 1994–5.* Legislative Assembly of Ontario, Commission on Conflict of Interest, June.

Flanagan, Tom. 1996. "Reform's Culture of Concealment," *The Globe and Mail.* 28 September, D2.

Fallows, James. 1996. "Why Americans Hate the Media," *Atlantic Monthly* 277:2 (February) 45-64.

Greene, Ian. 1988. "On the Brink of a Crisis?" *The Globe and Mail.* 12 February, A7.

Greene, Ian. 1989. *The Charter of Rights.* Toronto: Lorimer.

Greene, Ian. 1991. "Allegations of Undue Influence in Canadian Politics," in Janet Hiebert ed., *Political Ethics: A Canadian Perspective.* Vol. 12 of the research studies of the Royal Commission on Electoral Reform and Party Financing. Toronto: Dundurn Press.

Greenspon, Edward. 1995. "Job Advertised, but Saved for Party's Friend," *The Globe and Mail.* 6 February, A1.

Gutmann, Amy and Dennis Thompson. 1996. *Democracy and Disagreement.* Cambridge: Belknap Press.

Gwyn, Richard. 1996. "Endless Enquiries Smother Common Sense with Legalisms," *Toronto Star.* 6 September, A21.

Halberstam, David. 1972. *The Best and the Brightest.* Greenwich: Fawcett Crest.

Hampden-Turner, Charles. 1971. *Radical Man: The Process of Psycho-social Development.* Garden City, New York: Anchor Books.

Held, David. 1987. *Models of Democracy.* Stanford: Stanford University Press.

Held, Virginia. 1990. "Mothering versus Contract," in Jane Mansbridge ed., *Beyond Self-Interest,* 287-304. Chicago: University of Chicago Press.

Hiebert, Janet. 1991. "A Code of Ethics for Political Parties," in Janet Hiebert ed., *Political Ethics: A Canadian Perspective.* Vol. 12 of the research studies of the Royal Commission on Electoral Reform and Party Financing. Toronto: Dundurn Press.

Hobbes, Thomas. 1968. *Leviathan.* C.B. Macpherson, ed. Markham, Ont.: Penguin Books.

Howard, Ross. 1994. "Liberals, expect no favoritism," *The Globe and Mail.* 17 February.

Hutchinson, Allan C. and Patrick Monahan, eds. 1987. *The Rule of Law: Ideal or Ideology.* Toronto: Carswell.

Hughes, The Hon. E. N. (Ted), QC. 1994. *Annual Report of the Commissioner of Conflict of Interest 1993–4.* British Columbia, Commission of Conflict of Interest. June.

————. 1996. *Report of the Commissioner of Conflict of Interest 1995–6.* British Columbia, Legislative Assembly, Commission of Conflict of Interest. January.

Jamieson, Kathleen Hall. 1992. *Dirty Politics: Deception, Distraction, and Democracy.* New York: Oxford University Press.

Jennings, Ivor. 1959. *The Law and the Constitution.* 5th edn. London: University of London Press.

Jones, David P. and Anne S. de Villars. 1994. *Principles of Administrative Law.* Toronto: Carswell.

Kateb, George. 1981. "The Moral Distinctiveness of Representative Democracy," *Ethics* 91, 357-374.

Kernaghan, Kenneth. 1973. "The Ethical Conduct of Canadian Public Servants," *Optimum* 4:3.

———. 1974. "Codes of Ethics and Administrative Responsibility," *Canadian Public Administration* 17:4 (Winter) 537-541.

———. 1980. "Codes of Ethics and Public Administration," *Public Administration* 58.

Kernaghan, Kenneth and John W. Langford. 1990. *The Responsible Public Servant.* Toronto: Institute of Public Administration of Canada.

Kornberg, Allan. 1967. *Canadian Legislative Behavior: A Study of the 25th Parliament.* Toronto: Holt, Rinehart & Winston.

Kuflik, Arthur. 1979. "Morality and Compromise," in J. Roland Pennock and John W. Chapman eds., *Compromise in Ethics, Law and Politics.* New York: New York University Press.

Laframboise, H.L. 1991. "Vile Wretches and Public Heroes: the Ethics of Whistleblowing in Government," in Kenneth Kernaghan ed., *Do Unto Others: Proceedings of a Conference on Ethics in Government and Business.* Toronto: The Institute of Public Administration of Canada.

Langford, John and Allan Tupper, eds. 1993. *Corruption, Character and Conduct: Essays on Canadian Government Ethics.* Toronto: Oxford University Press.

Law Reform Commission of Canada. 1991. *A Consultative Document — The Determination of Refugee Status in Canada: A Review of the Procedure.* Law Reform Commission of Canada: February.

Liberal Party of Canada. 1993. *Creating Opportunity: The Liberal Plan for Canada.* Ottawa: the Liberal Party of Canada.

Lightbody, James. 1993. "Cities: The Dilemmas on Our Doorsteps," in Langford and Tupper 1993.

Locke, John. 1980. *The Second Treatise of Government.* C.B. Macpherson, ed. Indianapolis: Hackett Publishing Co., Inc.

Long, J. Anthony and Menno Boldt eds., with Leroy Little Bear. 1985. *The Quest for Justice: Aboriginal Peoples and Aboriginal Rights.* Toronto: University of Toronto Press.

MacDonald, David. 1991. "Referendums and Federal General Elections in Canada," in Cassidy 1991, 301-342.

MacEachen, the Hon. Allan J. 1973. *Members of Parliament and Conflict of Interest.* Ottawa: Information Canada.

Machiavelli, Niccolo. 1995. *The Prince.* David Wooton ed. and trans. Indianapolis: Hackett Publishing Co. Inc.

Macpherson, C. B. 1965. *The Real World of Democracy.* Montreal: C.B.C. Enterprises.

Malszechi, Gregory M. 1995. "He Shoots He Scores: Metaphors of War in Sport and the Political Linguistics of Virility." Doctoral Dissertation. York University. May.

Mancuso, Maureen. 1995. *The Ethical World of British MPs.* Montreal: McGill-Queen's University Press.

Marchak, Patricia. 1981. *Ideological Perspectives on Canada.* Toronto: McGraw-Hill.

McCormick, Peter. 1991. "Provision for the Recall of Elected Officials: Parameters and Prospects," in Cassidy 1991

McDonald, David C. 1981. *Report of the Commission of Inquiry Concerning Certain Activities of the Royal Canadian Mounted Police.* Ottawa: Minister of Supply and Services.

McLeod, D. G., QC. 1995. *Annual Report 1994.* Saskatchewan, Conflict of Interest Commissioner. March.

McQuaig, Linda. 1993. *The Wealthy Banker's Wife: The Assault on Equality in Canada.* Toronto: Penguin Books.

————. 1996. *Shooting the Hippo: Death By Deficit and Other Canadian Myths.* Toronto: Penguin Books.

Mill, John Stuart. 1972. *Utilitarianism, On Liberty and Considerations On Representative Government.* Toronto: J. M. Dent and Sons Ltd.

Mittelstaedt, Martin. 1994. "Gigantes Resigns as Housing Minister," *The Globe and Mail* 19 August, A1.

Montesquieu, Baron de. 1990. *The Spirit of the Laws.* Rev. Edn. New York: Colonial Press.

Nacht, David. 1990. "The Iran-Contra Affair," in Amy Gutmann and Dennis Thompson eds., *Ethics and Politics: Cases and Comments.* 2nd edn. Chicago: Nielson-Hall Publishers.

Nielsen, Eric. 1989. *The House Is Not a Home.* Toronto: Macmillan.

Newfoundland and Labrador, House of Assembly. 1994. *Annual Report of the Commissioner of Members' Interests, 1993–4.* April.

Newfoundland and Labrador, House of Assembly. 1995. *Annual Report of the Commissioner of Members' Interests, 1994–5.* May.

Osborne, David and Ted Gaebler. 1972. *Reinventing Government: How the Entrepreneurial Spirit is Transforming the Public Sector.* Reading, Mass.: Addison-Wesley.

Parker, William D. 1987. *Commission of Inquiry into the Facts of Allegations of Conflict of Interest Concerning the Honourable Sinclair M. Stevens.* Ottawa: Minister of Supply and Services.

Pateman, Carole. 1970. *Participation and Democratic Theory.* Cambridge: Cambridge University Press.

Piaget, Jean. 1932. *Moral Judgement of the Child.* M. Gabian trans. New York: Collier.

Polyviou, Ployvios G. 1980. *The Equal Protection of the Laws.* London: Duckworth.

Putnam, Robert. 1995. "Bowling Alone: America's Declining Social Capital," *Journal of Democracy* 6, 65-78.

Putnam, Robert. 1993. *Making Democracy Work.* Princeton: Princeton University Press.

Rand, Ayn. 1982. *Philosophy, Who Needs It.* Indianapolis: Bobbs-Merril.

Rawls, John. 1971. *A Theory of Justice.* Cambridge: Harvard University Press.

Richards, David J. 1971. *A Theory of Reasons for Action.* Oxford: Oxford University Press.

Rusnell, Charles. 1995. "Klein Broke the Rules, Political Scientists Say," and "Questions About Ethics of Stock Deal Linger Despite Clark's Report," *The Edmonton Journal.* 2 December, A1 and F1.

Salutin, Rick. 1996. "Ethical Issues Raised By the Copps Conundrum," *The Globe and Mail.* 10 May, C1.

Sartre, Jean-Paul. 1955. "Dirty Hands," in Lionel Abel trans., *No Exit and Three Other Plays.* New York: Vintage Books.

Sheppard, Robert. 1994. "Why Fault Politicians for Trying to Mediate?" *The Globe and Mail.* 11 August, A23.

Shugarman, David P. 1989. "Ideology and the Charter," in David P. Shugarman and Reg Whitaker eds., *Federalism and Political Community: Essays In Honour of Donald Smiley,* 307-326. Peterborough: Broadview Press.

Shugarman, David P. 1990. "The Use and Abuse of Politics," in Don MacNiven ed., *Moral Expertise: Studies In Practical and Professional Ethics.* London: Routledge.

Simpson, Jeffrey. 1988. *The Spoils of Power: The Politics of Patronage.* Toronto: W. Collins.

Smith, David E. 1987. "Patronage in Britain and Canada: An Historical Perspective," *Journal of Canadian Studies* 22:2 (Summer) 34-54.

Smith, T. V. 1942. "Compromise: Its Context and Limits," *Ethics* 53, 1-13.

Sniderman, Paul. 1975. *Personality and Democratic Politics.* Berkeley: University of California Press.

Sniderman, Paul, Peter Russell, Joseph Fletcher, Philip Tetlock and D. A. Northrup. 1993. "The Psychological Foundations of Prejudice: The Case of Anti-Semitism in Quebec," *Canadian Review of Sociology and Anthropology* 30:2 (May) 242-270.

Sniderman, Paul, Peter Russell, Joseph Fletcher and Philip Tetlock. 1996. *The Clash of Rights.* New Haven: Yale University Press.

Stanbury, W. T. 1991. *Money In Politics: Financing Federal Parties and Candidates in Canada.* Vol. 1 of the research studies of the Royal Commission on Electoral Reform and Party Financing. Toronto: Dundurn Press.

Stark, Andrew. 1992. "A 'Political-Discourse' Analysis and the Debate Over Canada's Lobbying Legislation," *Canadian Journal of Political Science* 25:3 (September) 513.

Starr, Michael and Mitchell Sharp, Co-Chairmen. 1984. *Ethical Conduct in the Public Sector.* Task Force on Conflict of Interest. Ottawa: Minister of Supply and Services.

Stenning, Philip C. 1995. *Accountability for Criminal Justice.* Toronto: University of Toronto Press.

Sutherland, S. L. 1993. "The Problem of Dirty Hands in Politics: Peace in the Vegetable Trade," *Canadian Journal of Political Science* 28:3 (September) 479-507.

Thompson, Dennis. 1993. "Mediated Corruption, The Case of the Keating Five," *American Political Science Review* 87 (June) 369-81.

Thompson, Dennis. 1987. *Political Ethics and Public Office.* Cambridge: Harvard University Press.

Tu Tranh Ha, 1996. "Liberals on Trial over System of Legal Agents," *The Globe and Mail.* 7 February, A6.

Trotsky, Leon. 1969. *Their Morals and Ours: Marxist Versus Liberal Views On Morality. Four Essays by Leon Trotsky, John Dewey and George Novack.* New York: Merit Publishers.

Walkom, Thomas. 1994. *Rae Days: The Rise and Follies of the NDP.* Toronto: Key Porter Books.

Walzer, Michael. 1973. "Political Action: The Problem of Dirty Hands," *Philosophy and Public Affairs* 2, 160-180.

Weber, Max. 1958. *From Max Weber: Essays in Sociology.* H. Gerth and C. Wright Mills trans and eds. New York: Oxford University Press.

Whitaker, Reg. 1987. "Between Patronage and Bureaucracy: Democratic Politics in Transition," *Journal of Canadian Studies* 22:2 (Summer) 55-71.

————. 1996. "The 'Bristow Affair': A Crisis of Accountability in Canadian Security Intelligence," *Intelligence and National Security* 11:2 (April) 279-305.

White, Theodore H. 1965. *The Making of the President 1964.* Toronto: The New American Library of Canada Ltd., Signet Books.

Williams, Sandra. 1983. "Conflict of Interest: The Experience of the American Congress," *The Parliamentarian* 64: 3 (July) 138–45.

Wilson, J.O. 1980. *A Book for Judges.* Ottawa: Ministry of Supply and Services Canada.

Zussman, David and Jak Jabes. 1989. *Vertical Solitude.* Halifax: The Institute for Research on Public Policy.

Index